The Road from Grimsby

Peter Pratt

Copyright © Peter Pratt 2014
Edited by Jenny Argante.

Cover design by the author and his daughter Tracey Cairns.
Thanks are due to artist Anne Harris [www.anneharrisart.net] for permission to reproduce her print of the Grimsby Dock Tower for the front cover.
Other photographs are from the author's family collection unless otherwise stated.

ISBN   978-0-9941107-8-7 (p/b)
ISBN   978-0-9941107-9-4 (Mobi)

Published by
The Little Red Hen Community Press
theroadfromgrimsby@gmail.com
64 Churchill Road
Judea
Tauranga 3110
New Zealand-Aotearoa

I dedicate this book to my beautiful wife, Patricia,
my wonderful children, Tracey and Damon
my grandchildren, Alex, Jack, Rachel and Emily
my mother and father, my brothers and sisters,
their children, and all my great friends.

The boy from Grimsby

Memories of the Old Cinder-Track

It was the name by the river I saw on the map,
near the street and the school
by the old cinder track

It was there we'd play football from morning until dark,
and copy the Mariners on Blundell Park
on the old cinder track

Under foggy street lights and cold autumn nights,
we'd play kick-ball-spy, steal an innocent kiss
by the old cinder track

Our houses are gone where our street used to be,
no patter of feet or old friends I see
on the old cinder track

Gone is our stadium of yesterday's dreams,
now a carpet of grass where our cinders once lay
on the old cinder track

Peter Pratt

Photo: Courtesy of Rod Collins

The Grimsby Fisherman's Memorial, a Trevor Harries sculpture in the grounds of St James Church, Grimsby, erected in memory of the town's brave fishermen.

Photo: Courtesy of Mike Whittaker
The Grimsby Royal Dock and Tower

Contents

Part Three: Shadows under the Sun

A Brief Word from the Author

These memories cover my first forty-years from my birth in 1936 to my departure in 1964 from England for Africa. My return to England in 1975 was eleven-years later making these important years of change.

My memories of people and places may have faded with time as, perhaps, their memories of me. Therefore I apologise for any missed or misspelt names. As far as I am aware, there is nothing here to offend; if there is, I can only ask to be forgiven.

I know many people will identify with my story – a memoir of progress from humble beginnings to a degree of personal accomplishment that I'm proud to tell.

It is by no means a complete record, and still I hope you will enjoy reading it.

Prologue

We shall not cease from exploration
And the end of all our exploring
Will be to arrive where we started

T.S. Eliot from 'Little Gidding'

One autumn day I drove south towards Lincolnshire, needing to breathe again the childhood air amid the landscapes of my early years. Once I reached the south side of the Humber on the M180, I was in familiar territory where rivers, woods, farms, oak and privet-lined country lanes and villages lay dreamily at the foot of the Lincolnshire Wolds.

I breathed a sigh of relief as I neared my birthplace, Grimsby, and its iconic symbol, the 312ft tall Dock Tower, came into view. The Tower was designed on the lines of the Palazzo Publico in Sienna, Italy, and built in 1852. Its sole purpose was to hold a water tank to feed Sir William George Armstrong's hydraulic system that operated the new dock's impressive lock gates.

Moments later I crossed Corporation Bridge, another familiar engineering feature that spans the Alexandra Dock. The bridge had always fascinated me when I was a boy, rising to let ships and barges pass from one dock to another.

Our town historians tells us there has always been some kind of thoroughfare on this busy waterway, going back to the 12th century, when Grimsby was used as a trading centre by the Scandinavians, who crossed the North Sea.

Edward, Prince of Wales, had opened the bridge in 1928 on the same day as he laid the foundation stone of the senior school I attended, Armstrong Secondary Modern.

Once over the bridge, I knew I was home where Corporation Road began with its labyrinth of streets and terraced houses on either side. Corporation Road ran through the heart of the West Marsh and was the backbone of the community. Here everyone shopped daily and snaking queues were a regular sight along the many shop-fronts. Women young and old, some dressed in headscarves, with shapeless dresses, and worn-out shoes, carried wicker baskets or hemp bags to hold their meagre rations. My mother shopped there long after the Second World War had ended, as food rationing did not entirely cease until 1953.

Corporation Road in those days was a cacophony of bell-ringing cyclists, with electric trams trundling and drivers of motor cars hooting loudly to warn of their presence. On workdays a wave of pedalling dockworkers, like a shoal of sardines, glided to the docks. They gave the Immingham Light Railway electric trams a run for their money as they clumsily rumbled down the Road. On foggy winter nights, the trams took on a ghostly presence, as their headlights poked through the evening gloom.

The 'Road' was also the constant route of lorries transporting fish offal - the skeletal remains of filleted fish - from the fish-dock to the bone meal factories. A fishy smell hung in the air daily. As Grimberians we were used to the smell with Grimsby being the biggest deep-sea fishing port in the world and this industry being the town's lifeblood. If a stranger asked, "Where do you work, mate?" the answer invariably would be "Down dock!"

It was years since I last saw the 'Road'. I got out of my car and stood for a moment, trying to visualise my past. In my head the clickety–click of the electric-trams, the sound of horses, straining to pull the loaded carts, the cries of the rag and bone men, the gaggle of queuing shoppers, the smell of fresh-fish and the jangle of bicycle bells came flooding back.

I opened my eyes to silence.

Gone were my mother's favourite shops: Howden's pork butchers, the whiff of homemade pork pies, penny savoury ducks (minced beef and spices.) The aroma of Glenton's freshly-baked bread and their delicious flaky-butterfly cakes. Prior's Post Office, where, as an 18 year-old apprentice I scrimped to save ten shillings a week to get married.

Gone were the grocers, pawnbrokers, cobblers and the barber shops. Brown's wet-fish shop where my mother would buy half a pound of cod's cheeks to bake fishcakes. The shoe shops, gentlemen's outfitters, ironmongers, drapers and furnishers had all disappeared. Yet they had all defied Hitler's bombers.

I walked across the road where Batty's Fish and Chip shop used to be and smiled to myself, remembering the time ash dropped off Mrs Batty's cigarette end as she wrapped my three-penny's worth of fried chips.

She smiled as she handed it over.

"Do you want any salt and vinegar on, duck?"

"No, thanks, Mrs Batty. The fag-ash is fine."

I sped out like Roger Bannister doing the four-minute mile.

Although Dr Cotterill was nearby, it was the legendary Mr Gooseman and his two chemists, Mr Sutherland and Mr Featherstone who were the preferred healers. They had a good manner with both young and old. My mother had more faith in them for everyday cures, as did a great many others on the West Marsh. At first glimpse on entering the shop, it appeared dingy with the underlying odour of different medications.

This was overlaid by the more pleasant aroma of Yardley's and Cussons soaps and eau de cologne. There as an apprentice I bought my first after-shave lotion; Imperial Leather, to hide the musty and pungent smell of the ships' bilges I worked in.

Reinecke's Soda Bar used to be on the corner of Rendel Street and Corporation Road, noted for its wonderful non-alcoholic beverages: sarsaparilla and dandelion and burdock. Reinecke's was a great meeting place for teenagers.

The Corporation Arms, better known as 'Kingies,' was my father's favourite pub. It was a known fact that fishermen were the heaviest drinkers and would get as much down their throats as quickly as possible, as usually they only had 48 hours on shore before they sailed again to endure fearsome conditions. Henry Morgan in *The Toughest Job in the World* confirmed the fishermen's hard and dangerous work.

It became evident to me that Yarborough Street where I grew up was long gone, renamed Ravenspurn Way. Now rows of smaller dwellings, with none of the familiar bay windows, doors or front gardens as of old. Here our mothers used to stand for a neighbourly chinwag as we played beneath streetlights. Gone too was the General Hospital and South Parade Methodist Church that overshadowed our street.

I parked the car in Earl Street and walked over the road-bridge crossing the River Freshney. The bridge still bears the Great Grimsby's coat of arms: the Grim and Havelock Seal, a black chevron with three boar's heads. I continued my walk beside the Freshney, the river of my boyhood. Here as a six-year-old I first fished with my twin sisters, using a strutting-net tied to a bamboo cane. Red doctors and sticklebacks were my targets, carried home in a jam-jar to proudly show my mother. There they soon died, as mother told me they would.

I loitered to look down at the river as it meandered under the bridge exactly as it did all those years ago. On the other side was my field of dreams, a grassless open field we called the cinder-track, now a cultivated carpet of verdant grass. That was where I kicked my first football, held a cricket-bat, ran the hundred yards, three legged and sack races, and built bonfires for Guy Fawkes Night and V. E. Day after we won World War II. Nearby my old primary school on South Parade, opened in 1879, seemed to be untouched by this modern age. Here I was taught the three Rs and stole a kiss from Pat, a 7-year-old blonde beauty.

Memories ambushed me until, as rain began to fall incessantly, I turned away to drive back into the country to Habrough, where I had arranged to visit my sister Irene. We always had so much to talk about, and I also took her to the Grimsby Cemetery. All our family are buried there: mother and father, our two sisters Brenda and Pauline and their husbands, and a multitude of aunts and uncles I had never known.

This particular occasion was special to both of us. Eighteen months previously, I had requested from the War Graves Commission that a formal headstone be placed where our dear brother Kenneth was buried in 1941. Kenneth was killed at only sixteen years old while serving in the Merchant Navy; a brother I barely remember as I was only five years old then. The bodies of Kenny and three other crew members had been recovered from the ship's wreckage and he had finally received his serviceman's headstone.

We both wished so much that our parents could have seen it.

Later I asked Irene if she knew how our mother and father had first met. She shook her head.

"You should visit Uncle Jim Griffiths. He would know."

She found his address in Cleethorpes and I tucked it away.

That evening I phoned David Holmes, my childhood friend. From primary to secondary school and after, David and I were inseparable and he had been best man at my wedding. He still lived in Grimsby with his wife Janet and I could not miss the chance of seeing him after so many years.

We caught up with the news and David gave me some old photos and notes on our early days in Yarborough Street. Like me, he was sad that our old houses had been demolished and showed me a roof slate he recovered from his family's home, No. 59. I hadn't realised he was that sentimental.

Part One:
Growing up in Grimsby

- 1-

69 Yarborough Street

My arrival came as something of a shock to my mother. After the birth of twin girls she was warned not to have any more children. Yet three years later I was born on 23rd June 1936 to James William and Elizabeth Pratt, then living at Boulevard Avenue, Grimsby.

My birth was no easier than that of my older siblings: James, Kenneth, Bernard, Irene, Brenda and the twins, Doreen and Pauline. Dr Cottrell sighed and, obviously worried, placed me, silent and unmoving, at the foot of mother's bed. The midwife picked me up by my feet and dangled me upside down. She slapped me twice on the buttocks.

"You squealed like one of Uncle Jim's piglets," my sister Irene told me.

Soon after I was born my parents did a flit to a bigger, three-bedroomed terrace house, with a grey slate roof in typical northern working-class style. 69 Yarborough Street was next door but one to South Parade Methodist Church. From the front door and across the street was the Grimsby District Hospital. In this street I spent the first twenty-one years of my life.

My four sisters took turns between work and school to keep me occupied, pushing me in a high-wheeled pram through the streets and along the banks of the River Freshney that meandered through the Boulevard (Duke of York Gardens).

"You were always the centre of attraction, Pete," my sister Doreen would reminisce.

As I began to take notice, they showed me how to feed the ducks and I would laugh at the other children playing on the Boulevard's swings.

During this novelty of a baby brother, my three older brothers, James, Kenneth and Bernard were either working or at senior school until the coming war took them away. I was the youngest and I cannot hope to accurately recreate the scenes and atmosphere of the first five-years of my life. I know as a pre-schooler I would play under the lilac tree at the bottom of our garden and watch with envy Nina our cat as she climbed among its branches.

She would lie there, waiting and watching, with her tail swishing back and forth. I didn't understand what she was up to, until my mother chased her away with a broom, scolding her for taking a sparrow into the house. Even now, the aroma of lilac brings back fond memories of long ago.

I was three when the Second World War began on 4th September 1939. At some stage, a band of workers delivered the Anderson shelter that was to be erected in the middle of our back garden. In the meantime, my six-year old twin sisters had other ideas and played slide with me on the curved metal sections left lying on the back garden lawn as the workers prepared to cut down our lilac tree.

"Pete, it was so funny," my sister Irene said. "We all stood gaping as mother threatened him with a garden spade."

The lilac tree was saved and was still blossoming well after I got married, seventeen years later.

Even our front garden railings were taken away in aid of the war effort – metal for munitions and essential equipment being in short supply. Pauline stood me on a chair in the front room and together we watched in wonder through the bay window as the workmen cut down our railings. Much to my delight, the gas-cutting torch created a burst of sparks like a Catherine wheel. To mother's dismay, as the railing fell apart, what remained was a row of metal stubs protruding an inch above the brickwork.

The same stubs proved painful and costly for me as I grew more adventurous. I would climb over the wall and graze my knees more often than not, or rip out the backside of my trousers on these sharp-edged remnants.

There were weekly visits from the ticket man, milkman, rent collector and insurance agent. By far the nicest was Mr. Wilson, the Co-operative ticket collector. Every Saturday morning, come rain, hail, snow or war, he greeted us with a cheerful 'Good morning, duck,' his voice echoing down the uncarpeted hall. I was always addressed as Snowball and he never missed out on giving me a sweet. He probably got them free when calling on Goody Taylor's 'sweet factory' in Corporation Road.

He would follow up on his initial greeting by politely doffing his trilby hat, and enquiring, "How's Elizabeth today?"

Did he have feelings for my mother? I don't know, but nobody else called her Elizabeth, not even my Dad.

With such financial obligations, our hallway over the years (and well into my teens) was the place for wheeling and dealing as Mam juggled her always stretched housekeeping budget. There were times she might have to miss going to the pictures, but if a Leslie Howard film was showing at the Rex, then one of the creditors got nothing but an apology.

Our front room was a forbidden place as far as we children were concerned, preserved only for aunts and uncles and family gatherings, Christmas, funerals and weddings.

Sparsely carpeted, the front room's centrepiece was a black marble fireplace surrounded with a brass curb and an ensemble of brass-handled fire-tools. The only time the front-room fire was lit was at Christmas time. While in secondary school, for a woodwork exam I made a fireguard - not to guard against a fire, but as a decoration. This was proudly placed in the hearth to hide the open grate.

I spent hours sandpapering its frame before the final touch of dark oak stain. Then my Aunt Emily made a pretty tapestry for its centrepiece of a girl on a swing in an English country garden surrounded by pink and white roses.

With the Second World War over, there were no more black-outs, so we were back to clear glass in the windows. All the strips of black sticky tape were removed, put there in case a bomb blast sent shards of glass flying like deadly arrows and causing serious injury. In peacetime the front room in summer was the best place to be as the afternoon sun shone through the bay window. In winter it was dull and shadowy, though still exciting to stand and watch windswept snowflakes highlighted in the glow of the street lights.

Our front room had by far the best furniture. The mahogany ornate plant stand in the bay window was never without a vase of fresh flowers. On the dark oak sideboard were displayed cut glass vases, a Japanese tea set, a silver-plated cake stand and a framed photograph of my parents' wedding.

The heavy oak sideboard's drawers held a multitude of linen tablecloths, crockery and silver plated cutlery that only showed their faces on special occasions – birthdays, Christmas and funerals. The only table, oak-polished and with extending leaves and six matching chairs, stood in the centre of the room, also with its vase of fresh flowers. The only comfortable chair was a well-worn leatherette armchair by the fireplace. Everything in the front room was dusted and polished weekly, down to the many casualties of time and wear like the threadbare carpet, broken ornaments or scratched furniture.

The bare wood floor of the middle room creaked with every step. Always unfurnished, it was a kind of oddments store, a place for bikes and old suitcases. From an early age, the middle-room was my Aladdin's cave, with boxes stuffed with books and toys from before I was born. My brother James' old school books in a leather satchel fascinated me, particularly one wrapped in brown paper and tied with string - *King Solomon's Mines*. Yet generally I was not into reading unless there were pictures or it was a comic.

Under an old coat I discovered something that made my eyes light up, an oil-stained wood box with J.W.P engraved on the lid. I didn't know these were my father's initials. I imagined that I had found a treasure chest like Long John Silver was searching for in *Treasure Island*. I was disappointed when I opened it and found it full of weird tools and nothing that resembled a cycle spanner.

My mother caught me surrounded with the content of the box.

"You'd better put all those things back, my lad. Father wouldn't be pleased if he knew you'd been rummaging in his things."

Not exactly the right thing to tell an inquisitive eight-year old.

Our evenings during and soon after the war were spent in the living room by the Yorkshire grate, the cosiest and warmest room in the house; the only room with a fire constantly lit and where mother did her baking. Above the mantelshelf was an over-shelf, an ornate mahogany affair with inset mirrors, with a clutter of ornaments, including jam jars for pens, pencils and mother's spectacles.

The only sacred ornament was a blue Delft jug that Mam cherished, with pictures of children in clogs playing by windmills. Though chipped and with a broken handle it was mother's favourite item. A collection of photographs showed Grandfather and Grandma Raper with their children. As far as I can remember, there were no photographs or ornaments of my father's family and the only picture of my father, young and handsome, was in his Royal Navy Officer uniform, taken during the First World War. His picture was set inside a border of nautical flags.

The living room table was used for all sorts of things besides meals from preparing them and cakes and pastry for baking; pasting wallpaper to playing games and ironing the laundry. Mam had a heavy iron that had to be heated on the fire-grate, until my sisters, now all working, clubbed together to buy her an electric iron that plugged into the living room light socket.

Standing on a chair to plug in the iron was not Mam's cup of tea. She distrusted electric gadgets and was physically unsuited for balancing on chairs. At first, my sisters would plug it in for her and as I got older and when they were not available I was trusted to do the necessary for her. The first time I did so Mam stood with fingers in her mouth ready to scream should I be electrocuted.

War or no war, the wireless continued to turn out a crop of names, but each night Mam tuned the wireless on to the BBC Home Service and its formal announcement, 'Here is the news' and then went on to talk about the Allies.

"That's us," Mam would say, but none of us recognized the other strange names: Tobruk, and El Alamein.

I would sit with my sisters and pore over the map of the world my brother James had left behind when he joined the RAF. We knew he was in Egypt somewhere as Mam had an air telegraph letter from him, sometimes with his sketch of a palm tree.

Later on, the same atlas gave me increased pleasure during my school's geography lessons, the only subject I enjoyed and where I was way ahead of everyone in my class.

When the BBC's Light Programme came on the wireless, we would be hushed into silence, especially if Anne Ziegler and Webster Booth were singing. Mam would sing along with them, as if in a world of her own, especially 'We'll Gather Lilacs.' It was unusual to see her relaxed from her everyday chores. Our favourites on the Light Programme were Henry Hall's Music Night and Tommy Handley's ITMA (It's That Man Again.) Probably such light-hearted programmes kept us all sane during the war.

When I came home from school at lunchtime I could hear the wireless even before I opened the backdoor. Workers Playtime with Arthur Askey and Elsie and Doris Waters, a pair of zany comediennes. Nevertheless, the BBC News and weather reports always took preference. One particular lunchtime we were all hushed into silence as the newscaster announced that Leslie Howard's plane had been shot down, with no hope of survivors. The following day, Mam read the headlines from the *Daily Mirror* in tears.

Leslie Howard was every mother's heartthrob in the 30s and 40s, famous for his role as the Scarlet Pimpernel and as Ashley Wilkes in Gone with the Wind. I only remember him as Mitchell, the inventor of the Spitfire in the film First of the Few, which we saw at the Rex on Corporation Road the year the war ended.

I always looked forward to Saturday night and a hot bath. In winter it was a delight to sit in the tin tub in front of a blazing fire, the bath water scented with Dettol. First Doreen and Pauline had their bath and afterwards would pour warm water over me while Mam gave me a good scrub. The bath was followed by toast and dripping and a mug of cocoa before we went 'up the wooden hill,' as Mam called the stairs. Everyone else, including my older sisters Irene and Brenda and my brother Bernard, took their baths in the privacy of the back kitchen, as I suppose my parents did.

There were times I would join the twins making rag rugs from odds and ends of fabric, or salvaging wool from old woollen jumpers and re-balling it ready to knit into hats, scarves and mittens. Those evenings the living room would become a hive of activity, while our mother sat listening to her wireless for any snippets of war news. Often 'Moaning Minnie,' the air-raid siren, would break the peace and signal a dash to the air raid shelter.

On top of the oak ex-gramophone cabinet, Mother kept an empty cocoa tin for pennies for the gas meter, and a hexagonal biscuit tin for pens and pencils, the rent book and the Co-operative dividend book. Similarly, another much bigger biscuit-tin held an agglomeration of bric-a-brac such a sewing needles, knob-pins, cotton bobbins, boxes of buttons of all colours and sizes and steel knitting needles.

As a small child, I would root in the tin as if it was a treasure chest, scoop a handful of buttons pretending they were gold coins, and spill them all over the floor. Doreen showed me how to play tiddlywinks. One time I sat there screaming, with a knob-pin stuck under my fingernail.

We had all our meals in the living room: no elbows on the table or talking while eating and always properly with a knife and fork or spoon. Mam had strict house rules, even to the extent of keeping a bamboo cane to hand, long enough to reach every corner of the table. This proper way of going on was demonstrated at all meal times, breakfast, dinner and tea. We were never allowed to eat anywhere else, but sat at the table even for our nightly bowl of Oxo, toast or cocoa.

For breakfast, Mother made sure we all had something substantial like porridge oats, shredded wheat or cornflakes, followed by toast with jam or treacle. Most of my school friends stayed for school dinners, but mother would not have that; she made us come home at lunchtimes. Most days there would be a cauldron of stewed rabbit and dumplings on the stove. What a pleasure to open the door to the aroma of thyme, sliced carrot, potato and onions. Our dinners were never without a pudding of some kind: rice, sago or steamed sponge, jam roly-poly and suet.

Sometime before the Second World War started, my brothers Kenny and Bernard made a vegetable patch and a chicken run. This came in handy during the war years when the nation was encouraged to 'dig for victory.'

Out came the hydrangea and roses and in went edible crops. We grew a seasonal variety of vegetables: cabbage, carrots, potato, lettuce and onions. Herbs such as thyme, parsley and mint grew wild along the back garden wall. As I grew older, my Mother showed me how to plant seeds and tend the garden and how to recognise a weed.

Mother was a believer in greens as the best medicine and made us drink a daily glass of cabbage water before we ate our dinner. The taste was awful, but she would say it was good for our complexion and for bowel motions.

After school we were offered drop scones or hot cakes warming in the hearth, for our high tea was an assortment of lighter meals: fish cakes, fried potatoes and beans or bubble and squeak with a fried egg on top. Saturday lunchtime after the war we had Batty's fish and chips. Saturday and Sunday teatime would be salads, cold meat, tongue, brawn and savoury ducks followed by trifle.

The scullery, painted with apple green distemper, was where everyone performed their daily ablutions winter and summer: bathing, brushing teeth and shaving, and even washing clothes besides general cooking on a four-ring gas stove. In one corner was the coal-fire heated copper used mainly for boiling clothes or filling the dolly tub. Under the back window at one end stood a huge earthenware sink with a cold water tap, the only means of water in the house.

On the windowsill stood a variety of jam jars for toothbrushes, an assortment of combs, hairbrushes, soaps, flannels, shaving brushes and hair cream. In the mornings the scullery was crowded with everyone trying to get ready for work, with us school children forced to wait until they had departed. Hung on the inside of the back door was an assortment of coats, hats and rainwear, with more down the passage by the side door to the back yard. Wellingtons and work footwear were never allowed inside the house, only plimsolls and best shoes.

Monday was always washday, no matter what the weather. Mam would don her pinafore and tie up her hair under a turban, before bending over the dolly-tub or feeding our clothing through the mangle. The scullery was awash with condensation running down the walls and the singing of the copper as it bubbled and gurgled. On rainy days, the living room was awash with steaming laundry hung on the clotheshorse: bras, stays, knickers, underpants, socks, hankies, stockings and the like.

On fine days, pegs between her teeth, Mother went along the line to hang out the washing. Billowing bedsheets flapped like a schooner's sails. Sometimes laundry had to be left out overnight and if it was frosty nights, they'd be stiff as cardboard next morning.

The terrace houses in that street, for all their faults, had a convenient labyrinth of passageways that ran around the back. Besides being our daily playground (and sometimes nightly) they were designed to help the likes of dustbin men and coalmen to deliver and collect. Mostly the dustbin men were a burly, flat-capped and motley gang, who wore leather shoulder pads. It was nothing unusual to find them hauling two bins, one on each shoulder, for return to the rightful gardens.

Likewise the coalman would haul a hundredweight sack of coal across his back in any season, smiling through his blackened face as he greeted us. He had been bringing us coal for many years, yet Mother never failed to remind Jack, Bannister's coal man, to wipe his feet before traipsing through her scullery to empty the sack of coal in the coalhouse. If she noticed there was 'slack' among the coal, she'd call him back without further ado.

The coldest place in the house was the lavatory, attached to the scullery but with a door facing the back yard. If there was a nor'easterly, it blew under the four-inch gap and gave no encouragement to linger unnecessarily. During icy winter nights, mother lit a paraffin-oil lamp inside to prevent the water pipes and cistern icing up. From the age of six or eight, I was given the job of cutting up newspapers into six-inch squares and punch a hole in one corner to thread string through and hang them on a nail inside the lavatory door.

In those days toilet paper was a luxury. I had only seen it once, while visiting my Aunt Lily in Louth Road, the posh end of Grimsby. There were two advantages to using newspaper: you didn't poke your finger through like you did with toilet roll paper, and it offered you a wide range of reading matter. The *Daily Mirror* and *Woman's Own* took some getting used to; ideally the *Dandy* and *Beano* comics were my favourites.

Oblivious to how long I sat there I would be called, "Have yer fell down the hole in there, our Pete?"

During the war years when Dad was home, which was not that often (him being a seaman), he and mother occupied the middle bedroom as I remember. However, while he was at sea one of my sisters or me would sleep with Mam, especially during the war. Mother's bedroom was the warmest as it was above the living room, the only room that usually had a coal fire lit and always in winter.

Sleeping arrangements were a game of draughts. Throughout my school years into my late teens, my sisters shared the front bedroom, as it had two beds, a dressing table and wardrobe. At some stage during my infant years, I remember sleeping in the bath in a corner of the back bedroom. The bath was never used as it should have been in all the twenty-one years I lived at 69, lying dormant with no water supply to it. This scenario only played out whenever our father and my three brothers were home at the same time.

When Kenneth joined the Navy and James went off to enlist in the RAF, Bernard and I had the back bedroom to ourselves.

I dreaded leaving the warmth of the living room to go to bed in winter. On cold and frosty nights I would often wake up to floral patterns inscribed in ice on the windows, inside and out. I would leap into bed, still wearing my socks, underpants and vest and, on extremely cold nights, wearing my balaclava and woollen jumper over my pyjamas.

In the dawn of the nineteen fifties came the DIY (do-it-yourself) craze. Time to get rid of the drab pre-war colours that made houses dark and miserable, and ours was no exception. Out went the dusty snip rugs, tattered coconut matting and floor linoleum. I relished the task of ripping up the lino with a claw hammer and nailing down loose floorboards found beneath.

After school I helped my sisters strip off the old paper. The painting and decorating craze went one step further; everything that had panels was 'flushed.' Within a few weeks, the ornately-twisted banister spells and hall doors were hidden behind panels. I could tell Mam didn't like all this new contemporary fashion. Nevertheless, the living room was vastly transformed with lighter colours and no snip rugs to trip over, but carpet almost wall-to-wall instead.

A new centre light with three glass shades was a great improvement, especially with no dirty flypaper hanging from it.

I came home from school, to see two council workers taking our Yorkshire grate down the garden path. Mam was on her knees by the hole where the grate had been, sweeping the living room floor, her arms, hands and face smudged with soot. A trail of soot led through the scullery and down the back garden path.

"That's the last time I have this mess," she kept saying, to no one in particular. It was not the mess that upset my Mam, but the loss of her pride and joy. Imagine if the Mayor of Grimsby opened the bonnet of his mayoral limousine and found the engine gone. Wouldn't there be hell to pay?

For two days, the living room looked like we had been bombed. Mind you, the change was a joy for me, as I hated the Saturday morning ritual of black-leading that iron monster. A few days later, we had a modern tiled fireplace with glazed grey and maroon tiles and an oblong Art Deco mirror hanging above it. Even my posh aunties, Lily and Emily, admitted the room looked cleaner and it meant less work for our mother.

In addition the room seemed bigger. The old carpet and snip-rugs were thrown out for the bin-men and a new carpet was laid, but we still did not have any hot running water or a real bath.

The year I started work, the Grimsby council built a public ablution block on the cinder track, opposite the hospital nurses' quarters. Each cubicle had a bath, mirror and wash basin, for a tanner (sixpence or two new pence) we were allowed twenty minutes. Over the time limit and a gruff voice would yell, "Are yer done in there? Others are waiting, yer know!"

To leave the ablution block was to run the gauntlet of wolf whistles from the nurses as they leaned out windows smoking a fag.

"All nice and clean, are we, ducky?"

Still the bath was worth the two-minute walk, especially after a game of football or a hard week's work in the shipyard.

-2-
Mam and Dad

My mother Elizabeth (Lizzie) Raper was born 14th December 1893 to William and Emma Elizabeth Raper in Thorold Street, Grimsby. My mother was the second eldest of four boys and four girls. Grandfather Raper, a fisherman, sadly died aged forty in 1904, leaving his family in near poverty. His oldest boy was only twelve and my mother ten years old.

At fourteen, my mother left school and worked in the Cosalt, braiding trawler fishing nets with her brother William (who later became a works manager on his return from World War 1.) Her mother insisted she still help with the daily chores even after working a nine-hour shift. It was a known fact in the family that my mother had an unhappy childhood.

My father, James William Pratt, was born on 15th March 1891, the oldest of the four children of his parents William James and Annie Pratt. Dad was born in Barcroft Street, Cleethorpes, but later they moved to Elsenham Road on the West Marsh, Grimsby. My father started his sea career as a fourteen-year old deckhand and trimmer on Grimsby trawlers. By the age of twenty-four he had progressed to engineer on trawlers and at the outbreak of World War I he joined the British Royal Navy Reserves. After further training in Portsmouth, he was stationed in the Mediterranean on board HMS Egmont and HMS Research, based in Malta.

As far as I know, none of my brothers and sisters knew a great deal about our grandfather James William Pratt, except that he was a bully to his children and more so to my Grandma Anne Pratt. As the story goes, he left his wife to live bigamously with another woman in Hull.

After Dad left the Royal Navy in 1919, he joined the Grimsby fishing fleet as a chief engineer and continued courting my Mam. They married in July 1920, and for the first four years lived with my Grandma Raper in Thorold Street.

Later my parents, with a growing family of their own - two boys and a girl – moved in 1924 into a three-bedroom, rented terrace house in Boulevard Avenue, Grimsby. Due to my father's heavy drinking it wasn't long before the family was living in near poverty.

My sister Irene recalls a time when our mother took Dad's dinner to 'Kingies,' the public house on the corner. She threw his dinner at him in front of his drinking cronies. Forever a mild-mannered man, he never uttered a word, but with gravy dripping down his best suit left the pub for home and went straight up to bed. Irene said the house was quiet for days afterwards. It came about that Mam didn't know he had already joined the Merchant Navy the day before and was celebrating his last drinking session with his friends?

I was two years old then and this was a turning point for my mother. Although Dad's trips were longer at sea it kept him off the booze and mother had a regular income coming in. Yet with the outbreak of the Second World War it became a great worry for Mam knowing Dad was on the Atlantic Convoy run: Liverpool, Canada and Russia. One in every three merchant ships was sunk in the war years.

I was five years old when my mother opened the front door to a Merchant Navy chaplain and a police officer. They had come to inform her that her son, my brother Kenneth, was killed in action aboard his ship the SS Rudby. I can only vaguely remember my 14-year-old brother Bernard and my three sisters as they sat crying with my mother in the living room. Word got round to Uncle Jim who brought Aunt Lily and Emily to help comfort Mam.

As the oldest of my siblings, Irene was relieved from her munitions duties. I watched while, still weeping, they sewed a black silk diamond to our coat sleeves.

There were visits from other relatives, many I had never seen before, and close neighbours rallied round to comfort our mother especially knowing my father was still at sea. Irene told me she had to write to let our brother James, with the RAF in Egypt, know the sad news.

"Tears fell on the letter as I wrote, sometimes smudging the ink," she said. "I must have written it several times over."

Kenneth's body was later recovered, along with three other crew members. Because he was almost unrecognisable, only my mother and my eldest sister Irene were allowed to see Kenneth. He was buried in Scartho Road Cemetery three weeks after my fifth birthday. That same night we had another severe air raid.

My parents were unable to afford a proper headstone for Kenneth. Irene told me decades later that she and Brenda planted a rose bush to mark his grave. Whilst assembling our family tree I wrote to the Commonwealth War Graves Commission requesting that a servicemen's headstone be placed in memory of Kenneth. They replied within a week apologising for their oversight and sixteen months later an official headstone marked his grave. This bore the Merchant Navy emblem and his name: Deck Boy Kenneth William Pratt S.S. Rudby (West Hartlepool) 29th June 1941 age 17, followed by Irene's inscription: 'Dearly loved son and brother. The Lord gave you and the sea took you away. God bless. RIP.'

My clearest memory of my mother goes back to when I was seven and the war was at its height. Though Mam was brought up in a strict Victorian manner, she did not adopt her own mother's unkind ways. How to describe her? My mother was stocky with strong but gentle hands - unless you riled her. Only five foot two inches, she was heavy-busted and wide-hipped with sturdy legs. She was strong and you knew it, but she could melt you with her gentle smiling eyes.

More often than not, she wore a wraparound pinafore and cardigan over a dress, winter or summer. Before going into the air-raid shelter in wartime, she would make sure each of us had our blanket, coat, scarves, gloves, mittens, hats and - in my case - a balaclava. Especially in winter when those steel Anderson shelters were icy cold, constantly damp and often flooded. As my mother used to say, "They're neither use nor ornament."

The 1940s and 1950s were the golden age of the cinema and make-believe. Going to the pictures was my mother's only social enjoyment while Dad was at sea. Tuesday and Friday evenings became a weekly ritual at the Rex cinema for my mother and Mrs Treacher, our neighbour and friend. It was at the Rex I first saw Errol Flynn as Robin Hood. Mam thought him too crude, wearing such tight trousers, especially when he kissed Olivia de Havilland. She would tut-tut to Mrs T who nodded in agreement, though I noticed, she appeared to enjoy every minute as she clapped her hands.

My sisters were unable to afford a proper hairdo at Rimmer's, the ladies' hair stylist on Corporation Road. I would watch them cut and wave their own hair with tongs heated on the living room fire, or set their hair in rollers. Doing Mam's hair was another kettle of fish. No matter how nice they made her hair look, she never went out without her headscarf. As for make-up, she wore only the slightest touch, a powder puff dab here and there followed by a thin film of light pink lipstick. She would say, "I don't want to look too garish."

Irene and Brenda tried their hardest to brighten her up, especially when Dad was due home. Mam preferred dark colours; her dresses plain dark blues and browns. Her best coat, the only one she possessed, was a pre-war ankle length walnut brown swagger. My sisters convinced her to buy more up to date styles, taking her to Richards in Freeman Street. Only in the early fifties would she wear fashionable clothes when Dad was home more often.

I was in my early teens before I had a full picture of my parents being together as man and wife. Dad would call Mam Liz, and Mam call Dad Jim. I had never seen her so well-dressed and happy. They would take me to the Palace Theatre or take a bus to visit Uncle Jim and Aunt Lily who lived on Louth Road. On those nights I would sit on Mam's bed and watch her getting ready. It was evident she was no Ingrid Bergman. She would frown at herself in the wardrobe mirror, giving her dress a tug here and a tug there, trying her hardest to flatten out any evidence of corsets. The nylon stockings Dad brought her from abroad made a change from her everyday lisle stockings. At least they hid the road map of varicose veins on her legs.

She would come downstairs, posh in a new floral dress and felt hat, with a string of pearls and earrings to match. My sisters would fuss around her with a powder puff and lipstick to add the final touches, Mam protesting, "I don't want to look like a tart, you, Brenda."

Now she more closely resembled her younger sisters, Lily and Emily. Aunt Emily was a widow; her husband George was killed falling off a crane long before I was born. Aunt Emily was a mild-natured, rosy-cheeked and dainty woman dressed usually in 'twinset and pearls'. She worked in the Regal ABC Cinema on Freeman Street.

After the war, there were no more cheap perfumes from the Gooseman's for my mother; nothing but the best. Her bedroom lost the acrid aroma of the 'gazunder' (commode) under her bed. Instead, the alluring aroma of Chanel, eau de cologne or Evening in Paris that Dad brought home would drift down the hall. Her smell of carbolic washdays was long gone as were the scuffed down-at-heel shoes. The pair of Branton and Blow's up-to-date black leather shoes with two-inch heels did nothing for her.

"These will take some getting used to," she mumbled, as I sat on the bottom stair watching her 'bedding' them as she tottered up and down the hall. "I think it's me bunions."

Every year Mam made a big thing of Christmas no matter what. The living room was decorated with coloured paper chains, Chinese lanterns and the Christmas tree she'd had from a little girl. On Christmas Eve we'd hang a pillowcase at the foot of our bed, waking up well before dawn to presents heaped on the bed: toys, dolls, little bags of nuts, sweets, oranges and apples, colouring books and comics. Santa, we were told, came down the chimney, so Mam always left out a mince pie and a glass of sherry by the hearth for him.

The Christmas of 1945 was one for us all to remember, the first time I'd known us gathered together, except for poor Dad, whose letter arrived from Singapore a week before Christmas. My brother Bernard, also in the Merchant Navy, arrived home Christmas week as did our James, whom we had not seen in four years.

The big surprise came as James introduced a new addition to our Pratt family circle: his wife Joy. They had courted before he was sent to Egypt in 1941 with 4,000 others in the troopship Dominion Monarch. Unknown to us they had married instantly on his return from Italy in September 1945. Mam was quick to show her disappointment that they had not let anyone know they were getting married and hardly spoke to either of them for two days.

Mam hated women smokers; she thought them common and was deeply upset when her new daughter-in-law Joy lit up. To Mum's annoyance, Joy sat in her fireside chair drinking Camp coffee, and made no attempt to muck in with the dish-washing. As a cooking instructor in the RAF, James soon made himself the centre of attraction. He had brought with him (thanks to the RAF larder in Abingdon) all the ingredients for a sumptuous Christmas dinner and the biggest turkey the likes any of us had ever seen.

Our last two chickens in the chicken run in the garden had a reprieve, as did Bernard's two pet rabbits, previously designated for our Christmas feast.

James had become more noticeable by his absences than by his presence, something that in due course, the family might also say about me!

Besides the gift of her family around her after six years of wartime turmoil, Mam's best Christmas present was the Grundig radiogram Bernard bought her. Throughout that Christmas Bing Crosby sang 'White Christmas' and 'Silent Night.' The snow that fell on Boxing Day made everything so magical. 'Red Sails in the Sunset' was another of our mother's favourite songs.

"Put that one on again, Pete," she would say.

We had the radiogram for several weeks before she got the hang of changing the records herself, sometimes forgetting to turn it off. We would find her sitting in her armchair by the fire in a dream world of her own. I knew she was thinking of our Dad and Kenny.

The following May of 1946 I went with Mam to meet Dad at Grimsby Railway Station after his eight months away at sea. When we arrived the station was crowded, mostly with returning servicemen in uniforms. Standing on the footbridge over the railway lines, I spotted Dad walking towards Mam as she waited anxiously amid the crowd. Dad suddenly appeared through the swirling steam from the train's engine with a porter wheeling a stack of suitcases on a wheelbarrow.

Smart in his navy blue suit, overcoat and trilby, and with the habitual cigarette in the corner of his mouth, Dad hadn't changed a bit. Oblivious to anyone around them Mam and Dad hugged each other. Dad took off his trilby and kissed Mam as Humphrey Bogart kissed Lauren Bacall in 'The Big Sleep.' They weren't the only couple embracing, either; but I had never seen them kiss like that before. Usually it was a peck on the cheek.

Then he saw me.

"Bloody hell, Liz, hasn't Pete shot up?"

He affectionately ruffled my hair, as he always did and handed me a small suitcase.

"Here, Pete, I think you can manage that one, but don't drop it. There's something special in there for your mother."

He winked at me and smiled.

Opening Dad's suitcases filled our house with excitement. There were presents for everyone: watches, perfumes and jewellery, nylons and silk night robes for the girls. Then he opened his small suitcase. Inside was Mam's present, wrapped in fine tissue paper, a Japanese tea set from Singapore. I usually got toys, but this time he brought me a pair of basketball boots and a baseball cap.

While Dad was home he was often slumped, snoring, in the fireside chair, the food on his dinner plate only half-eaten. Mam warned us not to make any noise after she helped him upstairs to sleep off the booze. He would come down and listen to the BBC 6 o'clock news before getting ready to go out again. On those occasions, we had to sit deathly quiet or be made to go out and play rain hail or snow. I envied my school pals down the street whose fathers were home every day.

Coming home from school I would often see Dad shaving in the back kitchen, dressed only in his long johns. All the hot water in our house came from filling kettles from a single cold-water tap in the back kitchen. The more I saw of my father the more evident it became that he was of only medium height and skinny compared to my brothers James and Bernard. His age did not occur to me then. Dad had a hard, weather-beaten face with a sharp bent nose and grey eyes. He had a warm smile and was quietly spoken. Although his hair was not thick, it was neatly groomed. Whilst home, he had it cut at Hobson's, the barbers on Corporation Road.

The first time I saw my Dad shave I watched in amazement as the tattooed women on his arms danced with every twist and turn. There were more tattoos across his chest from shoulder to shoulder and his back was decorated with a shamrock, rose and a thistle.

When he finished washing and shaving, he took his false teeth out of the jar of salt water, washed them under the tap and pushed them into place. It was a daily ritual for both Mam and Dad to soak their dentures overnight. Each morning as I brushed my teeth I would see their false teeth grinning at me. Their dentures were almost identical except Dad kept his near his shaving mug and Mam kept hers near the carbolic soap dish. Dad's were tinted brown from being a smoker and Mam would give them a scrub with carbolic soap before he came downstairs.

While Dad washed and shaved in the back kitchen Mam ironed his shirt, pressed his suit trousers and polished his shoes.

Fully dressed, he would adjust his waistcoat and suit jacket and ensure the Merchant Navy badge was safely pinned in his lapel. One final look in the hall mirror as he adjusted his tie and trilby before he gave our mother a kiss on the cheek as they hugged before he took a taxi to the Grimsby Rail Station. My father sailed from Bristol to Australia on the SS Culrain. He left in July1949 and did not return until January 1951.

The 1950s brought both joy and sadness to my parents and the entire Pratt family. My father arrived home to an ever-changing era. Not long after he returned from his long period at sea, my brother Bernard married Audrey, who a year later gave my parents their first grandchild, Andrea. Three years later Irene married; followed a year later by Pauline. In 1957 it was my turn, beating my other two sisters to the altar. Not to be outdone Brenda married John, her Austrian boyfriend and Doreen three years later married Basil, who came from the Ukraine after the war. Soon we were busy providing my parents with more grandchildren.

The 1950s were not entirely a kind decade, though. We were hit with another severe blow in February 1954 when my 27-year-old brother Bernard, also an engineer, was lost on the Grimsby trawler Laforey. The trawler was trying to avoid a heavy storm off the Norwegian coast and ran aground. All twenty crewmembers were lost in one of Grimsby's biggest trawler disasters.

The death of Bernard was a great shock to us all. He had been married only two years to Audrey, who was expecting twins the following week; they already had a beautiful one-year-old daughter, Andrea.

For days my poor mother couldn't stop crying. Sometimes I heard her whimpering late into the night.

(Fifty-seven years later Norwegian divers found and recovered the trawler's bell. The bell, although crushed, is still clearly engraved Laforey 1949. In 2011 with my late brother's family and over one hundred families and fishermen I attended the deeply moving memorial service of the bell's return to Grimsby. The bell is on display in the Fisherman's Chapel in Duncombe Street, Grimsby, alongside a list of the men who lost their lives on that day.)

With our house almost empty, my father retired in April 1958 aged 67. He had completed fifty-one years as a seaman visiting almost every known continent. If he had worked on a shore job - in a bank, for instance, or in an engineering works - he might have been presented with a gold watch or carriage clock besides a liveable pension.

At a loss without a rolling deck under his feet, and short of money with no reasonable pension to draw on, he took a part-time job, doing what he knew best and maintaining the heating boiler in the Methodist Chapel next door but one. Not to be outdone our mother volunteered to clean the chapel and polish the pews, whether to be near Dad or 'Him upstairs' I do not know!

In their retirement years, it was strange to hear them call each other Mam and Dad instead of Liz and Jim. I think they were happy to be together like normal pensioners should be as they had shown on a visit to Pat and me in Brighton.

But hardship and old age was taking its toll on both my parents. Unknown to anyone Mam was self-treating a weeping abscess under her left armpit and breast. My sister Doreen caught her one morning bathing it over the back kitchen sink. She and my other sisters immediately took Mam to the doctors. She had several months of radiation treatment that seemed to abate the tumour temporarily, but cancer got the better of her. My mother died in August 1963 aged 69.

My father was crippled with a severe stroke and died six years later. In his last years he was a pathetic figure, unable to talk or use his right arm or walk steadily. Neither of my parents deserved such indignity in their twilight years.

-3-
War, School and Castor Oil

World War II was in its second year when, aged five, I started my first day at school at South Parade Primary, only a five minute walk from home. My mother hugged and kissed me and put a penny for school milk into my hand, with a stern warning not to lose it. My twin sisters were told to look after me before mother watched us go from the front garden, with our gas masks slung over our shoulders. A sickly taste of the castor oil and orange juice she'd dosed me with lingered at the back of my throat as I held hands with my sisters to cross the cinder track.

At the infants school we had to address the women teachers as Miss and the men as Sir. That first day my teacher Miss Pringle told the class, "If you want to go to the toilet, you raise your hand and say, Please, Miss, may I leave the room?"

Each day she made sure we drank every drop by examining each bottle before we put the empties back in the milk crate. Some days we would play in the sandpit hoping to build the best sandcastle, or build houses with wooden blocks that bore the letters of the alphabet. While in the playground we had to wear a coloured band around our body. To warn us playtime was over one teacher rang a bell as a signal for us form a straight line in our colour group before returning to the classroom.

My first teacher Miss Pringle had a kindly smile and spoke softly like my Aunt Emily; perhaps that is why I liked her. Each morning she played the piano at morning assembly and we all sang 'All Things Bright and Beautiful,' my favourite tune when I sang at Sunday school.

One morning another much older teacher came into our classroom holding a ruler. It was our head mistress Miss B, who wore thick-framed spectacles. She was bigger than Miss Pringle and spoke louder and with more authority. I can picture her as she stood there, gigantic, in front of the teacher's desk; her hair in a bun spiked with what looked like knitting needles, in black belted jacket and heavy black shoes.

"Good morning, children!"

With hands on hips, she stared around the classroom at our upturned faces. The classroom fell silent.

"Good morning, children!" she repeated, even more loudly.

We found our voices and chorused, "Good morning, Miss."

Miss B came over to me at the big table and told me to sit at a two-seater desk in the front of the class. I sat next to a girl with curly white hair whose name was Pat. We became good friends while we were in the infants, and would leave school together as Pat lived in the next street to me.

The classroom was large enough to hold many children, two to a desk, I can't remember exactly how many, probably up to forty. There was a large wooden table on one side of the room and many double-desks with seats in neat rows. The windows that overlooked the cinder track were large and square and swivelled from the centre. Around the walls were other children's drawings, paintings, posters of the alphabet and numbers in various colours. As we went through season to season, the flowers in vases on the window sills changed to suit. I remember daffodils, pussy willow and sticky-buds from the horse chestnut tree. Lessons in spelling at school were an agony of frustration for me as was stringing a few words together.

When the school doctor visited to examine and immunise us, he found that I had a gummy ear infection and referred me to the hospital. I often suffered with earache and runny ears, and

Mam would put a drop of warm olive oil in my ears and plug them with cotton wool and would send me on my way. On visiting the hospital, they found I had an abscess or something. A doctor stuck a needle inside my ear, promising it wouldn't hurt.

"Your screams were loud enough to wake the dead," reported Irene.

Waking up one morning for school I found my eyelids stuck. I thought I had gone blind and woke Doreen and Pauline, Brenda and my brother Bernard with my yells. (We shared a bedroom.) Mother rushed me across the road to the hospital emergency department. The nurse told her an eye infection had gummed them together. She wrapped lint around a spoon and dipped it in hot water before holding it on my eyes to melt the gum.

"It won't hurt, ducky," she said.

She was the second liar I had met in that hospital. I only stopped screaming when I found I had not gone blind after all. I was sent home wearing an eye patch and with two days off school.

One day during those first weeks at school I asked to leave the room. Instead of going to the cloakroom, I ran home to my mother, who quickly dragged me back by the coat collar, her hands still wet with soapsuds. She was extremely cross, especially as she had to apologise to the headmistress, who was not such a likeable person, it would seem. Besides that, I had interrupted my mother while she was in the thick of doing the washing.

Miss B took me back to my classroom, but not before giving me a rap on the knuckles of each hand with a wooden ruler. My punishment was not only for leaving school without permission, but also without my gas mask. Afterwards, Miss B always seemed to have it in for me. My moment of escape did not end there. When I returned home from school that same day, escorted by my two sisters, Mam gave me a spank on the bottom with her slipper, a weapon we all felt at some stage in our growing up. I stayed in the bedroom for the rest of the day with pencil and paper to practise the Alphabet. My term 'in the dog house' as Doreen called it ended with the distinct wail of 'Moaning Minnie,' the air-raid siren and a dash to the bomb shelter in our back garden.

It's an understatement to say school was a nightmare for me. I hated the discipline. I wanted to be free, out in the playground or on the cinder track. I only liked playing ball games and skipping around the maypole in the playground. Anything but sitting, bored, at my desk. Each morning Miss Pringle called the register, where we answered 'Here' to our names. This was followed by a daily gas-mask drill and a walk to the air-raid shelter.

My gas mask was the ugly black rubber type with a Perspex window and a bulky filter that resembled a pig's snout. I envied the children who carried the red 'Mickey Mouse' type gas masks, with its big eyes and ears. Nonetheless, they all had the same nauseous smell of rubber and a visor soon fogged up by anxious breathing. As the war raged on, the Luftwaffe came in waves and the air raids became more regular.

On one horrendous air raid our school was bombed, luckily in July during the summer holidays. It was the summer of 1943 when Grimsby experienced one of its worst-ever bombings. With sirens blurting out their warning, still in my pyjamas, my four sisters and I, wrapped in our blankets, traipsed behind Mam to the communal shelter at the corner of the street. Our own Anderson shelter was flooded more often than not especially with the heavy rainfalls that summer.

The night-sky was a latticework of searchlights criss-crossing each other as they sought to pinpoint the German intruders. Bernard stopped and pointed skyward so we could see a plane lit up in the beams. Our mother soon dragged me inside the shelter, as the orchestral drone of enemy planes came closer and the symbolic crump-crump of our anti-aircraft guns retaliated. We trembled with fear as we huddled down in our blankets like frightened mice. There were several tremendous ear-shattering explosions, followed by a nerve-racking shudder and then darkness.

For a while it was pitch black as the shelter's lights went out. Mr Treacher came, our Air Raid Warden, and shone his flashlight around to check if everyone was all right. By then there were more flashlights lit, and thankfully there were no physical casualties as far as I can remember. The all-clear siren sounded and we all returned to our homes in the strange orange glow of the raid's aftermath, a scene we became used to in the following years.

The following morning revealed the damage after a savage air raid across the West Marsh. Dixons Paper Mill was aglow with incendiary bombs and several houses by the River Freshney in Haven Terrace had been demolished. The streets reeked with the acrid stench of burning wood and cordite that seemed to last forever. On that particular night, several people in the town were killed, including a school friend of my twin sisters and his parents.

So it was not the hospital that had been bombed, as we had first thought, but our school, South Parade. At the time, I had not realised the dangers my teachers faced with their nightly task of fire duty. Luckily no one was injured or killed during the school's bombing. My hopes of an extended holiday were short lived, as I soon found out. We would be attending another school until South Parade was repaired.

The twenty minute walk to Victoria Street School led us over the Corporation Bridge to where, earlier in the war, Victoria Street itself had been severely bombed, turning shops and houses into blackened naked shells. As we walked past the bombed sites, we were warned not to collect shrapnel – the metal fragments – because they might be a butterfly bomb. Those were unusual small winged bombs, somehow attractive, but deadly to touch.

That first day as we walked to Victoria Street School I was amazed by the sight of the Corporation Road Bridge lifting up to let a ship pass through. I had never been this far away from home before, and it became something of an adventure to watch for different ships along the docksides and, in the distance, the Grimsby Dock Tower rising high above everything else.

Later that year on returning to South Parade School after its repairs, I had a new teacher, Miss Kemp. She noted my good drawing skills, but was bewildered by my inability to grasp the simplest spelling or the basics in arithmetic. Slowly and laboriously with her help I learned the two times table, the alphabet and spelling words. She had the class chanting the alphabet in a sing-song rhythm along with thirty odd other infants.

Although I also enjoyed sport, in those early two years of school my favourite subjects were drawing, crayoning and painting. Often my pictures were displayed on the classroom wall.

"You must take after your brother Jimmy," Mam said. He was clever and good at art. But you must do more reading, my lad."

Inevitably, for Christmas, instead of toy cars and aeroplanes I got colouring books; that year I also got a well-worn copy of *The Swiss Family Robinson.*

Although my mother herself didn't attend church, she made sure that we went every Sunday at Methodist Church next door but one to our house. My Sunday school teachers Miss Pringle and Miss Nelson told us Bible stories and played the piano as we sang 'We Plough the Fields and Scatter' during the Harvest Festival. At the end of the year if your attendance card was full with the blue stars stamped by the teacher on your attendance card you received a prize, usually a book.

In our echoing School Hall, the headmaster was more like a police officer than a teacher, and a mean hand with the cane. Still only eight, I found the junior classrooms more daunting than the infants' - no toys, no sandpit and no nursery pictures pinned to the walls.

Instead there were times tables and letters of the alphabet forming a frieze around the room. My early weakness at figures and spelling was aggravated when I entered the boys' school following my sisters' departure for Armstrong Street, the senior school. Thoughts of the cane disturbed me, yet I still could not master those basic elements. Therefore I found it heavy-going for my first two years, especially as the emphasis was on arithmetic in our build-up to the eleven plus entrance examination.

Fortunately, school was not all work. Popular playtime and after-school games included cigarette cards. Inside packets of popular cigarettes were collectable pictures of the famous: sportsmen like footballers Frank Swift and Stanley Matthews; cricketers Norman Yardley and Bill Edrich and such film stars as Errol Flynn and Humphrey Bogart. Sometimes the cards featured motor vehicles and trains. By collecting and swapping the cards you could make up sets. Doreen, a proper tomboy was above average at winning these cards and had a shoebox full.

We would stand them up against a wall or road -curb, while kneeling a few feet away and take turns flicking a card at them. Any knocked down became yours. This was a highly competitive game that sometimes ended in a fight.

As cigarette cards became scarcer, we would flick our school milk bottle tops instead. With a hole for the straw, they were easy to hang on a length of string hooked to my belt or hung around my neck. My sister Pauline used them to make pom-poms or bobbles for the woollen hats and tea cosies she knitted.

At the start of autumn 'conkers' was another competitive game we played using nuts from the horse chestnut tree. We'd go in gangs down Littlefield Lane and around the cricket field to find the best crop. Once a good tree was located, we'd throw a heavy piece of branch up to knock the conkers down. This was something else Doreen excelled at, and she showed me how to drill a hole through the conker with a meat skewer and then thread them on a length of string.

While your opponent stood holding his or her conker at arm's length on the end of the string, you'd whack theirs with yours, trying to break it. The aim of the game was to make yours a 'oner' or 'twoer' or more dependent on how many your conker could break.

Doreen had all the secrets and showed me what to do. She soaked them in vinegar overnight, then baked them briefly in the oven. Once I had a 'fifteener' before it got shattered.

The winter before the war ended I found Nina, our cat, floating in our flooded Anderson shelter. I ran inside the house crying for Mam, who hooked out her lifeless form using the garden rake. We gave her a tearful burial under the lilac tree, Nina's favourite perch. We missed her - the house didn't seem the same without her bringing birds and mice to the back doorstep. However, my Mam was determined she was not having another cat and kept putting off my requests for a replacement.

One of my happiest memories is when Uncle Jim and Aunt Lilly visited us soon after my ninth birthday. They handed me a cardboard box and inside was a six-week old puppy.

"He was the brightest and friendliest in the litter," said Aunt Lilly, "so we named him Chum."

As I picked Chum up he licked my face – the start of a long and happy friendship. My mother knew all along that Uncle Jim had a dog for me and that was the best kept secret of the war. Chum was a cross-breed, his father a Border collie and his mother Sally Uncle Jim's Springer spaniel. He was all black, except for white patches on his chest, the top of his nose and his forepaws.

As Chum grew older, he grew feathery chaps on the backs of his legs like a spaniel and a long wispy tail. From day one he had us all in stitches with his antics as he plodded after me, stumbling over the rag rugs and tripping over the back doorstep. Although she was fond of Chum, Mam wouldn't allow him upstairs. Every night he watched me climbing the stairs and come morning he would lie in wait on his bed of old coats or inside a tea chest, his makeshift kennel. Sometimes I'd find him waiting for me with his head resting on the first stair-tread.

Chum was a quick learner, and by the time he was six months old we were playing many games together. Each day after breakfast, Mam let me play games with him in the garden before I left for school. I taught him to sit, shake hands when I said hello and stay while I hid, then whistled for him to track me down or find a ball at the command 'seek'. Uncle Jim showed me how to train him.

"You must reward him, Pete. If he gets it right, always have a biscuit in your pocket and give him a piece."

If it was a nice day my mother tied him to a length of old clothes–line to our lilac tree while I was at school. That gave him a fair run of the back garden. As we both grew older, she would let me take Chum out for walks tied to a string lead. We would run across the cinder track and walk along the banks of the River Freshney.

When I could trust him not to run off, I'd let go and throw a branch into the river. At first, he just stood there and barked, then he'd run along the bank following the river's flow. Finally he'd pluck up his courage and dive into the water, retrieve the stick, jump out and place it at my feet. Panting, with his pink tongue lolling to one side, Chum would look up at me with anxious amber eyes. His tail swishing the ground, he would let out a whimper, then pirouette excitedly on his back legs, eager for more.

On his third birthday he was run over by a lorry and died. I buried him alongside Nina under the lilac tree.

At 3pm on Tuesday 8th May 1945, Winston Churchill's voice came over the radio. Our mother hushed us all into silence as we all listened to his broadcast.

"The war in Europe is over. Germany has surrendered."

Mam burst into tears of happiness, hugging me and my four sisters. Almost immediately, the victory celebrations began. We ran into the street where everyone went crazy, singing, dancing, kissing and hugging friends and strangers. Flags were flying and bunting was strung across the street from house to house. Church-bells were ringing, vehicles honking their horns and from the nearby docks came the long dull hoot–hoot of ships' foghorns.

My best pal David, who lived only a few doors away, came running around to tell me that his brother Kenny would be coming home. David's family were already stringing flags and bunting around the front of their house. Kenny had endured four years in a German prisoner of war camp, not knowing he had lost his brother Leslie, who had fought in the desert campaign against Rommel at the battle for El Alamein.

All the families in Yarborough Street contributed what they could afford to make the street party that followed a success for the children. Trestle tables and chairs were set out along the street. All around me were happy faces smeared with jam and jelly. Each of us was given a brown paper bag with a stick of liquorice to dip into lemon sherbet, boiled-sweets, an apple and orange, and a balloon.

David and I got a toy parachute each with caps (the kind you put in a toy gun) to put in its 'bomb.' When I threw it up, the parachute sailed down and hit the pavement with a bang loud enough to make us jump. I suppose we were all still a little war-shocked.

After the street party, we were all marched in an orderly file to the Queen's Cinema to see George Formby in 'Get Cracking,' followed by cartoons.

That night, the cinder track was jam-packed with civilians and service personnel in uniform: Army, Navy, Air Force, police constables and hospital staff from across the street. A carnival atmosphere ensued and the finale of the day was the victory bonfire. From surrounding streets everyone brought their old furniture and rubbish and piled it up. The highlight was the burning of an effigy of Hitler strung up and dangling from the cinder track's sycamore tree.

Before dusk fell, he was tied to an old chair set on top of the bonfire and lit to chants of "Burn! Burn! Burn!" We cheered as the fire spluttered around his figure and sang and danced as the flames consumed him.

Three months later on 6th August 1945, the first atom bomb was dropped on Hiroshima and another on Nagasaki three days later. The Japanese finally surrendered on 14th August 1945 and VJ celebrations began.

Now the Second World War was finally over.

-4-

1945 and All That

To a greater extent than other Grimsby suburbs the West Marsh was a proud and thriving community. In its heyday it was a unique shopping area with Corporation Road the main thoroughfare. Most of the residential streets including Yarborough Street ran more or less at right angles to its left and right. Furthermore the West Marsh was divided by the River Freshney, which flowed eastwards down from the Lincolnshire Wolds and meandered through the West Marsh, the Boulevard (the Duke of York Gardens) and into the River Head.

We were lucky as children to have tennis courts, a bowling green, a play area with slides, roundabouts and swings and a football pitch at the Boulevard. In addition, the Grimsby General Hospital was nearby, as were churches, schools, public houses and workingmen's clubs and picture houses.

Yarborough Street where I grew up had activities of its own, with horses and carts seen daily hauling sacks of coal or beer barrels for the Jubilee Working Men's Club and Kingies, the corner public house. Nor was it unusual to see milkmen, gypsy hawkers, rag and bone men and police constables on their daily rounds. We knew nearly everyone in the street, at least by sight if not by reputation, and respected most.

The wider community stretched further left and right. To include children from nearby streets we formed teams on the cinder track to play against each other, mostly football and cricket. There would be dares as to who could climb the sycamore tree the fastest and highest or competitions to catch the most fish from the River Head or the River Freshney. We found so much to do, mainly in order to take our minds off the worries of the war years.

After five years of wartime turmoil and blackouts it gave me a strange excitement when the street lamps were relit. Before the war I was too young to remember them. The pale pools of light they cast enabled us to play out longer when winter loomed. After school and my evening meal my mother let me join in the street games, hide and seek, cricket and football with my pals. My older twin sisters joined other girls, skipping and chanting rhymes or hopscotch.

What I enjoyed most was kick-ball-fly, especially if it was my turn to kick the ball and hide. I wasn't so thrilled when it was my turn to fetch the ball while the others hid behind walls, down passages or among front garden bushes.

The hours after school passed quickly and before I knew it, it was 8 o'clock and time to go home in answer to my mother's call. It was reassuring to know that there would be no 'Moaning Minnie' to wake us in the dead of the night.

At weekends I played football and cricket almost all day on the cinder track at the bottom of our street. This open area of ground, almost the size of a football pitch, was set between South Parade School, the River Freshney and the general hospital, with sycamore and oak trees around its perimeter. Its surface of crushed cinders with hardly a blade of grass left us vulnerable to grazes and bruises.

Furthermore, we were forever repairing our leather footballs due to the cinder track's abrasive surface as well as our boots and plimsolls. But it seemed our elbows and knees came off worse. Often I would arrive home grazed, bloody and black from the cinder track's dust.

The older gang members arranged matches against other street gangs. At first, there were no strict rules or number of players as we bundled our coats for goalposts. One day there was a big match so we set out a rough pitch using sand from the sandbags around the street's now disused air raid shelter, where not too long ago we had huddled like frightened mice, waiting for death!

Our games often drew the attention of the local police constable, known as Ginger. One time standing by his police box, he seemed to be taking a more than normal interest. He was a huge man with a bushy ginger moustache that seemed to hinge with his sideburns as he spoke. With his cape neatly folded over one shoulder he was watching us; and we were watching him.

Finally he took off his helmet and bicycle clips and leant his bicycle against the sycamore tree. He strode towards us, looming larger as he drew closer. He blew his whistle and we were about to scarper, thinking we were in trouble for taking the sandbags.

"Here," he said, smiling, "I'll referee you laddies and while I'm at it I'll explain a few rules. Remember, when you play any sport it's only fair to play by the rules."

Once he was satisfied we knew what we were doing, he got on his bike and pedalled away, whistling.

The cinder track, besides its use as a sports ground, was a considerable asset to our community. Here we had built our bonfires following the end of World War 2 for VE and VJ celebrations. For years after we held our Guy Fawkes festivities there; it became a yearly ritual for all the families in the surrounding streets. When I was older, I would join in raids on the bonfires in nearby streets bonfires, with two of our gang left behind to guard our own. Come the big night when any families with young children would gather round and the adults would set off their fireworks.

We would roast potatoes in the dying embers and the following day the remains would still be smouldering. I would dash out before going to school to rake the ashes for any coins that might have been lost inside old couches and the like.

When I was eleven, being a member of a street gang was a big thing. Mainly there were seven of us: myself, Derek, David, Brian, Eric, Barry and Bernard.

One of our gang came up with another prank this time to play on the neighbours we didn't like. During the dark autumnal nights we exchanged their front garden gates by lifting them from their hinge-pins. This not only rankled the house owners, but the postman, newspaper boy and especially if the gates had the house number on. Tying tin cans to front door handles, we'd bang on the door and hide behind walls or gardens, close enough to hear the disgruntled house-owner.

"If I catch you bloody lot, you'll be in for it."

Our forays got more daring as one of our gang found out that our street's grocery store stocked their van the night before an early morning delivery. I wasn't too fond of this idea, as my mother shopped there, but as a gang member I couldn't back out. I didn't relish the idea of being caught and spending time in a remand home. Worse still, if my Mam found out it would be more than a slipper slapping. The 'raid' turned out to be a dare more than anything. You couldn't call it a break-in because the garage door was never locked. Furthermore, we didn't take anything away.

We sat in the van helping ourselves to tinned fruit and Carnation milk, something I had never tasted before then. Now every time I open a tin of Carnation milk those innocent naughty boy escapades come guiltily flooding back. We ended that one night of petty pilfering by sharing a bottle of lemonade, dumping the empty in a neighbouring dustbin. We never left any clues.

Derek was the oldest, and for an eleven year old the brainiest in our gang. He was clever at making things work and even repaired a wireless for our clubhouse in later years. Besides his interest in electronics, he played the violin, taking lessons half-heartedly every afternoon after school, while his younger sister Rhonda practised the piano.

Although Derek lived in the same street as ours, his home was posh. The family had a bath with hot running water and carpets and fine furniture as well as the piano. I had seen a piano before at my Aunt Emily's house as she played it sometimes. Derek's was different, a pianola with a music roll inside. Though it looked like a piano you played this instrument's selection of tunes by pressing down on the foot pedal. No need to use the keyboard. As both Derek's parents worked we often had the run of the house.

Derek was always fascinated by things electrical and once unscrewed the light switch cover while we were playing blind man's bluff. With a scarf over my eyes I was feeling my way around the walls in the back kitchen and got an almighty shock when I touched the exposed socket. The pain shot down to my feet, knocking me to the floor. Somehow, his father got to know what we were up to and banned us from his house.

After tea, our evening meal, we would meet in Derek's garden shed to plan our evening's activity. It's amazing what antics young boys can get up to. Soon after dark we would sneak a packet of Woodbines through a cracked windowpane from Gales Newsagent and for the first time I tried smoking. That didn't last long as after the third raid they fixed plywood over the crack.

The winter of 1946–47 brought two major hardships: bread was rationed for the first time and coke and coal were in short supply and the nearby-bombed buildings were already stripped of their wood doors, staircases and window frames. I would go out with my twin sister Doreen and my best friends David and Eric and root around the bombed buildings. We would come home reeking of old plasterboards and soot.

Desperate for wood, we were unaware of how dangerous those buildings were or that, should a policeman catch us 'looting', it could have meant a term in the remand home – a feared institution of correction.

Mother hushed as the BBC news came over the wireless.

"Today Aneurin Bevan, the Minister of Labour, has passed the National Insurance Act in Parliament."

What this meant was beyond me and it seemed that even my mother couldn't understand exactly how the benefits would help her. However, that news was the birth of the National Health Service.

In January 1947 there was a ferocious snowstorm. Traffic vanished and everything came to a standstill as snow seemed to fall endlessly. At the same time the Labour Government nationalised the ailing coal industry. The weather remained bitterly cold for weeks with snow above the windowsills. Snowdrifts were 5ft deep and 2ft icicles hung like stalactites from roof gutters and windows frames. There were nationwide power cuts and as well as restrictions on the electricity supply coal was still in short supply.

The council cleared the streets, which meant lorry loads of snow being dumped on the cinder track. Within a week it began to resemble the Swiss Alps, and we had enormous fun building igloos and ski slopes for our sledges. One afternoon after school I saw Eric Broadly trying to skate in his hob-nailed boots on the

River Freshney. It was a strange but beautiful scene to see the river and the willow-trees sparkling with frost.

On the way home from school, we sucked icicles broken off from house window-sills, and engaged in snowball fights, sometimes splattering the trams as they trundled by. Once I was chased down Freshney Street by a conductor. He soon gave up running after me as the road surface was like glass. That same day after tea, several of us made a huge snowball, at least six-feet across by rolling it around the school playground.

One of the gang had a brainwave and shouted, "Let's stuff it inside the doorway of the woodwork classroom."

By the following morning it had frozen solid and it took hard digging by the teachers to remove it using spades and picks. Feeling guilty, we joined them.

Because there was no let-up in the wintry cold and the shortage of coal my mother gave my sister Doreen enough money to hire a handcart and to pay for three sacks of coke. Wrapped like Scott facing Antarctica, I walked with my twin sisters and my two best friends to get two long-handled flat carts from Bannister's and pushed our way along frozen streets to the Gas-Works. We left home at 7am to avoid the heavy traffic of trolley buses and motor vehicles in Victoria Street ('Top Town.') This was the posh shopping area in Grimsby with banks, building societies, huge department stores, the Gaumont Cinema and restaurants.

The queue at the coke-house was endless, mainly women and children wrapped in headscarves and balaclavas revealing pink dripping noses as they stamped 'wellied' feet and blew on raw fingers. There was every kind of conveyance from prams to homemade trolley carts, anything with wheels that would carry away coke to keep their homes warm.

I had asked Mam where the gas works were where the coke was made.

"You can't miss it," she said. "Just follow the smell!"

She was right and it was nauseating, like rotten eggs. I helped holding the sack under the chute while a coke-worker pulled a lever to release the measured amount with sudden whoosh followed by a cloud of black dust until the sack was full.

We loaded six or eight sacks and arrived home two or three hours later frozen to the core, noses pink and an icicle of frozen snot from nose to balaclava. Our reward – besides a warm living room – was pocket money enough to go to the cinema for Saturday's 'tuppenny rush' matinee with enough left over for a penny packet of broken biscuits from the biscuit woman in Somersby Street.

We were lucky that within a few minutes walking distance from our house - south, east, west and north - we had a choice of four cinemas: the Rex on Corporation Road, Queen's in Alexander Road, the Chantry (bug-hut) and the Savoy in Victoria Street, which was the largest. When we were not able to go to the coke-house for our pocket money we reverted, in desperation, to pilfering. Not thinking then that this was an offence, we took empty beer and lemonade bottles from the rear of the Jubilee Working Men's Club.

This petty theft allowed us sufficient cash to go to the Saturday matinee. My claim that we were robbing the rich to feed the poor soon ended. One Friday night a burly barman saw us from the men's urinal. We were too fast for him, still in the throes of doing up his trousers and forced to dodge the broken bottles we dropped while evading him.

The Savoy cinema was where I first saw Larry 'Buster' Crabbe, an American Olympic swimming champion who starred as Flash Gordon in 'A Trip to Mars.' My all-time favourite, however, was Johnny Weissmuller as Tarzan, another US Olympic swimmer and winner of five gold medals. I envied his African adventures and claimed one day I would go there. He thumped his chest like a gorilla, yelling 'Umgawa!' while swinging from tree to tree to rescue Jane from the perils of a giant crocodile. As time went on I found him disappointing when he appeared in a safari suit as Jungle Jim.

During these childhood fantasies, my other idols were Errol Flynn as Captain Blood or Robin Hood, Roy Rodgers and Hopalong Cassidy. When our gang left the cinema, we would re-enact the exploits of our idols, tight-roping and climbing walls, jumping fences among our street back-passage ways and climbing trees in the boulevard. During our re-enactments, there would always be an argument, sometimes leading to a fight, as to who would be the hero. More often than not we would all end up with cuts and bruises from someone's sword or bows and arrows.

The summers were hot and it hardly ever rained... or so we all like to remember. With that dreadful winter behind us that summer of '47 was full of wonder and excitement, and my first long journey without my mother (except for the times that I stayed at Uncle Jim's on Louth Road.) Mam waved me off with a sixpenny-piece in my pocket, a bottle of cold tea and a wedge of jam sandwiches. I heard her yelling down the street to Doreen and Pauline, "Look after Pete."

Mother had given Doreen our train fare to 'Meggies,' a local name for Cleethorpes, Grimsby's seaside town. The resort was a huge favourite with day-trippers from the Midlands - Sheffield, Leeds and Nottingham. I boarded the train with the twins and my best pal David for my first real adventure. After the train left the station, my sister Doreen pulled a leather strap to let the window slide down and poked out her head.

With her blonde hair blowing in the breeze, Doreen beckoned me to join her.

"Come on, our Pete; come on, Dave. Take a look."

The wind grabbed at my hair and both David and I screamed with delight. Even more exciting was the sight of the train as it curved around bends and my first glimpse of the powerful engine. I soon pulled my head back when a cloud of smoke filled my lungs, making me cough and splutter. Pauline was not as adventurous as her twin and lifted her eyes from her book to tell Doreen to close the window. The ticket collector, tall and skinny in his dark blue uniform and peaked hat, slid open the door and warned us to behave and not to open the windows.

Only then did I hear for the first time the wheels singing, clickety-click, clickety-click, as the train gathered speed. Even today with all the modern technology, that same old song has never changed its tune and I still get a buzz, travelling by train. Train journeys are relaxing and it is thrill to whiz by other villages and towns through the ever-changing countryside.

Before reaching Cleethorpes, we passed the fish docks and the smoke houses, where cod and herring were processed. Anyone visiting Grimsby by train knew without doubt when they had arrived by the fishy aroma. Within minutes, the docks were left behind and the scenery changed to row upon row of terraced houses like ours. Pauline mentioned that in one of those houses our mother was born.

The train came to a stop at a halt near to Blundell Park. I knew then we were in Cleethorpes, as that's the home ground of Grimsby Town's football team, the Mariners. It was a well-known fact in Grimsby that when the Mariners played 'at home,' they were really 'playing away' as their home ground is in Cleethorpes.

We were not the only visitors to Cleethorpes, as we soon found out. The promenade and the beach were crowded with hundreds of them, few of whom sounded anything like us. We could have been anywhere in the world, but that is what Cleethorpes is noted for, holidaymakers and day-trippers. They came from, Leeds, Nottingham and Sheffield and talked with the queerest accents...

"This is reet good, in't, our lass?"

"Gis another tanner!"

"Tek tha shoes off, or yer'll be gettin' wet through."

"Ey up! How's tha doin, young 'un?"

They might have been English, but they definitely sounded foreign to me.

We had to walk half a mile to the beach the first time I saw the sea. With my sandshoes slung around my neck and my short trousers rolled up, I followed my sisters, who had tucked their dresses up into their knickers. None of us had bathing suits with us, so swimming was not an option but we did the next best thing.

I left my trousers on the dry sand with my sisters' dresses and we had a great time splashing in and out the shallow pools around the wave breakers. Sometimes there'd be small crabs trying to burrow away to hide by scooping the sand around them. We were enjoying ourselves so much we forgot about the tide coming in and almost lost our clothes before the fearless Doreen waded in and rescued them before they floated out of reach. I could only imagine, with some trepidation, what Mam might do if she ever got to know about this escapade.

To dry out we wandered through Wonderland, a vast indoor fairground, or watched day-trippers roaming the amusement arcades. Games spewed out loads of halfpennies when a coin was inserted at the right moment and other machines where you put in your money and a silver ball popped up. Flick the lever and it would hurtle round before it mysteriously disappeared along with your money. You could go out on the Cleethorpes boating lake at sixpence for half hour. David and I would hire a skiff, the sleekest boat on the water, and have great fun with the sculls, until the loudspeaker announced, "Come in, 49, your number is up."

There was no end to the enjoyment to be had at Cleethorpes, but at a cost when money was hard to come by. Sometimes if we spent our return fare, we faced a long walk home.

-5-
Out and About

The seasons during my childhood seemed to dominate our every action, where we went and ruling our lives. From when I was twelve to fifteen what mainly comes to mind is football and fishing, although there were many other good things to do in those days – the kind of things boys got up to, that is!

At secondary school, to become a member of the school gang, I had to pass a few tests; not schoolroom tests, but gang dares. First I had to carve my initials on the inside lid of my desk, knowing if caught it meant three strokes of the cane. The biggest and boldest dare was to scale the school's six-foot high wall and bring back a tuppenny loaf of bread from the bakery next door. This was the best dare as I got a share of the crust.

Passing all the tests I became a member of the gang and by then was conditioned for all kinds of mischief. Yet none of us ever surrendered completely to becoming ruffians like some of the poorer kids in the school, who invariably ended up in Borstal (a type of youth detention centre.)

As we got older, we ventured further away from the hustle and bustle of town life and no longer played among the bombed out buildings. None of us had bicycles until later on, although my best pal David had a tricycle when he was an infant. I only learnt to ride my sister's bike when I was ten, and she soon took it away from me because I kept falling off.

With the gang of David, Brian, Barry, Derek, Bernard and Eric I roamed the nearby countryside. These expeditions were so different from the walks I had been on with my sisters.

Sometimes we hiked to Hewitt's Wood down Peak's Lane hunting rabbits or bird nesting. There was no one to bother us as we tramped over fields or raided apple and pear orchards...

On those outings, we would take a pop at squirrels, crows and rooks with our catapults. I can't remember us hitting any squirrels, I am pleased to say; only the occasional crow. I know it sounds cruel, but I suppose that is what boys did then. Barry, the oldest gang member, had a good collection of eggs in a box padded with cotton wool.

In the spring when we went bird nesting he would remind us to take one egg only, and only if there were three or more in the nest. Myself, I wasn't interested in 'egging' - fishing was what I liked best. Frog spawning was another popular pastime. What fun it was to watch the tadpoles hatch into frogs. The most prized trophy was a newt. I never did catch one and envied those who had.

Getting to Bradley Woods, one of the prettiest picnic spots in that part of Lincolnshire, was a boring four-mile walk through housing estates. In spring, the lane would be in full bloom with horse chestnut, flowering into 'sticky-buds,' pussy-willow and ash and beech regaining their seasonal lustre. The woodlands hosted an ocean of bluebells and necklaces of daffodils, a welcoming glow below hazel, birch and oak.

The best and most fearless climber by far was Eric, until he broke his arm falling off his family's pigeon shed. Eric could climb a tree like a monkey and it was he who usually tied on our 'Tarzan' rope. We'd strip off our shirts and, bare-chested, take turns to swing across, yodelling like the jungle boy, and pretending river below was infested with crocodiles.

As the day wore on, scratched and with mud up to our armpits, we would make our way home, but never before picking bunches of wild foxgloves, bluebells, sprigs of pussy willow with white furry buds and horse chestnut sticky-buds about to flower. These bouquets took some of the sting out of my Mam's temper when she saw me in muddy shirt, scuffed shoes and ragged trousers.

Sometimes with the gang, I would explore the muddy creeks near Grimsby Docks or by the Humber Bank. The creeks were formed by the rise and fall of the incoming tide and here I first tried my hand at blob-line fishing. With four hooks tied at intervals along the line, each baited with a piece of cod's head, I would hurl the weighted line out into the creek. I always brought home something from eels to dabs, but my mother would throw them into the pigswill bin. She never gave me any encouragement – perhaps for good reason, a warning to stay away from docks.

There was one scary moment when I was almost cut off by the incoming tide. We'd been fishing on the mud flats with the gang and before I realised it the incoming water had encircled me and I was stranded on the mud bank. Barry threw me his rope to haul me back and, plucking up courage, I waded knee-deep in slime and mud to shore. With every step a gaseous odour puffed out of the mud, making me nauseous as it sucked my feet. A man shouted at us from the jetty.

"Get yer sens out thar, the tide's coming in, you silly little buggers!"

He was telling me something I already knew. With a struggle I came out unscathed, though my jersey and trousers were splattered with the black, foul-smelling mud. As I rested on the bank I worried what Mam would do to me, especially when I realised I had lost a wellington in the mud. I didn't dare go back in for it and my blob-line fishing over the creeks ended then and there.

One day, word went round the school that a 'Blows' barge was off loading peanuts at the River Head and it wasn't long before the surrounding streets were empty of kids. The workers had knocked off for lunch and dozens of youngsters were already swimming across to Blows Wharf were the barge was tied alongside to bring back bags of peanuts.

For non-swimmers like me one gang had a rope to guide them from the quay to the barge. Not to be outdone, I asked David if his Dad had any rope in their shed. He ran home returning with a coil of twine that the trawlers' fishing nets were made of. Hardly a rope but better than nothing.

By then another member of our gang had arrived. Barry, a keen swimmer, was soon across and tied a much stronger rope to the barge. Using an old shopping bag, we filled it with peanuts. By then my sister Doreen had appeared and, being a good swimmer, helped us get more. After several trips across, I lost my grip on the line and sank to the bottom of the Haven like a stone. I could remember bubbles above me floating to the surface. I came around laid in the bottom of a sea-cadet's rowing boat - luckily they were practising as they often did in Alexandra Dock and dragged me out, vomiting dock water.

It is an understatement to say Mam was not best pleased at the sight of me as I stood in her clean back kitchen, shivering, while my clothes dripped dirty dock water. When Doreen told her what we had been up to there was an element of panic in my mother's fury. Doreen helped my Mam fill the zinc bath with kettles of water for her to wash me down.

By then I thought my Mam had calmed down, until Doreen told her the full story of how I was rescued. With a face like thunder she turned on me with her slipper and that was definitely a time you wanted to be elsewhere. I was sent up the wooden hill to my bedroom with no supper.

A few weeks after my tenth birthday and the following summer after the Second World War ended, I spent two weeks of my school holidays at the home of my Uncle Jim and Aunt Lily. Their two-story house, a big, white-painted semi, was the last house on Louth Road, and overlooked open farm fields on the outskirts of Grimsby. This was the first of three summer holidays with them. I don't think this was a punishment, but more to get me away from the street gang for a while. Certainly, it did the trick; but inflamed my desire in later years to seek greener pastures.

Uncle Jim and Aunt Lily had the front bedroom; my cousins Barbara and Pat were in the middle bedroom and little Jimmy and I shared the room next to the bathroom. Besides a bath, there was a toilet and washbasin exactly as pictured in the movies. From the bedroom window, I had never seen so many birds and white doves flitting in and out the trees. Each day Aunt Lilly would feed them scraps from the breakfast table. I was amazed how tame the blackbirds and doves were, eating out of her hand.

My aunt and uncle had a huge front garden and the back yard was busy with roaming chickens, ducks, geese and a pigsty. They also had a small orchard with apple, plum and pear trees and rows of green vegetables, potato and salad plants.

My Aunt followed the same daily routines as my mother, washing clothes, baking breads, fruit scones and her Yorkshire curds - the best I had tasted. Unlike our pantry, here there were jars of homemade jams, pickled fruit and slabs of cheeses. From the ceiling hung legs of ham, rabbits and pheasants.

I looked forward to my summer holidays at Louth Road with little Jimmy only a year younger than me, Barbara four, maybe five years older and Pat two years older. They would take little

Jimmy and I to pick brambles for a pie and mushrooms for our breakfast.

In the late afternoons, I would help my cousins feed the pigs. Uncle Jim did not come home from work until late from the docks because he would collect food leftovers as pig swill from the neighbouring houses.

My last summer holiday at Louth Road was after my twelfth birthday. I went reluctantly as by then I was more into angling. On my last week there Aunt Lilly said I had to go with little Jimmy to help out on the farm where my cousin worked as a land girl only two fields away. This was my first taste of real work for one shilling and sixpence a day, a good sum of money for me then.

Harvesting saw us forming hay stooks, hot, sticky and back-breaking work, but at the end of the day it was satisfying to see the fields dotted with hundreds of straw 'pyramids.'

Some of the other schoolchildren were older than me, including two girls, one of whom I took a liking to. She was almost two years older than me and our conversation was limited as she wasn't a bit interested in either fishing or football – only the players, it seemed.

On my last day at the farm, heavily scented with lavender, she wrapped her arms around my neck and kissed me full on the mouth. I thought she was playing a game until she said, "I'll see you at the back of the hayloft."

Then I couldn't help but remember what my cousin little Jimmy had warned me of.

"Stay clear of her, Pete. Mum won't be pleased if you've been up to something."

For that reason I left as usual with little Jimmy and with my virginity intact. We raced each other across the fields. The crackle of the corn-stubble under our feet frightened the skylarks, blackbirds and crows that chattered and flew every which way. Happily, crazily we crashed through thistles and leapt across dykes to see who would be home first, arriving panting, sunburned and happy, with scabbed knees and elbows.

Aunt Lilly laughed at us. I could only imagine what my mother would have thought. Before supper we always had a hot bath, and it was heaven to breathe in the steamy antiseptic aroma of Dettol.

Before bedtime Aunt Lily made us her homemade milkshake: lemonade and fresh cream whisked to a froth. Most nights in bed Jimmy and I played a game of I Spy or snakes and Ladders. Although Aunt Lily was not a church person, she made us kneel by the bed and say a thank you prayer.

Returning home after my two weeks in the country, I missed the bright summer mornings filled with the call of the cuckoo and the nightly tu-whit, tu-whoo of the owl and, most of all a real hot bath and what might have been after that first kiss!

It was Herbert, one of our neighbours, who first got David and me interested in the real ways of freshwater angling. He was a friendly, quiet chap who worked for Faulkner's Builders down our street as a labourer and gravedigger He showed us there were many choices of tackling up and how many lead shot to suit water depth, so the float would sit upright in the water. I soon found out there was more to this fishing lark than meets the eye.

After several visits to Chapman's pond in Cleethorpes and now confident with the fishing rod, Herbert took David and I to Killingholme Ponds near Immingham. The three of us boarded the electric tram to Immingham Docks, an exciting journey and our first time out of Grimsby. Arriving at Immingham Docks, we crossed the lock gates.

The rough track was tricky as David and I stumbled after Herbert carrying our tackle boxes. One slip and you could tumble down onto the mud flats or, if the tide was in, the Humber Estuary on our right. The foreshore was littered with flotsam; tins, bottles, driftwood and dead seagulls.

Herbert called a halt near the Immingham Creek and we all sat as he rolled another a fag by an old monument shaped like an obelisk. I scrubbed the muck of the inscription, hardly legible - something about Pilgrims. David read it out.

"From this creek the Pilgrim Fathers first left England in 1608, in search of religious liberty. This granite top stone was taken from Plymouth Rock, Massachusetts, and presented by the Sulgrave Institute of U.S.A. Engraved on it: 'This Memorial was erected by The Anglo-American Society of Hull in 1924.'

I asked Herbert, "Have we found a long lost treasure?"

"Nah! Grow up, lad," he said, lighting up. "It's been there years. Best be getting on now before the sun gets too high or the fish'll not bite."

All those years ago, the Pilgrim monument meant nothing to me, but it came back to haunt me decades later on a 'Fly-Drive' holiday in New England USA. I was with my wife Patricia and two friends in New Plymouth, Massachusetts where the Pilgrim Fathers had landed in 1620 after their historic sea journey in 1608 from Lincolnshire.

On one of my many visits to my sister Irene, I found that the monument had since been relocated from Killingholme Creek. It now stands in the park opposite St Andrew's Church, Immingham, in Lincolnshire, England.

My first glimpse of the Killingholme ponds was breath-taking with its mirrored surface reflecting the summer sky. Two swans glided in as we walked down the bank to the water's edge. With feet outstretched in the forward position, they made a perfect landing and paddled towards us inquisitively.

"Those buggers there will ruin our day," said Herbert.

He ran to the water's edge swinging his arms like a windmill to shoo them away. The cob stopped several feet away, stretched its neck and rose in protest almost out of the water, flapping his wings. He gave us one last piercing glare before settling down with his mate to paddle to the island of reeds in the middle of the pond, with a peek every now and again to check on our whereabouts.

Excited, I sat down on my tackle box and baited up, using a maggot for starters. With my float sitting some yards out, I threw a few more maggots in the water as a tantaliser to attract the prey, as Herbert had once shown me. The first thing he did was to light up his hand-rolled cigarette and the primus stove to brew a mug of tea.

David had aptly nicknamed him 'Belisha' after the new beacon (always lit up) on the pedestrian crossing in our street. Thus was an annoying feature so close to house windows with its orange globe blinking all through the night.

Herbert made us each a plate of baked beans with a fried egg on top to dip our bread in. Ah! This was the life. During the course of the day we all caught a variable array of roach, perch, bream and chub, none of substantial size. All too soon the sun dipped below the trees, our sign to leave and catch the last tram back to Grimsby.

Over the following weeks, we cycled to Tetney Lock ponds, North-Thorsby and finally to Brigg to fish the River Ancholme, a pretty river active with houseboats painted all colours of the rainbow. Of all the sports, I have participated in over the years angling is never far from my mind wherever I lay my head.

-6-

Long Trousers and Acne

After I failed the eleven plus exam in the following September I started at Armstrong Secondary Modern School. The school was a sprawling red brick building with square windows overlooking the playground. Mostly these windows were left open summer and winter, but there were times when they were hurriedly closed due to nauseating smells from the Pywipe fish offal factories and the acidic fumes drifting from the titanium plant on the nearby Humber Bank.

The change from women and men teachers to all men made a big difference to my view on life. That first morning in Armstrong's vast playground thronged with hundreds of boys much older and taller than me was a frightening sight. Most of the bigger boys wore long trousers, and it was a relief to me that most in my class still wore short trousers. Mam had insisted I must wear out my short trousers before they could be replaced with long.

"Money doesn't grow on trees, you know!"

A phrase often heard in our house.

Mr Horne, the school's headmaster, stood massive and god-like in his dark worsted suit, well over six-foot tall. Once a British army sergeant major, he was known to mete out caning with military precision. Although I never had the honour of facing him for such punishment, I had heard tales from those that had. In his office were several canes and after some deliberation and sizing the culprit up he'd select one and make a few practice swings, then it was two whacks on each hand – never any less.

I had spent my first eleven years mostly among women - my mother, four sisters and primary schoolteachers. Those first few days came as a shock, finding myself so suddenly in a male world. Armstrong Secondary Modern was more formal. Here there were no homely smiles or being addressed by our first names. Older boys seemed to double in size overnight, with prominent Adam's apples, gravelly voices and faces of festering acne poking through the first stage of stubble. Cigarette smoke would drift from behind the lavatory block where, if they were caught they would happily share a fag with the teacher.

Beyond the 8-foot high brick wall that divided our two playgrounds the girls could be heard as they skipped or played netball. There was some forethought in building such a wall, as on one side were budding young women and on the other side horny young men.

Being shouted at and caned seemed part of our learning culture. Did most teachers see us as monsters that needed taming? Moreover, the school took great pride in its sporting events. We had one of the town's strongest swimming teams as proof, besides a strong interest in football and cricket.

Generally, we had a different teacher for each subject and these teachers had their own different styles, and methods of punishment. However, I have never regretted being a pupil at Armstrong and I agree with the opinion expressed by fellow pupils at a school reunion I attended.

"They turned us boys into honest and responsible men."

Most of our teachers were ordinary folk, some were ex-servicemen, but they all demanded respect and respect is what they got.

My first form teacher in my early years of senior school was Mr Hollingsworth, who taught English according to the curriculum. Unfortunately my grammar and spelling was never up to his standards, as indicated by all the red ink used to correct my exercise book. My maths book was also similarly marked, and both usually ended with, "You must do better" scrawled across the page. Although I was a reasonable reader and did better at art, my dealings with vulgar fractions, decimals, Pythagoras's theorem and mensuration was another matter.

If anyone got out of line and as a last resort, Mr Goulding would growl, "Fetch me my mahogany, lad." This was a length of polished mahogany, once a chair spell. Three whacks across the backside and you certainly took more care in your work. I did hear that he had other means of getting results by throwing your exercise book out of the classroom window that opened out on to the girls' playground. To retrieve the book meant you first had to ask permission to go into this forbidden territory.

Goulding would allow the class to stand on their seats and encourage them to cheer as the culprit picked up his book. The girls would stop their netball game and giggle as they did so. I found the physical pain was easier borne than this humiliation.

Some of my happiest moments at Armstrong Street were spent on the playing field and as goalkeeper for the school's second team. This was the closest I came to winning respectability in sports. Mr Holmes, best known as Max, took us for sports and PT lessons. Although not tall, he was athletically thickset. Max was coach for the first team in football and cricket. He had played as a younger man for Grimsby Town 'Mariners' football team and was also a keen cricketer, the sport he preferred.

Max instructed us on the technical rules and tactics of football and cricket before taking us out to the nearby Duke of York Gardens or Boulevard, affectionately referred to as the 'Bully.' His talks and blackboard diagrams on cricket and fielding positions always baffled me. Silly mid-off... short leg mid-off... mid-on square leg ... slips. (They still do.)

Max knew I found it all boring.

"Right, Pratt," he would say, "if you don't want to learn how to adhere to the rules of the game, you'd better take up knitting."

Invariably I would find myself as wicket keeper, a position that suited me best at cricket, as did playing goalkeeper for the school's second eleven.

It was a proud achievement for the whole school when the swimming team under Mr Lees wiped the board from 1949-51 taking the Telegraph Shield and the Maddock Cup. Swimming was something I never enjoyed, mainly because I suffered with severe ear infections, therefore my mother discouraged me from attending any swimming sessions.

A favourite lesson that served me best at the start of my working life was woodwork, taught by John (Knobby) Armstrong. Knobby was a jolly sort, ginger-haired and ruddy-faced, and different from any other teacher, perhaps because of the fumes he inhaled from the glue-pot that was always on the boil. On the other hand, his manner was not to be taken lightly. If he found you were not paying attention, a mallet would fly your way preceded only by the curt shout of 'Catch.'

We'd all duck, not knowing were the missile was aimed. After I left school and taking up metalwork in a local shipyard those practical lessons in woodwork taught me to be creative with my hands and mind. Entering the woodwork room the whiff of freshly sawn timber, glue, methylated spirit and polish had always taken me into a different world.

Geography and history were the other useful lessons I enjoyed during my last two years at Armstrong. Geography was a joyful classroom journey through Europe, visiting France, Spain and Rome. History, was also taken by the same teacher and somewhere between those lessons was gardening.

Mr Herbert, our gardening teacher, was a pleasant man. I cannot remember him ever raising his voice or using a cane. Without resorting to threats or violence, he still got results. The school's allotment was a fifteen-minute walk from the school across the River Freshney. He made us walk the half-mile two abreast in an orderly fashion carrying our gardening tools over our shoulders, military style. To some it was a good get out to snatch a crafty fag. For me, it was an escape from sitting in a stuffy classroom.

I did not mind gardening lessons as we were learning what I already knew, thanks to my mother - how to set out vegetable plots for growing potatoes, carrots, cabbages, beetroot and lettuces from pots and seeds and prepare to replant them out in neat rows as they strengthened. In the classroom we learnt about the properties of soils, acidic and alkaline, and what that meant for growing healthy plants, much of which went over my head.

Seasons passed and standard by standard I stumbled my way through vulgar fractions, algebra and the decimal system. I suppose I was a slow learner, as my final school report stated. I had found it all too easy to go unnoticed if I sat at the back of the class. Nevertheless, I had good reports for the more practical lessons: sport, art, woodwork and gardening. Surprisingly, geography, too, my favourite subject, I loved poring over maps.

For my thirteenth birthday Mam took me to Lawson and Stockdale, a posh department store in Victoria Street or 'Top Town' as we called it. I was fitted out with a pair of light grey long trousers for best and dark grey for school, a white shirt, grey V-neck Fair Isle pullover, grey socks and black shoes. It was the first time that I had been in this store as usually we shopped in the Co-op. Lawson and Stockdale was an eye-opener. There, Mam was referred to as 'madam' and me as 'young man,' by the assistant who measured me up for my trousers.

When you signed the bill and paid for it, a metal canister whisked both away by an overhead wire system, returning the canister within minutes from the office overhead with change and a receipt tucked inside.

Round about then I started to support the Grimsby Mariners at their home games instead of going to the Saturday film matinee. My sisters knitted me a scarf and bobble hat in the team colours, black and white. Along with Dave Holmes and Barry 'Fatty' Maxstead and others in our gang I watched the game from the sixpenny 'boys' stand.' We had a good view of the ground from there, but it was like an icebox in winter if a nor'easter was blowing, as the ground, close to the river Humber, was exposed to the elements.

I didn't care how many goals Tweedy let in; he was still my hero. He could pluck an incoming ball out of the air with ease, sometimes with one hand and kick it down the pitch for the waiting Billy Cairns or Tommy Briggs. Early on, seeing the likes of George Tweedy and later on Wilf Chisholm wearing the famous red jersey prompted me to be a goalkeeper.

When I was selected to play goal for Armstrong's second team, my sisters clubbed together and kitted me out with new football boots, socks and shorts for my thirteenth birthday. What an honour to wear the school's colours and badge. Playing for the school's second eleven made my last two years at Armstrong's the best.

1951 was the year I turned fifteen and left Armstrong Street Secondary Modern forever, along with two of my pals from a neighbouring street. I had not been the brightest pupil, and I was grateful to have an engineering apprenticeship waiting for me.

"There's no going to sea for you, my lad," Mam had declared. "Your Uncle Jim's got you in as an apprentice boilermaker down dock."

On my last day I shook hands with most of the other teachers, but it was Mr Hotchkin, my final form teacher, whom I respected the most. I remember that last day how he wrote with speed and energy on the blackboard, emphasising each word as he wrote to a silent class:

"You will succeed if you put your mind to whatever you do.

If at first you don't succeed try, try again.

Don't be afraid to ask for help.

To learn best look, listen and digest."

Four weeks before leaving Armstrong School, I had told Mr Emerson, for whom I worked delivering groceries that I would be leaving to start an apprenticeship at the Humber Graving Dock. Nine months before I had taken this job over from a school pal, Derek Pindar. Derek had also left to take up an apprenticeship as an electrician. On my last day, I thanked Mr Emerson for giving me the opportunity to work for him. He gave me my final pay packet and a box of groceries for my mother, as he so often did each Friday, and wished me luck.

When I arrived home, I handed Mam the box of groceries and my final pay packet. She counted it as she always did.

"Mr Emerson has given you a bonus, Pete, an extra two weeks' wages."

My mother had opened an account for me at Prior's Post Office the week I started work at Emerson's. The following day she handed over the savings book. Unknown to me, she had been putting away the money from my delivery round each week.

"This is yours now, our Pete, and it's up to you to keep saving a little each week for the future."

The balance was almost ten pounds, more than enough to get what I wanted from Dynes' cycle shop. Before I started my apprenticeship, I had gone in and bought the latest model, a gold, drop-handle Rudge racing bicycle equipped with a three-speed gear system.

Now I was ready to be a working man.

Dad back from Australia (1950)

Mam in Gale's sweet shop, Yarborough Street (1958)

My brothers and sisters

James, Air-Gunner (1940)

Bernard, Merchant Navy (1950)

Irene (1940)

Brenda (1950)

Pauline and Doreen (1950)

Kenneth's Headstone (2004)

Going fishing to Tetney Lock with David Holmes
(Yarborough Street 1951)

Goalkeeper with Little Coates Under 18s football team.
Grimsby Intermediate League Cup winners (1952-3) with
Alf Rowbottom, Manager - Roger Howard far left. front row.

St Aidan's Church, Cleethorpes   Patricia & her father Alex (1957)

Our families outside St Aidan's Church

With Pat & her twin brother Les and his wife Jean (1959)

Café Dansant, Cleethorpes with Christine Turner, Patricia , Geoff Doncaster, Pat Reynolds, Steve & Babs Farman & Bill Turner (1960)

After the 1960 Mr Cleethorpes Competition with Pat, Dave Stroud, Pat Reynolds (Miss N. E.Britain), Colin Bush & John Brown

With Al Maggs & David Reed, Brighton Beach (1963)

Patricia with Colin and Gwenda Bush (1964)

Patricia with Manorbe Gym lads. Mr Britain Show, London (1964)

Farewell to Grimsby (1964)

-7-

A Proper Job

The Grimsby Humber Graving Dock was a twenty minute bike ride from our house in Yarborough Street and on 12th August 1951, aged fifteen, I started my first proper job there on nineteen shillings and sixpence a week.

During my first years, in the Grimsby and Immingham ship-repair yards, I worked aboard a variety of sea-going vessels: a Royal Navy minesweeper, merchant ships, dredgers, tugboats and the Humber paddle-ferries.

In my final year as an apprentice, I worked in a variety of chemical factories: British Titans and Courtauld's along the Humber Bank between Grimsby and Immingham. We were mainly on maintenance and new installations. At times it was so toxic working among pigments used primarily in paint manufacture. On hot-days there would be signs of the pigment coming out of my pores. In those times there was no health and safety training.

At 6.30 am on that wet August morning I met up with my uncle Jim Griffiths.

"You OK, Pete?"

I nodded.

"Right. What you're about to take on is not like delivering groceries; it'll be hard work, but you'll be all right. Ask for Johnny Longthorn, the boiler-shop foreman. Johnny's an old friend of mine and he's expecting you.

When I asked the time keeper for Mr Longthorn's office he pointed ahead.

"You'll find him up that flight of steel stairs."

I knocked on the door marked Foreman and poked my head around.

"I'm looking for Mr Longthorn."

"Wait downstairs, son, Keith here will be with you shortly."

Mr Longthorn waved me away.

Keith Waterhouse, the boilermaker's charge hand, showed me around the works. I was in for a rude awakening. The noise was ear-splitting and sparks sprayed out wherever you walked from welders and oxyacetylene-burners.

"Don't look at the welders without a shield, son, or you'll get 'arc-eye', then you'll end up with eyes like piss-holes in the snow."

Keith chuckled.

Carefully we picked out a path between groaning machines where groups of workers bawled instructions to each other above the constant crunch and thump of machines. Steel plates thicker than my thumb were being sheared as if cutting butter. Being there soon had my nerves on edge.

Half the size of a football pitch, the boiler-shop bustled with men and machinery. In the fuggy atmosphere of dust and acrid coke-fumes from the open furnace sweat-soaked workers busily formed the ships' frames. From where I stood, some ten-feet away, the heat was almost unbearable. I never gave it a thought then that one day I'd be doing the same type of work.

Keith gave me a full tour of the shipyard's other departments: the machine shop, shipwrights, coppersmiths, plumbers, rigging, paint and blacksmiths.

"The Graving Dock's the best engineering company in the area," he assured me, "and you'll soon learn the practical side of the work. Whatever trade you choose, never be too proud to ask, that's how you learn. At some stage in your early apprenticeship, Pete, you'll be expected to attend night school, and join the Boilermakers Union."

Before I knew it, the whistle blew for the mid-morning tea break. As if by magic, a congregation of filthy, ragged workers milled around the poky canteen, laughing and joking. Serving them was a skinny, wrinkled old chap called Frank.

"Tea's thrupence," he informed me. "Oxo is tuppence, son."

Bemused in my new surroundings, the sound of the works horn still ringing in my ears, I took the mug of steaming tea he handed to me.

After my first day in the shipyard, Mam was aghast at the sight of me.

"Whatever have you been up to, our Pete? You're all mucky; just look at yourself in the mirror!"

I knew I was filthy, but I wanted to show my mother and sisters I was a working man now. After a wash, I sat down to my tea with sisters throwing questions at me left, right and centre.

"How much do you get?" was the first.

I couldn't answer, as I wouldn't know myself until Friday or so I thought, not realising we had to work a week in hand!

During that first week I got to know other would-be apprentices around my own age and those that were about to complete their apprenticeship. Eddie, a riveter; Arthur, a caulker and Mike, a burner. I was the only one out of the new starters, who chose to be a plater – a steel fabricator. All equally nervous to begin with, we melded into a happy and friendly bunch over the following five years.

That first year went quickly as I was shunted from trade to trade. We worked alongside skilled tradesmen so we could get a taste of the different trades. My first task was as a rivet catcher - handing red-hot rivets to the riveters and assisting the platers, even though they had two labourers working with them, a normal practice in shipyards. A welder usually worked by himself, with a labourer between several hauling their cables.

In the main during our first year we were 'gofers,' running errands to the stores, carrying tool bags, rivets, bottles of gas and oxygen, nuts, washers and bolts by the thousand.

The same month I started work in August 1951 Brenda Fisher, a secretary on the Grimsby Docks, swam the English Channel and set up a new world record for women. On her return to Grimsby the town rose to celebrate her triumph; it was like V E Day all over again.

Grimsby's Mayor, Alderman W. Harris, paid tribute to her achievement, was quoted as saying, "There are 50 million people in this country and only half a dozen of them could swim the Channel."

Our champion was front-page news in all the national newspapers. *The Grimsby Telegraph* described her as 'The Queen of the Channel.' That year a new tugboat was named 'The Brenda Fisher'.

Working with the riveting squads was something I had to get used to now. As each rivet was knocked down, fumes from burnt pitch and oakum in the watertight joints stung my sinuses. In the ship's tank it was hot and filthy as I crawled through manholes to pass over the red-hot rivets, using long tongs for the holder-up.

My efforts paid dividends as on paydays I was often slipped a couple of shillings from the riveting squad. There was no doubt in my mind that riveters had the toughest job in the shipyard. Shipyard workers in general, men with a much-needed skill, generally brought home better money than many other everyday tradesmen around town – and deservedly so.

Life in the shipyard was not all serious though; for the first few days, being wet between the ears, I was easily caught out and despatched to fetch a bag of blank washers or a left-handed hammer. On one occasion I was sent for a long stand.

"Aye, wait over there, lad," said the ginger-headed storekeeper said, chuckling.

Half an hour later, the head storekeeper asked what I was waiting for.

"A long stand, sir."

He blew his top.

"Tell whoever sent you to bloody come here himself. Now fuck off!"

The jokes made our days a little happier and rarely harmed us.

Being late for work at the shipyard was no option especially for a new starter. For me it was always a race to get to work on time and this one particular morning was no exception. It was raining like billy-ho, a typical English gloomy November morning. With the fear of being late, I pedalled like the clappers down Fish-Dock Road. I knew that I had to beat the early morning fish train before the railway gates closed.

I nipped through the gates as they were closing by mere inches and that's when my gallant effort came unstuck and the road's broken and uneven cobblestones got the better of me. In my haste, I lost control of my bike's front wheel as it slid left, then right. Before I knew what was happening I had tumbled over the handlebars.

I awoke to the smell of antiseptic in the Grimsby General Hospital, my head hot and throbbing.

"You're awake then," said the nurse, as she checked my pulse and stuck a thermometer between my swollen lips. "We thought you'd never come round."

I was shocked when I saw my reflection in the glass water jug on the bedside cabinet. My head was swathed in bandages like Boris Karloff in 'The 'Mummy.'

"You've been lucky," said the nurse. "No bones broken."

She wouldn't believe I'd only crashed a bicycle. However, the laceration on my upper lip left an, ugly grey scar and even now, I have to be careful shaving. I was lucky no teeth were broken, although my front bottom teeth ripped into my lower lip. The tip of my nose had been cut as both elbows and knees in a mess. I nearly screamed when the nurses had to dig out the gravel.

Two weeks later, I limped out of the hospital, as bad as Joe Louis after Rocky Marciano beat the shit out of him, with plasters on my upper lip, forehead and elbow. My Rudge racing bike was worse off than me, leaning forlorn and twisted against the back yard wall, front forks bent, front wheel out of kilter and minus its spokes.

A week after leaving hospital, I borrowed a wheelbarrow and took my bike to Sidney Dines' Cycles in Fildes Street from whom I had bought the bike only six months previously. He inspected the damage, tut-tutting.

"Yes, it can be repaired, lad, but it could cost you eight quid, at a guess."

We did a deal for me to pay him five shillings a week. He smiled and took off his horn-rimmed spectacles to clean them with his handkerchief.

"Your bike will be ready in two weeks."

Good news for me, as the bike was my best companion and the only means of getting to work, other than getting the trolley bus. Even then, I would have another mile-long trek over the goods yard.

The dry dock, built in the style of a terraced amphitheatre, was in area about the size of a football pitch. In effect, it was a huge concrete bath with high concrete steps around three sides. Daunting at first glimpse, and a spooky experience when I descended the steps, fortunately unaware that only the lock gates were between me and millions of tonnes of dock water.

The stern of the SS Bury, an old tramp steamer of the London and North Eastern (LNER) line, loomed massively 60 foot above me, an awesome sight for a fifteen year old. I had never dreamt I would one day see a ship from a fish's point of view. I followed Kevin and his mates under the ship's bottom. Being six feet tall to their five foot eight inches, I had to stoop further to pass beneath the ship's keel as it rested on timber blocks a mere five feet high.

Adding to all the hidden dangers ship repair work was filthy and foul-smelling. Inside a ship's hull its bilges can harbour a festering sedimentation gathered over many years, especially in old tramp steamers like the SS Bury. With the noise of pneumatic riveting all around, it can be claustrophobic at first – but that was life in the shipyard industry.

With my bicycle accident behind me, I was assigned to Kevin, the yard's senior apprentice. Although I had been a year in the yard, it was the first time that I had worked down the dry dock with a plater. I followed Kevin and his two labourers, Sid and Bert, down to the base of the dry dock, wondering what task we'd be set now.

As it transpired our job was to number each of the vessels hull plates from stem to stern and keel and upwards to the level of the ship's deck. Luckily, the rain had stopped, but rainwater still ran in rivulets, dripping on us when we least expected it. Numbering was so the surveyor could identify which of the ship's hull plates where to be renewed.

Soon the ship became a throbbing bustle of men and equipment. Miles of compressed-air tubing, electric welding cables and ropes were strung from shore to ship. More led down sides of the dry dock and snaked along decks, through portholes and manholes. In no time, the SS Bury sat forlorn, its hull plates stripped off, resembling nothing so much as a chicken carcass after a ravenous Sunday dinner. The vessel was surrounded by scaffolding and staging where a multitude of workers from riveters to painters each performed their set tasks. We were bombarded with a cacophony of rattling riveters, caulkers and paint-chippers wielding pneumatic machines. Over the years, I almost grew accustomed to the noise; turning a deaf ear, as the saying goes.

When I reached sixteen, I was initiated into the Boilermakers Union as an apprentice plater. There were many of my fellow workers there to witness the event and I was given my apprenticeship 'Black Book' of rules and my union attendance record. To choose your trade was a major decision, as there are so many different skills in the Boilermakers Union, but a plater, my Uncle Jim told me, was the 'cream' of the yard. In the old days, they wore bowler hats and took precedence over other workers, being employed as 'gaffers.'

There was no end to the pranks going on in the shipyard with the workers always keen to take the piss out of someone or other. One welder, asked me to stand on a plate while he tack-welded the joint.

"Ha'way, hinnie!" he called.

But I couldn't move; he had tack-welded my boot steel heel plates to the ship's steel deck. When I finally wriggled my feet out of the boots, they became the centre of attraction, especially when a caulker, Robbie, offered to chisel them free. My boots shot one way and the heel-plates another. Mother was not too pleased when she saw the state of my new boots, now in need of immediate – and expensive - repair.

Kevin winked.

"I know how you can get your own back on Hammer, Pete."

I followed him to the shipyard's ablution block. The separate cubicles did not have individual lavatory pans, only a single communal trough, a bit like a rain gutter, that ran along the back of the six cubicles. During the mid-morning tea-break we saw Hammer go in to read his newspaper. Kevin lit a rag of oily cotton waste and floated it on a piece of paper towards Hammer's cubicle. The air was loud with yelps and curses!

"Who the f***s done that? Ha way, man, ya buggers."

And Hammer shot out with his trousers around his ankles.

My last two years of my apprenticeship, I was transferred to the Humber Graving Dock's Immingham Yard. Immingham was one of the biggest commercial ports on the East coast and HGD had a huge steel-fabrication workshop besides its two dry docks. Working at the Immingham Yard I learnt other skills than those I had acquired in the ship-repair yard. The move furthered my knowledge and experience in steel fabrication. Working with different steel sections and forming intricate developments from engineering drawings was what I came to most enjoy and found it more interesting than crawling around ship's bilges.

Jack Ramage was the fabrication shop foreman who always found time for his apprentices. He instructed me in different methods in developing all manner of structures from raw steel plates, girders and tubing. He also taught me how to read engineering drawings and make templates.

Jack must have seen my eagerness to learn. My main worry was my lack of ability in maths and soon it was obvious to Jack that I was largely ignorant in that subject. He kindly gave me a City and Guilds textbook on *Sheet Metal Work and Development* that included simple maths formulas appertaining to the work.

90

"If you follow the rules in there, Pete," he said, "you'll not go far wrong."

I did my apprenticeship among an extraordinary society of men and as I grew older, I grew more confident and streetwise. It was different from growing up among school pals and four older sisters, because now I was among men whose talk was of horseracing, card games, beer, women and sex on a daily basis and in a language bluer than a summer's sky.

It was an education to listen to their conversations. Though it was a hard road into the world of the work, my apprenticeship made a man of me and was worth every single tear, cut and bruise.

Those five years opened a new world for me, a world I didn't know existed. My qualifications became a passport that would take me anywhere I wanted to go.

-8-
In Safe Hands

Roger Howard, my friend and fellow-apprentice at the Humber Graving Dock, asked me if I would like to be goalkeeper for their team. Little Coates Juniors played in the Grimsby Intermediate League for the Under-18s, an ideal step-up for school leavers.

One training session under the watchful eye of Alf, our coach, we were jogging past the Tin Mission, which among its other church activities was also used as a dance hall. The sound of music attracted my attention and, no, it was neither 'Jesus wants me for a sunbeam' or the Boys Brigade at practice.

The Tin Mission, an iron corrugated structure was run by Father Fagan of the Church of the Good Shepherd in Little Coates on the West Marsh. Father Fagan stood for no nonsense, in or out of the hall, and especially on dance nights. There were no exceptions; he was jury, judge and executioner and as he also ran a boxing gym he gave anyone caught fighting the chance to settle their differences at his boxing sessions. If not, they found themselves banned from the mission's dance nights.

The Mission Hall had a resident band of lively musicians. The Roy Waterhouse Four was comprised of drums, sax/trumpet, piano and double bass, and offered a good variety of modern music. During their breaks, the latest hits were played on gramophone records, vinyl 78s. Favourites included Guy Mitchell 'Singing the Blues' or Rosemary Clooney with 'This Old House' and Johnny Ray's 'Cry' and 'Walking My Baby Back Home.'

These dances were held every Saturday evenings, the girls outnumbered boys but I was eager try my hand at dancing. Getting into the rhythm wasn't as easy I thought it would be and it soon became obvious that treading on too many toes meant I was constantly rejected as a partner. The lonely walk back across the dance floor to the jeers of my mates after yet another refusal was embarrassing.

However, I was determined not to give in and enlisted the help of my twin sisters, Doreen and Pauline. During those home lessons, Doreen assured me that the basic steps of the waltz are not that different than those for other dances.

"You just quicken them up a bit, Pete, as you listen to the beat of the music."

She also showed me an advertisement in the *Evening Telegraph* for 'Stevenson's Ballroom Dance Lessons for Teenagers.' I shared it with my best pal, David, who was equally keen to try it.

For one shilling and sixpence per lesson we enrolled with Mr and Mrs James Stevenson's Modern Ballroom Dance Classes and were soon tackling those basic steps to Victor Sylvester's modern waltz played on a vinyl record player. Our first lesson was to dance with a piece of card between our own and our partner's stomach. If the card dropped, you weren't dancing close enough.

"You must concentrate and connect with your partner," we were told. "Dancing is about closeness."

For obvious reasons, I dared not let our other mates know that David and I had to dance together due to there being a lack of girls that first night. We must have looked a right comical pair, me six feet and David almost a foot shorter.

Over our first six dance lessons we progressed to the slow slow/ quick quick/ slow tempo of the foxtrot and quickstep, sometimes with older women or, if we were particularly lucky, girls our own age.

My first encounter of being partnered with an experienced and mature ballroom-dancer came sooner than I anticipated. This time my partner was elegantly dressed. I can't recall her name but she was classically glamorous in a flowing, sequined blue frock, her red hair tied back in a bun. During my first week at Stevenson's I had noticed how effortlessly she moved around the dance floor, reminding me of Ginger Rogers dancing with Fred Astaire.

My dance partner smiled and whispered, "Relax, you can hold me closer, ducky, I'll not break."

She clasped my left hand and eased my right hand onto the small of her back. It seemed an age as we stood there waiting for the tempo. With my arms up and shoulders set wide, it was as if I had left a coat hanger inside my jacket. Suddenly she moved in, I felt the heat of her body and could almost taste her perfume.

With her persuasive movements of body and legs, she was able to guide me around the dance floor, instead of me leading her. We danced to a Victor Sylvester modern waltz, followed with a slow fox trot. As a fifteen year-old who was still green behind the ears, I had never danced this close with such a sensual female before. I was worried in case, as she pressed close, she felt something unintentional.

However, over my last three lessons at Stevenson's I was shown the double reverse turn, with a heel pivot and reverse turn which took a lot of concentration. I knew then I would never become the greatest of ballroom dancers as I found the technical tactics too difficult to digest. After eight weeks I left the dance school, satisfied I was now confident enough in the waltz, foxtrot and quickstep and anticipating what was in fact delivered, many enjoyable years on the dance floor.

94

On Saturdays after a hectic and often muddy game of football, my mates and I would visit other Grimsby dance haunts besides the Tin Mission. The Wellington Rooms and Manor Café had a live band of sorts - piano, drums, saxophone or clarinet and piano accordion - or the latest hits played on a vinyl record player. The rooms all had a familiar musty odour of alcohol, cigarette smoke and perfume. I found the girls usually outnumbered the boys and often preferred dancing together. It became a competition with the boys to butt in and split them up.

For my sixteenth birthday, my sisters Doreen and Brenda took me to Alexander's in Freeman Street for a new suit. They chose a double-breasted gabardine in midnight blue - full drape, the latest style. I also had a new white shirt and tie.

With my eye on a particular girl, and a nervous adjustment of the tie, I would walk across the dance floor.

"Please can I have this dance?"

Usual the girl would smirk and reply "Nah!" followed by an outburst of the usual girly giggles.

Bernard, the most experienced in our gang, put me wise.

"You're trying too hard, Pete. You're not at the dance school now. Never say please!"

I changed my chat-up line and adopted a more positive approach.

I held out my hand.

"Do you want a dance?"

To my amazement it worked first time.

Bernard said the Alexandra Rooms – 'the Alex,' as it was known locally - was far better than the other places. There were Wednesday and Saturday 50-50 dance nights: the waltz, quickstep and foxtrot were still my favourites and I was in trouble if they played Latin American or the 'old time' numbers like the Boston two-step, veleta, Gay Gordon or St Bernard

('Doggy.') The 'Polly Glide' (Palais Glide) was the easiest and got everyone on the dance-floor singing 'Show me the way to go home' as we whirled round the dance floor arm in arm.

The bandleader Len Bowles played drums, backed with a saxophone, clarinet and piano-organ. As his signature tune, Len bashed 'Won't You Come Home, Bill Bailey?' and included in his repertoire the most up-to-date jive numbers. The band supported a good-looking singer Johnny Sutherland and as the music switched rock 'n' roll, that's when Johnny had us bouncing and bopping.

Although I was brought up with four older sisters, mixing with other girls of my own age in the dance halls was different. They came in their taffeta dresses or tight-fitting pencil skirts, high-collar cotton blouses or figure-hugging sweaters to jive and twirl around the dance floor. The 50s craze for hair was a ponytail or held back with a slide and the ends flicked up. As the music jazzed up, white ankle socks and black velvet pumps for jiving or bopping replaced the usual high heel courts. Singing smooch numbers, Sutherland had the girls swooning, especially to the likes of Al Martino's "Here in my Heart."

The summer of 1952 and barely a month after my sixteenth birthday, I was at a summer dance in the Boulevard with the gang. I told Bernard I wasn't feeling too good and left my mates to dash home with severe stomach pains. In the early hours my stomach was on fire and I vomited into the bucket prudently positioned by my bed. Bile and blood splattered my pyjamas, the bedsheets and the bedroom floor. My moans and groans woke my sisters and mother, whose maternal instincts kicked in and warned her I was seriously ill and she immediately sent Doreen for Dr Evans.

After he examined me and took my temperature, he scribbled a note and once again Doreen was sent off, this time across the street to Grimsby District hospital for an emergency ambulance. There, surrounded by doctors and nurses, I was asked to pee into a bottle, which proved difficult and extremely painful. The nurse held up the bottle of urine, the colour of Cherryade and I heard shouts for an enema. Two nurses came running, one with a long rubber tube she promptly shoved up my backside. My stomach was bursting as warm fluid pumped into me.

A nurse held my hand, whispering, "Try to relax, duck, and breathe deeply, but do not pass anything – try to hold it. You're doing fine."

The last thing I remember before I blacked out was my worried mother, standing helplessly by and watching what they were doing. Although I was sixteen, I was still Mam's baby.

I came round seven days later, my eyes flooded with daylight. For a moment it frightened me, not knowing if it were another dream – no, a nightmare. I tried to sit up, but was restrained by a sharp searing pain from the tube up my nose. I lifted the bed-sheet to a foul-smelling odour from the green bile weeping from another tube in my stomach. I couldn't remember how long I had been there, only nightmares of black-robed and hooded people gathered around a gallows. That picture has stayed with me ever since.

I dreamt of the flies I had caught as a boy to feed the spiders, dreams that haunted me for years.

"Oh, you're awake."

The curtains swished open. Matron and the other nurses came in for a look as a dark-skinned doctor checked my pulse. He smiled.

"Looks like you will be kicking the ball around quicker than we thought."

Later, my big sister Irene told me I had been at death's door. The ward sister told her, "If it wasn't for your Pete being so fit and healthy, he could easily have died."

I had survived peritonitis from a burst appendix. Friends and family rallied around my bedside almost daily, hoping that I would wake up. Irene said our Mam prayed every night in the Methodist Chapel down the street. This all happened while my father was at sea. Seemingly, all our family grief comes while Dad is away, with our mother left to pick up the pieces.

Two weeks out of the coma, I was rushed down to the operating theatre again after developing an abscess on the bowel. Yet again I survived.

With my feet back on earth again, I began to take notice of my surroundings. Nothing much had changed on the ward since my bike accident. The sickly aroma of antiseptic, beds made when you wanted to lie in them, the smell of bedpans and piss bottles. Food trolleys shunted from bed to bed with steaming jugs of tea. For breakfast I was fed a heaped bowl of thick porridge oats, ladled out like wallpaper paste. Thankfully, a spoonful of Tickler's raspberry jam made a big difference.

On the other hand, I was never short of company as most of my best pals visited daily. Derek, I heard later, almost passed out the first time he saw me lying pale and motionless with tubes in every which way. While I was in the coma, he had asked Matron if he could play his violin as he knew I liked to hear him play.

"No, you cannot, young man. This is a hospital, not the Palace Theatre."

After ten weeks in hospital, my strength improved and I was able to walk freely about the Yarborough Ward. Finally I was home, shocked by the stranger in the bedroom mirror. The illness had taken its toll. I had lost almost 28lbs in weight and was thinner than ever. I could have come out of Belsen, the infamous World War 2 concentration camp.

Flicking through my brother Bernard's old boxing magazines, I envied the muscular physiques of boxers and wrestlers. Unable to afford real chest expanders, I improvised using two old bicycle inner tubes and performed bicep curls and chest pulls. When he saw me struggling with the home-made chest expanders, Bernard bought me a set of Terry's with a book of exercises. He was always a fit-looking young man and had been a keen boxer once; often fighting in the working men's clubs around Grimsby.

Before Bernard was married, when I was a young lad, we shared the back bedroom. I would join him shadowboxing and exercising, mainly press-ups and sit-ups. I think it was due to Bernard and the exercise regime he instilled in me that I pulled though my illness. I still have that urge to be fit today.

While still recuperating from my operation, I was mooching around Freeman Street Market while my mother did her shopping. A *Health and Strength* bodybuilding magazine caught my immediate attention. On the cover was a picture of Reg Park, last year's Mr Universe (1951). I was mesmerised by his size and muscular physique. As I flicked through the magazine, there were weight-training schedules by Reg Park, Steve Reeves and many other famous bodybuilders. That little book inspired me to take up weight training. I wanted a body like Reg Park. I wanted to be Mr Universe.

Once back at work, I secretly made a pair of steel dumbbells, crude, but they did the job. Craftily I hung them piece by piece around my neck and cycled painfully home with them under my raincoat. Following the training exercises in the *Health and Strength* magazine and drinking four pints of milk a day, my bodyweight shot up. Within several weeks my strength improved and my pectorals and biceps were growing bigger and firmer. When I started football training again even my team-mates noticed an improvement. Mam would shout up the stairs, "You be careful, you Pete. I don't want those contraptions coming through my ceiling."

With my mind on weight training, I knew I could be another Reg Park if I set my mind to it.

Wanting somewhere to go in the evenings other than dancing and the cinema, Bernard Kendall came up with a brainwave. He knew Wray's Store in our street had an old storeroom above their garage. Bernard did the negotiations and the seven of us rented it for seven shillings and sixpence a week. I made more weights and an exercise bench by copying one I had seen in the *Health and Strength* magazine. We still had plenty of room for the table tennis table we bought second-hand from our old school teacher Max Holmes. Brian rescued an old settee and armchair from going onto a bon fire.

Derek, an apprentice electrician, sorted out the electrics and from a stack of old wall bricks David, being a bricklayer, rebuilt the broken-down fireplace. We all mucked in and collected second-hand furniture and carpets to make our club comfortable. Bernard acquired an old His Master's Voice wind-up record player and a stack of vinyl 78s. After the dance at the Alex or a night at the movies it was a good opportunity to invite our girlfriends into our clubroom.

Although I had weight training on my mind, the following spring and end of our 1952-3 season, playing for Littlecoats Juniors, we won the Grimsby Intermediate League Cup. That was the highlight of my football dreams. We had a great team, managed and trained by Alf Rowbottom and it was a shame we were now too old to continue another season in that under 18 league.

In the summer of June 1953 we let the street hold their Queen Elizabeth's II Coronation celebration party in our club. At the same time, though we were as yet unaware of it, another big event took place when New Zealander Edmund Hillary had conquered Mount Everest. That following week we had to close down our clubroom. We assumed it was a complaint from the lady across the street who we'd spotted spying on us taking our girl friends in the club.

The early 1950s was the dawn of the Teddy Boy era, and the Frank Sinatra style, double-breasted, full drape suits were out. I had a pea-green gabardine suit tailored, with a velvet collar and patch pockets. The coat fell almost to my knees, with 14-inch drainpipe trousers, my one and half-inch crêpe-soled green suede shoes (brothel creepers) looked like tugboats. Much to my Mother's tut-tutting and 'whatever next' comments as I sat at the dinner table. Every Saturday I had my hair 'bop' styled into a DA (duck's arse) at Frank Cripsey's Barbers popular with the in-crowd. After his creations Cripsey applied 'bop juice' a kind of setting lotion of his own formula. A final blow-dry brought it to a cardboard stiffness not even a nor'easterly could wreck.

The new dance craze, "The Creep" was all the rage, soon banned by Alex's organisers, who claimed it was too sexy. Yes, I was one of the first to be banned for three weeks and caught after three warnings. Reg, a formidable ex-paratrooper, was the dance hall's door attendant. Before he handed out interval pass-outs, he'd warn us, "Back before ten or the doors will be closed." We all knew Reg stood no nonsense, and we respected him for that.

It was on my first night out for some weeks after my brother Bernard had been lost at sea. Bernard Kendall and Roger Howard-my best friends pulled me out of my gloom and urged me to go to the Alexandra Dance Hall with them.

"Pete, it will do you good."

He was probably right and it was about then that I began to take more notice of Patricia. That night she was at the Alex with her girlfriends, Jean, Margaret and Valerie, whom I also knew.

-9-
"May I have this dance?"

How Patricia and I came to be together was fate. We were a happy bunch of teenagers, who would meet at the Alex Dance Hall or in Reinecke's, a soda bar on Corporation Road. Reinecke's was the local teenagers' hideaway and noted for their range of non-alcoholic beverages - lime, peppermint, dandelion and burdock and sarsaparilla. Set on cradles behind the long oak bar were several wooden barrels, from which the delicious cordials were drawn.

The bare wooden floor, cosy cubicles, marble top tables and smoky hue gave Reinecke's the allure of a Wild West saloon. May and her husband Ron would tune in the wireless to Radio Luxemburg 208 for the latest hits played by DJ Pete Murray.

The first time I saw Patricia she was going out with Brian, another member of our street gang. Brian was about to follow my best friend David, who was already doing his National Service in the British Army, a two-year compulsory scheme that all men turned eighteen had to serve. If you were serving an approved apprenticeship, you were deferred until your 21st birthday. Before Brian left I wished him well as we all did while in Reinecke's on his last night. I told him not worry about Patricia as I would escort her safely to the bus stop. Brian glanced at me, unsure what to make of this. He knew my reputation with the opposite sex!

After the dance at the Alex the following Saturday night Patricia was saying cheerio to her friend Margaret who was leaving with Bernard. I asked Pat if she would mind me walking her to the Palace bus stop were she caught the bus home to Cleethorpes. We talked about films we had seen, what music she liked and where she worked. After that first time I looked forward to walking with her again, inwardly hoping to make it a regular thing.

Patricia was pleasant and quietly-spoken with sparkling hazel eyes and chestnut hair sometimes held back by a slide. She was always fashionably dressed, mostly in a pencil skirt and blouse that showed off her petite figure. Besides I enjoyed dancing with her as she guided me along and tolerated my occasional lack of sequence with the music. She was different from the other girls I usually chased after. Those first few weeks I thought about Patricia daily.

Finally, as we walked over the Corporation Bridge for the fourth time, I plucked my courage.

"Do you fancy going to the Rex to see 'White Christmas, Pat?"

(A film everyone was talking about that starred Bing Crosby and Rosemary Clooney.)

I had mentioned this idea to my friend Bernard.

"I could ask Pat's friend Margaret to make up a foursome," he suggested. "Then it won't look so bad if Brian gets to know."

After our clandestine meeting at the Rex, I saw Pat as usual at the Alex the following Saturday with her friends. We had the last dance together something that had rarely happened before. When we left the dance hall for our usual walk to the bus stop, I asked Pat if she'd like to go to the Regal cinema.

"What's showing?"

"The Last Time I Saw Paris."

I didn't let on that my Aunt Emily who worked there could give me free tickets. Pat hesitated, then just before she boarded the bus, "I'll see you outside the Regal then, Peter."

She smiled. From that moment, we both knew what was happening, our friendship was not so platonic friendship any more. Over the following weeks it was the Regal on Tuesdays and the Queen's cinema on Sundays and the Alex on Saturdays. As the weeks rolled by we met in addition each lunchtime on the corner where she worked, as it was on my route back to work. When we'd been going out for three months it dawned on me that Pat was the girl I wanted to be with forever.

I never spoke with Brian again. In fact, I can't even remember him returning from the Army.

Being with Patricia helped take away the agony of losing my brother Bernard. Since that awful day we heard he'd gone down with his ship, I would lie in bed thinking of his poor wife Audrey, his little daughter Andrea and the twin sons he had never seen. I was in a state of amnesia during that period as if a part of my brain didn't want me to remember! Sometimes I would look at their photographs, hoping some thread of memory would return and allow me to piece together how life was in our house then. How did my sister-in-law, cope and my own parents, sisters and brother for that matter?

Years later I found the courage to track down Audrey (who had married again), my niece Andrea and my nephews Bernard and Anthony. No one will ever know how pleased it made me that we were reunited.

After the Easter of 1954, Patricia and I had begun a wonderful courtship. Through spring and summer, our Sundays were filled with cycle trips to Cleethorpes. We would sunbathe and picnic among the sand dunes or stroll along Cleethorpes Promenade; such happy times. After some weeks, Patricia introduced me to her mother Minnie, her brother Alec and sisters Joyce and Renee as they picnicked by the Cleethorpes boating lake. Like my own, Pat's father Alex was mostly at sea, working as a skipper's mate, so I never met him until months later. Pat and her twin brother Leslie are the youngest in their family and I first met Leslie with his girlfriend Jean at the bathing pool in Cleethorpes.

I still managed to play football every Saturday and train three nights a week with the weights. I had joined the Torrington Street Gym to progress my aspirations in bodybuilding. Although money never came easy, both being apprentices, we somehow managed to go dancing and to cinema, with more time for both now my night school course had ended.

Eventually, my friend Bernard married his girlfriend Yolanda and they asked Patricia and me to be witnesses. At the time I didn't know what that meant, until we had to sign the marriage certificate in front of the registrar. Sometime afterwards, Bernard joined the Merchant Navy as an engineer and we lost contact with him and Yolanda.

I proposed to Pat the night her sister Joyce married Neil, her Danish boyfriend. We both had too much drink and because Pat was unused to alcohol, she staggered off to the toilet. She vomited in violent gushes, moaning, "Never again." I had never been in that position with a girl before. I thought if I asked her to marry me, it might make Pat feel better. It did. Almost immediately she turned to me and put her arms around my neck and kissed me.

"Yes! Yes! Yes!"

Eighteen months later on Patricia's nineteenth birthday we went to Hewitt's the jewellers in Victoria Street Grimsby's 'Top Town'. Pat's eyes sparkled like the diamond solitaire she chose and she kissed me. That night we celebrated our engagement and her birthday in a small restaurant above Palethorpes Jewellers in Victoria Street. The thirty pounds bill for the ring and the evening meal made a hole in my savings, but Pat had made me the happiest man alive.

As I was expecting to be called-up for National Service the following year, our wedding plans soon came to fruition. Patricia and I were married at St Aidan's Church in Cleethorpes on June 1st 1957. Patricia's father Alex escorted her down the aisle, as he had his other daughters Renee and Joyce. As we stood side by side before the vicar, the Reverend A.H. Hurt, with me in a Cecil Gee pale blue suit I turned to look at my bride, stunning in her white brocade wedding dress. My sister Doreen was bridesmaid and my childhood friend David Holmes was my best man.

The entire affair was costly and took some organising, as we were both still in the last year of our apprenticeships. What made matters worse was that neither of our parents could afford to contribute anything towards our wedding costs. Nevertheless, we were madly in love and nothing could change our minds. After a reception for fifty of our family and friends at the County Hotel in Cleethorpes, we left for the train station, followed by our guests, who showered us in confetti.

After a hot cloudless day, the train whisked us to Manchester and then to Llandudno North Wales and the start of a wonderful honeymoon. We went on coach journeys, sunbathing on the beach and walking the Big Orme, but not too far up, as I wanted to conserve my strength for other activities. (Anyway, it was too hot.) In the evenings we strolled along the seafront and stopped at a pub, where it seemed strange to hear the locals chatting in a language we couldn't understand. I had never thought about how different Wales was to England and wondered if they understood us – it was obvious they did, when we came to pay our bill.

Those first two evenings as dusk descended we returned to our hotel-guesthouse for our evening meal then retired to our room. We had seen each other almost nude before, making premarital love, but still had to get used to fully undressing in front of each other, as both of us had a modest upbringing. Some nights were quite hot so, we would lie on the bed in just our nightwear and listen to the dull drone of a ship's horn, the murmur of the incoming tide and the unmistakable screech of seagulls at first light. Excluding our lovemaking, the highlight of our honeymoon was a coach tour that whisked us away through the rugged Welsh valleys, Conway Castle, Betws-y-Coed and Swallow Falls.

All too soon, our honeymoon was over and we returned home and our daily work routine – this time as husband and wife. As planned, we settled in with Pat's parents in Brereton Avenue, Cleethorpes. This was largely because I was about to be called for my two years National Service. With that in mind we had decorated and furnished the downstairs middle room and took over the upstairs back bedroom that was Patricia's anyway. Pat's brother Les had flown the nest so there was ample room. Although we all shared the bathroom, my boyhood dream had come true. For the first time in my twenty-one years I could have a real hot bath in comfort.

Three weeks after we were married and two days after my twenty-first birthday, I boarded the train to Lincoln for my National Service medical. As I looked around me at the thirty other young men, I was confident I would pass. Playing football every weekend, dancing, and weight training three, sometimes four times a week, I assumed I would waltz through the health tests. But it was the hearing tests and anxious expression of the doctor that worried me. He shone a light inside my ears and then asked me to stand in the far corner of the room and repeat what he said.

After I had given him a blank look or stuttered out wild guesses, it was obvious to us both that I had a hearing problem.

Another doctor who had held my testicles in his hand at alternate intervals and invited me to cough asked about the scar on my abdomen.

"I had suffered a burst appendix when I was sixteen."

"You look pretty fit, but does your abdomen give you any problems and do you have breathing problems or is that a bad cold you have?

I answered no to his first question, then added, "I get clogged sinuses now and then. The chemist gives me drops for it."

The doctor tilted my head back and shone another light up my nostril, then probed with a stick with lint on the end, twisting it. He fished out a string of 'spaghetti' – four inches of yellow mucus.

"You have a polyp. You had better see your doctor when you get home. Does this give you any breathing difficulty?"

"Not at all," I lied. "I play football regularly and I'm a keen weightlifter."

"That will be all," he instructed me. "You can get dressed now and go."

The blow came with the arrival of a letter two weeks later, confirming I was grade four and exempt from National Service. I was disappointed, especially at the thought of continuing shipyard work. I didn't want to end up like my Uncle Jim, working in the same old shipyard all my life. I wanted to see the world, like my father and brother James.

After my ordeal with the National Service medical, I saw my own doctor about my sinus problem and he referred me to a specialist at Grimsby District Hospital. I was told I had acute sinusitis. The following month I was admitted for an operation, where they sliced through the inside of my top gum and drilled through the bone above and behind. I woke up with a bandage under my nose that was tied with a bloody great bow. In the ward were three more in a similar get up, four Easter eggs with panda-blackened eyes and faces bruised and swollen. Several nurses thought they recognised me from when I had my appendicitis operation.

After my first year as a journeyman, I was made redundant along with many others in the shipyard. This was not a good start to married life. Fortunately, Pat still worked full time at Burnett's Printers.

A year after we were married Pat's father, aged 57 died suddenly from a massive heart attack. Minnie was beside herself and woke us both up at 1am that Sunday morning. We didn't have the luxury of a telephone, so I ran in my pyjamas to the Park Street telephone box and dialled 999. The ambulance man shook his head as he closed the ambulance door and confirmed that Alex was dead.

It was left to me and Pat to tell her mother, although I'm sure she already knew that her husband had died. I left Pat with Minnie and took on the daunting task of cycling around the town to let her sisters and brothers know.

Pat's father had been a happy go lucky man who readily accepted me into his family. He was typical of most fishermen and liked his ale, cigarettes and food in that order. Alex, before and after Patricia was born, brought their family down into near poverty due to his heavy boozing, as did my own father to his family before I was born.

It was not until Pat and her brothers and sisters started work that the family managed to live normally.

Patricia once told me that during their early schooling, she and her twin brother Leslie often had to share shoes so one of them could attend school. Yet for all the poverty of Pat's upbringing, it did not affect her ability to be in the school's A stream.

Many months went by after the passing of Pat's father before life in number 59 returned to some kind of normality. It was not long after that Buster, her spaniel, died too.

-10-
The Big Band Sound

I first met the late Geoff Doncaster in the Grimsby Health Studio. He would glide along the gym floor in his tan slip-ons, a music folder and LP invariably under one arm and sporting a big grin.

"Hi, fellers, be with you in a jiff."

He would change into his tracksuit and start with squats before getting busy on the bench press, continuing his training routine.

Geoff, although a regular gym member, had different aspirations from me. At the time, Geoff occasionally sang alongside fellow vocalists Vic Gerrard and Sandra Brown with the Bob Walker Orchestra, the Gaiety Ballroom's resident band. As I got to know him more, I realised Geoff was a big Sinatra fan down to his marrow. He sang Sinatra songs as his hero sang them, with all the theatricals.

After one training session, Geoff invited me, Terry Brown, Peter Jarvis and Steve Farman to his home. His bedroom was like a record shop, with *Melody Makers* and *Capitol Review* magazines and record covers pinned around the walls. He had hundreds of 1930s, '40s and '50s vinyls: Dave Brubeck, Dizzy Gillespie, Count Basie, Duke Ellington, Oscar Peterson and modern jazz. Mel Torme, Ella Fitzgerald and a selection of Frank Sinatra photographs. His record collection was seemingly endless.

Geoff played Ella's 'Lullaby of Birdland,' her silken voice drifting around the room as we sat cross-legged drinking cans of Long Life lager. Geoff started to nod and click thumb and finger together, and we followed suit, nodding heads to the rhythm. Geoff pretended to play the drums and we, too, began to 'play' imaginary instruments along with Ella's scat singing. Geoff had me hooked on jazz. Gone were Elvis, Bill Haley and Tommy Steele.

Geoff was infatuated with Patricia Reynolds and soon they became engaged, that same summer. Geoff and Roger Woodliffe organised a summer week at Cleethorpes, Humberston Fitties. Our chalet was close to the sand dunes and in sight of the sea. If you needed the toilet, it was a fifty-yard scramble down the garden.

By coincidence all the three girls were called Pat! We referred to them as Pat 1, 2 and 3 and being gentlemen, we let them share the only bed while we camped out on the floor in the lounge-cum-kitchen. Patricia and I were the eldest and married, and she stood for no shenanigans.

We had a great, happy-go-lucky week. In the evenings we would walk over to the pub for a few drinks, though none of us were heavy drinkers. We took early morning dips in the sea as the first fingers of light appeared and generally frolicked around the boating lake like young children. Pat Reynolds fell in, laughing and giggling. You'd never have guessed she was Junior Miss Britain.

Our general buggering about was dampened only when the rain came down. Apart from that, it was like our school days back again.

Many decades later, in his early seventies, Geoff developed diabetes, unrecognised and therefore treated too late. He had to have half a leg amputated and the shock knocked him for six as it did his friends on his behalf. Geoff had two passions: singing and weight training. After Geoff had a prosthetic limb fitted, he became a recluse, or so we were told.

So, settled as we were 140 miles north in Middlesbrough, Pat and I took time off work and drove down to Grimsby. We persuaded Geoff to spend a week or so with us. We had a great time together and it was good to see him smiling again.

Although it took time, he appeared to be accepting his plight and with the help of his gym friends and close friend Jill, he started singing again. Not long after he finally cut a disc of his favourite songs and then knuckled down to singing and some light weight training with Terry and John.

One of our greatest gifts on our golden wedding anniversary (50 years) was Geoff and our Grimsby Health Studio friends turning up to help Pat and me and our family celebrate. Geoff got up on stage alongside Alex, our 16-year-old grandson, who had joined in to play his guitar with the band. Taking the microphone, Geoff glanced at us with a big smile, just as he had over forty ago in the Cafe Dansant and sang our favourite song, 'You Make Me Feel So Young.'

Over the years, before his illness, he became one of Grimsby's best-loved jazz singers. Sadly, his illness got the better of him and this brave man died on 8th April 2010.

It was through Geoff that my taste in music changed from be-bop to the big band and jazz, as did my style in clothes. Out went the Teddy Boy look, DA hairstyle, pea-green suit, drainpipe trousers and brothel creepers. I now wore a single-breasted jacket, with patch pockets tailored for me at Fred Woodliffe's, a gentleman's outfitters, in silver grey flannel, dark blue trousers and oxblood slip-on shoes and a crew-cut hair style. Pat bought me a pale blue knitted Slim Jim tie.

In the 1950s and 60s, Thursday night at the Gaiety Ballroom was Big Band Night, hosting an array of visiting bands: Joe Loss, Ted Heath, Ivy Benson, Jack Parnell, Syd Phillips, Johnny Dankworth, Cyril Stapleton, Eric Delaney, Mick Mulligan, along with George Melly, Dr Crock and his Crackpots and the zany Temperance Seven of 'You're Driving Me Crazy' and 'Pasadena' fame.

The Ray Ellington Quartet, however, was Pat's favourite and mine. He had a wonderful personality and his catch phase in that gravelly voice - 'That's nice!' – would be followed with a grin as wide as a piano keyboard. He accompanied great vocalists: Valerie Masters, Marion Ryan and Susan Maughan (who sang 'Bobby's Girl,' a major hit.) Ray's catchy voice was often heard over BBC Radio's Goon Show.

The first time Patricia and I had heard the famous Ted Heath Band was at the Gaiety. We were both madly in love and aglow with excitement as the band, the biggest this side of the Atlantic, opened up with 'You Belong to Me' with Dickie Valentine. The Gaiety had one of the biggest dance floors in England. Either side of the room were booths with table and chairs. Parallel was a corridor known locally 'Passion Alley.' No need to explain what those occupants got up to.

That night, there were two thousand people packed in the Gaiety Ballroom and more queuing outside. Accompanying Ted Heath's Band were vocalists Dickie Valentine, Lita Roza and Dennis Lotis.

After the week at Humberston Fitties with our new circle of friends, Pat and I went out with Geoff and Pat Reynolds, Roger and Pat Woodliffe most Saturday nights. After a few drinks at the P&M – the Pestle and Mortar - we moved on to Grimsby's Gaiety Ballroom or the Cafe Dansant in Cleethorpes. Our love of dancing and good music was never far away and it was good to take a break from the gym, work and football and spend time with Pat and our friends. Although Roger was not into weight training like me, we played for the same football team on

Saturdays or sometimes watched the Grimsby Mariners play at Blundell Park.

We became firm friends with the Woodliffe family through Roger and his wife Pat. From then on, I had my jackets, suits and shirts made to measure by Roger's father Fred. Besides being a post-office, their shop was a man's outfitters on Grimsby Road, Cleethorpes. Pat got on well immediately with Rogers's mother Peggy. Although in her 50s, much older than us, she was a wonderful person with vibrant good looks. She would ask us to come round to their apartment at the rear of the shop for snacks and also invited us to their Christmas Eve party. With Dave Brubeck's 'Take Five' or the bird-like sounds of Ella Fitzgerald or Lena Horne drifting softly in the background, the drinks flowed like a tide coming in.

Both Pat and I were almost paralytic that Christmas Eve. After wishing everyone a merry Christmas we made the fifteen minutes' walk home in the early hours of a crisp and frosty Christmas morning, and crawled into bed as dawn was breaking. Pat's mother Minnie was awake, sitting in her fireside chair to enjoy her morning Park Drive fix. I could see she was none too pleased at the state of her daughter. I got up still groggy to give Minnie a hand cooking the goose or there would have been no Christmas dinner that year. Pat has always made a big thing of Christmas where everything has to be just right. Crackers to pull, cards artistically displayed, all the trimmings, a tree full of toys and perfectly wrapped presents tied with ribbons, waiting under the tree. She has never altered to this day and I would not want her to.

By 1960 work started to pick up in the shipyard and took out a bank loan to buy David Holmes's Lambretta scooter. Now mobile I could get around quicker to the gym, work and Cafe Dansant than by cycle or bus. I also used the Lambretta when I went fishing on the occasional weekend, sometimes taking Pat along. Wearing our matching red and white crash helmets we could easily be mistaken for Ladybirds.

In the following November, with our friends Steve and Barbara Farman, we spent two nights in London. As it was too expensive by rail, Pat asked her brother Alec if he would lend us his Humber Super Snipe. He readily agreed, as we already had tickets for the show 'Blue Magic' starring Tommy Cooper and Shirley Bassey. Alec thought the world of Pat, his younger sister, and wouldn't hear of us travelling to London in Steve's Ford panel-van. Steve, the only one with a driving licence, relished the idea of driving such a powerful car. It was a massive change from crouching on boxes in the back of Steve's rattling panel van, though we had still managed to get in some good laughs on our nights around town.

Beside the variety show on our first night, we spent the following afternoon at Regents Park Zoo. I wanted to see the zoo's most famous resident, Guy the Gorilla, a 500lb silverback, who was indeed was massive. With fingers bigger than a banana, he could amazingly unwrap a Werther's Original toffee as fast as any human. What also caught my eye was the size of the lions the first time I saw them. I was poised to take a photo when, as I thought, it started raining. Only it wasn't rain, but the bloody lion pissing over me. Not only was it my lost moment resulting in no photographs, but Steve's party piece for over fifty years.

Knowing I was in and out of work Steve got me a job two nights a week as a door attendant or bouncer, as some prefer to call them. Steve introduced me to Harry, the Café Dansant's manager. He was a slight five-foot six individual, with a pleasing calm appearance. Forever the gentleman he greeted everyone with his unassuming smile, the kind you expect from your bank manager! He was always immaculate dressed in a black evening suite, black bow tie and hair slicked back with Brylcreem. At first glance, he reminded me of George Raft, the film star, so often seen as a nightclub owner. Like Raft, Harry was surrounded by four heavies, hired to keep the peace in his establishment.

The door attendant's job only paid £4 a night, though a ticket fiddle could double that. Besides, admitting a further two dozen or so extra customers helped to boost the bar takings, so everyone benefitted. As there was no overtime in the shipyard and I was more often out of work than in, the extra money supplemented my meagre dole money.

My time at the Cafe Dansant was not without its moments. Friday nights were special, when the dance hall could be hired for private company functions. Those nights when a free bar invariably brought trouble. As the town's pubs closing time was 10.30pm, we would get the odd drunkard trying to get in and that often led to a fight inside and out.

As a team, our bouncers looked out for each other, especially if a brawl turned nasty. Troublemakers often thought nothing of head-butting ('the Glasgow kiss') or slugging you with a beer bottle or a chair.

Afterwards back in the gym we would laugh about the previous night's events.

"You should have seen John. He had this guy in a headlock who was squealing like a stuffed pig. And Steve had a woman on his back while fending off her bloke, who'd just been bashing her."

Because of such a night, I came before a judge on a charge of assault. I had 'accidentally' hit a chap, breaking my knuckles in the process and knocking him out cold.

The judge peered at me over his spectacles.

"You must weigh all of fifteen stone, Mr Pratt. Compared to Mr Harvey here, it was clearly no contest. But having said that, I can assume you are primarily employed to keeping the peace and to protecting the welfare of other users of the said establishment against inebriated trouble makers."

The judge turned his frosty gaze on Harvey.

"Case dismissed."

Then, to me, "All the same, Mr Pratt, I do not want to see you here again under similar circumstances."

-11-
Aspirations of a Bodybuilder

I was well into dancing and played football but knew they would not give me the body I craved after seeing the likes of Reg Parks in the *Health and Strength* magazine. I had lost two stone in bodyweight after my operation for peritonitis the year before. The after-effects of ten weeks in hospital was to leave me in a poor physical state overall and that was the primary reason I became interested in weightlifting and bodybuilding.

While at our local dance hall the Alexandra Rooms, I could not help but notice one particular lad. When he took off his leather motorbike jacket, his biceps were bigger than cricket balls stretching his short-sleeved shirt to bursting point. Likewise, his open neck shirt emphasised his pectorals and broad shoulders. Clearly he was a weightlifter of sorts.

Although Barry had a rough gypsy appearance, once you knew him you found out he was a pleasant chap with a ready smile and a twinkle in his good eye! He was not what you would call good-looking, due to his face colliding with a gravel road when he came off his motor bike. His nose was in the process of recovering from hours of necessary plastic surgery.

My girlfriend Pat, knowing I wanted to join a gym after our street clubhouse closed down, urged me to ask him where he worked out.

"It's obvious he's a bodybuilder, Peter," she said, "so go on then."

'I'm a member of the Torrington Street weightlifting" gym." He held out his hand. "Barry Vickers. Come round anytime.

We're looking for members. Have you done any weights before?"

"Pete," I replied. "No, not in a real gym, just mucking about really."

"I'll be there on Monday night. Come along and meet the gang and we'll see what you're made of, Pete."

The Torrington Street Gym in Grimsby was easily found from the street below by the clang of metal. I opened the gym's door to the grunts and groans of occupants busily exercising in the gloom of two light bulbs hanging from the rafters. The gym was compact, no more than 40ft x 20ft. An incline bench, lat machine-pulley, bench press, squat stands and an abdominal board took up most of the floor space.

The gym's walls were decorated with exercise charts and framed pictures of past Mr Universe winners posed in different attitudes: John Grimek, Steve Reeves, Reg Park and John Lees, a Mr Britain winner. Barry Vicars, whom I had met at the dance hall, had just finished exercising on the bench press. He shook my hand and introduced me to the other members. There was Pete Jarvis, whom I had seen earlier squatting with what seemed an enormous load of weights. Terry Brown was on the lat, a pulley contraption for developing the *Latissimus dorsi* and back muscles that I had seen in bodybuilding magazines. John Dent was sat curling a dumbbell and stood up to welcome me, towering four or more inches over my six foot frame.

John was the club's secretary and enrolled me for the weekly sum of 2/6 pence.

From then on I started training every Monday, Wednesday and Friday. John gave me a beginner's schedule after I told him I had only trained at home with a pair of dumbbells and chest expanders. On that first night, I must have done too much on the squats as I could hardly pedal home on my bike. When I got there I told my mother I had joined a bodybuilding gym.

"Thank God for that." She looked up at the living-room ceiling. "So now you can get those contraptions out of my house before your father comes home. He'll not stand for those rattling above his head. I hope this new rigmarole doesn't interfere with your night school. Your father or Uncle Jim won't be too pleased if it does."

I soon settled in with the other gym members. We discussed different training methods and health foods. John Dent introduced me to healthy eating: fresh fruit, brown bread, raw eggs, honey, skimmed milk and brewer's yeast powder, a good form of vitamin B complex that bodybuilders need for strength and muscle growth.

Great quantities were out of the question for me as most foodstuffs were still on rationing and I was on apprentice wages. And as my Mam often reminded us, "Money doesn't grow on trees, yer know."

My sisters then were a boon, helping me with a few shillings here and there, and free milk from Brenda who delivered milk for Clover Dairy."

John was an encyclopaedia of knowledge regarding healthy eating and exercise. In those early years most of my training methods came from John or the *Health and Strength* and *Iron Man* magazines.

Patricia would occasionally meet me afterwards outside the gym after babysitting for her sister Renee. After my work-out we would walk our bikes to John's house, which was nearby. John's wife Myrtle always made us feel at home with tea, cheese and biscuits while John showed me his collection of bodybuilding magazines.

It was from watching John weigh his food that I realised what a life-threatening disease diabetes must be. I had never known anyone else with the disease and asked him more about it. He told me he was diagnosed type1 diabetes at 17 years-old.

John continued entering physique competitions well into his sixties winning five trophies and is still training into his eighties. He sent me a *Grimsby Telegraph* photograph in 2001 taken with his second wife Frances and nurses. He had been awarded the Allan Nabarro Medal presented by at the Diana, Princess of Wales Grimsby Hospital behalf of Diabetes UK, in recognition of John's courage and perseverance in living with diabetes for over fifty years.

A year later, with the Torrington Street gym membership increasing and extra equipment added, we had to move premises. The owner feared the floor would not stand the amount of weight, a valid point considering his delivery van was parked in the garage below. A vacant room was found at the back of the Red Lion public house. Not the best place for a gym with the reputation that bar had, but we had no choice. John Dent's friend Harold Myers, once a weightlifter himself, obligingly helped us transport the gym equipment on one of his trucks.

Our temporary gym was never without its moments. Being at the rear of the town's most notorious boozing bar the gym attracted inquisitive drunken fishermen and prostitutes. We would hear the clatter of stilettos on the outside metal stairs and the door creak open for the girls to have a peek. Just for fun, we were tempted to let them have a go with the weights, but had been told by the manager of the pub 'Strictly NO Women.'

After our usual two-hour session pumping weights, Terry, Peter and I, perhaps with two or three other club members, often went into the Red Lion's bar for a beer to cool down before going home. The knowledgeable Terry would engage in repartee with the girls who now and then sent us over a pint perhaps as a tantaliser for a different kind of trade.

Our time at the Red Lion was short-lived as the amalgamation with the Castle Street Gym came to fruition. In the summer of 1956, the Grimsby Health Studio was born, in a vacant storeroom above Hewins and Goodhand Builders Merchants in Eleanor Street. The new gym was four times bigger than our previous gym and, as word got around Grimsby, we doubled our membership in the first two months.

The following year Pat and I were married and soon after started a women's section on Tuesday and Thursdays evenings. My wife joined as did several other members' wives and girlfriends, especially when our youngest member Patricia Reynolds was crowned Junior Miss Britain.

A year after opening the Grimsby Health Studio, the club bought extra weights and a chrome-plated Olympic barbell. Several members wanted to try the three Olympic lifts – clean and press, snatch and clean and jerk. The club had a good weightlifting team under trainer Pete Ready who was the areas official weightlifting referee: Peter Lockwood, Bill Turner, Terry Brown, Bill Tansley, Peter Jarvis and Colin Bush, all of whom competed in county competitions.

Other members wanted to train just to keep fit - Steve Farman who was once an amateur boxing enthusiast, Jimmy Blastland and Leon Marklew to name a few.

I joined NABBA (the National Amateur British Bodybuilding Association) so I could enter their competitions and had *Health and Strength* magazine delivered by post. Along with John Dent, John Brown and Pete Jarvis I entered my first bodybuilding competition, Mr North East Britain, held at Leeds City Hall.

The club organised a coach as we had our wives, girlfriends and gym members to support us. From my recollections none of us took a place, but it was good experience. I was nervous at the thought of posing on stage in front of hundreds of people, but kept telling myself this was what I had wanted to do.

I realised then to achieve my ambition of becoming Mr Britain or, better still, Mr Universe, I needed a great deal of training to match up to the other contestants. Backstage there must have been twenty or more bodybuilders pumping up or doing floor press-ups, while others dolloped oil on themselves and fellow-competitors. It was overpowering to stand beside the likes of Ron Oakley, Tony Emmett, Malcolm Stringer and Ted Gutterage, all evidently experienced in such competitions. George Greenwood, editor of *Health and Strength* and Oscar Heidenstam, secretary of NABBA, were two of the judges.

After first discussing my situation with Pat she agreed for me to take Dan Doran's postal tuition bodybuilding course. A week later the first instalment arrived, suggesting a split routine training four nights a week. For breakfast, cereals, porridge oats and bran type followed with a skim milk shake, honey or molasses, two raw eggs and a tablespoon of Complan, a good cheap protein powder, available from any chemist. For lunch and dinner, eat plenty of meat, fish, pasta, vegetables, salads and fresh fruit. After six months, my strength increased and my bodyweight went from 165lbs to 190 lbs. It was not long before my family, work colleagues and football team noticed the transformation in size my physique was taking.

Bill Turner, a well-known Grimsby market trader and fruitier and Harold Myers, a haulage contractor, generously drove us around the country to enter competitions. Sheffield, Leeds and Nottingham were the most popular. They were the only members in the gym who owned motor cars; most of us had bikes.

In the spring of 1959 the town's major cinemas, the ABC Regal and Cleethorpes Ritz cinemas approached our gym asking if we could give a bodybuilding display at the premier of the new film Hercules starring the legendary Steve Reeves in the lead role. Reeves had won the1950 Mr America and Mr Universe and was a bodybuilding legend. Together with John Brown and Peter Jarvis, I took part in the posing displays, which was followed by our weightlifting team demonstrating the three Olympic lifts. Our nightly displays proved a great success and continued for a further three weeks.

The club organised a coach trip to London for the 1959 Mr Universe competition held in the Victoria Palace Theatre. After the show in the Russell Square Hotel ballroom there was a get-together function to meet some of the world's best bodybuilders. One of the most amiable and interesting was American Bill Golumbick, who sat with Pat and me discussing training and diet. He mentioned adding an avocado pear every day to his diet. I didn't know what an avocado was until then. He told me there is more goodness in one avocado than in a 2lb beefsteak...

"But don't pass the steaks up, Peter," he laughed.

In later years I found avocados plentiful in Africa and even now in New Zealand are always added to our salads.

Vince Geronda was another American we met. Even at the age of 44, his unique style in posing and his fabulous physique was the best in the show! Pat still has his signed photograph in our album.

In the summer of 1960, our gym organised the Mr and Miss Lincolnshire competition held at the Cleethorpes Pier. We invited Len Sell, the current Mr Universe and Junior Mr Britain, Dave Stroud, to act as judges for the posing display. Our own

Patricia Reynolds, Junior Miss Britain and newly-crowned Miss North East Britain added Miss Lincolnshire to her titles that day. John Brown, one of my training partners, won the Mr Lincolnshire to add to his third place in the Mr North-East Britain.

My wife Pat surprised me by entering the Miss Lincolnshire competition, and although she was a worthy contender, it was her first and last.

The turning point in my bodybuilding aspirations came after I met Derek Manthorpe (who owned the Manorbe Gym in Brighton) at the 1960 Mr Midlands in Manchester. I admired Derek's articles in the *Health and Strength* magazine and was impressed by his methods of training. He trained George Cox and Adrian Heryet, both Mr Britain winners and Universe contenders. Derek said I had good potential and suggested I should try his postal training schedules and emphasised a strict style.

"You have to concentrate and feel the muscle you're working," he told me.

The following week Derek Manthorpe's training schedules arrived, rotated every six weeks along with specialist advice on diet, especially 'No sugar.' Within ten weeks my physique took on a new look, lighter in bodyweight and more defined. Derek told me I must continue to practice posing as well, flowing slowly and smoothly from one position to the next, then tense and hold. Balance is all important as well as posture. You look straight ahead, never down.

Knowing the Mr Lincolnshire Competition was three months away, I worked out four nights on my full training schedule in the Grimsby Health Studio and three nights mainly on abdominals and calves in the Barcroft Street Gym it being a five minute walk from our house. While training in the gym I wore plastic bloomers under my tracksuit to retain the heat. Sometimes I would feel a trickle of water (sweat) as it leaked down my legs.

I was in the best shape that I had ever been after shedding 14lbs in three months. My physique became leaner, with sharper muscle definition and I had a good natural suntan thanks to a wonderful early summer. Pat complained saying I was too skinny, but I felt great - fit and confident. It was hard work travelling thirteen miles to and from Immingham in a smoke-filled tramcar, almost an hour there and back daily, but thankfully I had a job.

After nine months' training under Derek Manthorpe, the hard work paid off. I won the1961 Mr Lincolnshire competition held at the Winter Gardens Ballroom in Cleethorpes. Earl Maynard, the current Mr Universe judged, and later gave a posing display. As always, Earl astounded us with his magnificent physique. Pat Reynolds judged the Miss Lincolnshire competition and presented me with the Mr Lincolnshire Trophy.

The following week I entered the Mr Adonis competition held in Scarborough in the Holiday Town Parade, a regular Saturday night variety show visiting Britain's main seaside resorts. The winner would receive £25, £20 for second place and £15 for third, so it was worthwhile entering when my weekly wage in the shipyard was ten-pounds. Besides the Adonis, there was a Beauty Queen and Fashion competition. Disappointingly, I wasn't placed, but stayed over with the lads for the Saturday night show to see who won.

Unexpectedly, one of our women gym members was there and we spent the night together. Two days later, we both absconded to London on my Lambretta. Our affair had started while I was a bouncer at the Cafe Dansant, where I became infatuated with her. Running away with her was the most selfish and stupid act I have ever committed. To this day, I don't know why or what came over me because I still loved Pat more than any man could.

Pat eventually found out where I was working through my old firm Humber Graving Dock, possibly through the Boilermakers Union, and discovered we were in London. She came with my parents to the boarding house in Catford South London where the woman and I were staying. I got the shock of my life to see my Dad with Pat standing by the roadside near where I worked. I stopped my Lambretta and Dad came up to me with a raised hand as if to hit me, but quickly withdrew it.

Back at the boarding house, I had never felt so ashamed when I saw my poor mother, her eyes red with crying and worrying over where I was the past two weeks. The boarding-house landlady wasn't too pleased either to know she had harboured two married runaways.

The following day before I saw my parents safely on the train to Grimsby, my father made me promise this would never happen again. It was known in the family his own father, my Granddad, had left his family for another woman. Maybe my actions brought back unpleasant memories for him.

After my lady friend caught the early train back to Cleethorpes, Patricia and I stayed in London at the boarding house for a few more days to discuss our future. We visited Brighton for the day to see Derek Manthorpe at the Manorbe Gym and shared with him intention to move there one day. Though it was late in the day when we arrived back in Grimsby I had to see if Mam and Dad were OK and to let them know Pat and I were going to be all right.

We had been married then four years and the turning point came sooner than expected. After finding myself in the dole queue again I saw a job offered at a steel fabricators in London. Ironically, it turned out to be the same company, Farmers Engineering, where I had worked previously during my moment of madness. Farmers offered me four months' work, which was all I needed as a stepping stone to Brighton and a better future for Pat and me. Knowing that I would be travelling to and from London, the Lambretta scooter was no longer an option, so I exchanged it for a more powerful motorbike.

Instantly everything changed for us.

In London again, I was lucky to find good lodgings with Mr and Mrs Adams near to work. Every other weekend I rode to Cleethorpes on the motorbike to spend time with Pat and her mother Minnie and to visit my own parents in Grimsby. I found that nothing had changed except me. At times, I felt like a stranger in my own town. Knowing we were going to move to Brighton we had to ensure Pat's mother was comfortably placed when we left, and at some later stage she moved in to stay with her daughter Joyce and family.

Pat made all the arrangement for our final, removal to Brighton from Cleethorpes. I don't think we realised at the time what a huge and costly decision we had made in transferring from one town to another and how difficult it would prove. For example, neither of us had ever lived more than four-miles away from our parents, sisters, brothers and friends. We had always known the people around us and it never occurred to me how Patricia felt, especially leaving her mother behind. However, Pat had older sisters and brothers to take care of Minnie, probably better than we could have done, and I had four married sisters who all lived near to our parents.

-12-

Brighton

I met Pat at London's Kings Cross rail station and we stayed one final night at Mrs Adams where I had lodged for the last four months in Lewisham. The following day we left for Brighton on my motor bike, its luggage rack piled high with our suitcases. Arriving in Brighton we stayed with Derek and Louise Manthorpe for three days until our household goods arrived from Cleethorpes.

That gave Pat and Louise time to get to know one another and explore the town's famous lanes and the Royal Pavilion with its Indian architecture, domes, towers and minarets, built by the Prince Regent (George IV) in 1787 as a seaside retreat. We continued along the sweeping two-mile esplanade and pebbled beach to Hove, with its Regency townhouses and posh hotels such as the Grand. That first week in Brighton was like a second honeymoon until reality struck. We had to find work.

Three weeks before Christmas 1961, we moved into the ground floor apartment at No. 45 Hampstead Road in Preston Park, a quiet suburb of Brighton. Derek had already introduced us to the proprietor Mrs Hall to take over Derek's remaining two years' lease. Mrs Hall was a tall haughty type who occupied the upstairs apartment. As she worked in London, we only saw her on her two weekend visits each month when she collected the rent.

The only fault we found there was no means for us to have a decent bath. We could wash at the back kitchen sink or ask to use Mrs Hall's bathroom upstairs on her weekend visits. I soon let her know this arrangement was most inconvenient, which came as a surprise to her. Before signing the lease I asked if we could at least install a shower for our own private use. With a curt nod, she agreed and without further ado increased our rent by another pound, making it a total of £16 a month. Putting up the rent another pound might not seem much these days, but it was an enormous amount then. Our past combined earnings of £15 a week had left us struggling to save anything. At least Patricia and I were together and, for the first time in our four years of marriage, in our own place.

Our flat at 45 Hampstead Road was set high above Preston Park in a long line of terraced dwellings only a few minutes down from Preston Park railway station and the busy London Road into Brighton. The window of the front room (our bedroom) overlooked The Drove, a pretty tree-lined street and a treacherous 1-in-4 incline that even motor cars groaned while ascending. Each side had handrails to assist pedestrians along the pavements. Even the fittest, including me, had to take a breather halfway.

Walking down was easy, but having to walk back up again was another matter as Pat soon found out. Out exploring the town she found she had to carry her groceries and the 14lb bag of coal nuggets for our fire. This was the reason we ended up installing two gas fires on the never-never in our flat. A television was the final touch to our new home. The one great advantage was the wonderful view of the rolling Sussex Downs.

As always Patricia organised all the decorating as she had an artistic flair for colour schemes, whether for her own clothes or curtains, wallpapers and paints. Furthermore, she was a dab hand with a Singer sewing machine. In fact she could turn her hand to almost anything and always enjoyed a challenge. Our furniture from Cleethorpes arrived and the bedroom suite and lounge furniture fitted in perfectly. Luckily the rooms were similar in size to those in Pat's mother's house.

We felt strange without her at first, not seeing her mother around and active as she rode her sit up and beg bicycle, with the fumes of a Park Drive cigarette trailing behind her. For all her little faults, Minnie was no trouble and good company for Pat. I suppose that I did spend too many evenings in the gym and then as a door attendant at the Cafe Dansant. While we were starting over in Brighton I did often wonder if, after the other woman episode, our days will ever be the same again.

Second to me getting a job a Christmas present for Patricia was on my mind as we were hard pushed for money. So not only what to get her, but with what. A few days before Christmas with a last ten-shilling note burning a hole in my wallet I saw a ring for seven shillings and sixpence in a jeweller's window on Western Road.

"Pure antique copper, sir, vedy, vedy unusual and extremely well crafted."

The salesman spoke with a musical flowing Bombay accent and with a reassuring bobbing of his head. When Patricia opened the little present on Christmas morning she seemed over the moon with the ring and wore it almost every day for years. And I was more than happy with my present - socks, hankies and a silk tie. We were kindly invited for dinner at the Manthorpes, our quietest Christmas ever since their classical taste in music was not ours.

In the snowbound new year of 1962, we both started work, Patricia started at a printer's in Heyward's Heath, a fifteen-minute train journey. I thought it was a brave decision on her part, as back in Cleethorpes she only rode a bicycle to work and had never been on a train until she was twenty. The weather was abominable, snow and ice everywhere making trains and buses late. Three days into her job, Pat saw another advertisement for a bookbinder's assistant at Graphic Arts Printers that was only a ten minute walk from our flat down The Drove. She was more than qualified and got the job immediately.

Before Christmas, the Boilermakers Union told me to report to Smiths Structural Steel in Horley. I hadn't a clue where Horley was and he told it was a half hour's train journey from Brighton. Snow was falling thick and fast so it actually took an hour and half due to the inclement weather. Arriving at Smiths for my interview less than half the workforce had turned up. Six hours later I arrived back home, miserable and sodden wet, but most annoyed that even Smiths works manager whom I had spoken to before the holidays hadn't come into work either.

It's funny how things turn out. That same evening in the gym Derek introduced me to another member, Ernest. He was a retired engineering consultant who proved most obliging. He gave me his business card and suggested I get in touch with Mr Boyes, General Manager at the Phoenix Iron Works in Lewes. My interview with Mr Boyes went well and he introduced me to his workshop manager and foreman. The workshop employed a workforce of about thirty men and contained a varied mix of metal-forming machinery (radial-drill, plate guillotine, rolls, break-press, hole punch and angle iron cropper) besides the usual welding machines. Some of the machines were new to me, but I soon adapted to their usage not realising then exactly how useful this knowledge would be in the years to come. At least I was no longer crawling through filthy bilges in the bowels of a ship.

So after my first winter and as the weather improved I started riding my motor cycle to work. It was a pleasant ride along the Sussex Downs and furthermore it saved me time in getting to the Manorbe gym after work. Pat settled happily in her job at the printers only a short walk away. While I worked out in the gym, Pat would prepare our evening meal to be ready by seven after which we usually sat and watched television.

My first year at the Phoenix Iron Works flew by as I settled in with the friendly bunch of workers, one of whom left to migrate to Africa. That's when the seed was sown and from then on I habitually scoured Thursday's *Daily Telegraph* situations vacant for overseas work as he had done.

The Manorbe Health Studio had two gyms, one of them under the Brighton Ice Rink on West Street. This was where most of the everyday, no airs and graces, rough and tumble lads trained using the heavier weightlifting equipment. I trained there with Al Maggs, the current Mr Wales, and Adrian Heryet, who was Mr Britain. Adrian later on became a Mr Universe runner-up three times over and later held the title of Mr Europe and Europe's strongest man. Adrian had only been training two years before he won the Mr Britain title. He was extraordinary, a natural like Reg Parks and Steve Reeves, both Mr Universe winners.

Adrian's physical transformation during the three years I knew him was incredible. He had film-star good looks, and was shy, soft spoken and unassuming person, always with a ready smile. As a working class lad like many of us - Adrian erected television aerials with his brother. Like many of us he took up the sport before we knew Anabolic steroids existed. We were natural bodybuilders. The only supplements I took were vitamin B12, Vitamin C and pure wheat germ oil, vitamin E and my daily Complan protein milkshake.

Although our training regimes were taken seriously, especially before physique competitions, it was inevitable that occasionally we would break the rules. We shared jokes and performed pranks on one another, which would not be appreciated in the businessmen's and ladies' gym up the road. There the atmosphere was tranquil, the equipment chrome-plated, with comfortably padded workout benches, carpeted floors, a full body sunlamp and steam cubicles.

At times, I was asked to supervise there to relieve Derek and Dick from the long hours involved in running both gyms. This also gave me the opportunity to understand how a professional gym was organised, a learning curve that came in handy for me in later years.

Our new life in Brighton was not all work and gym. We kept the weekends free so Patricia and I could spend time together. During the good weather we could visit the beach and on Saturday nights go dancing and to the movies on Sundays, when we could afford to, that was. With our first year in Brighton under our belt, we were both enjoying our work and quickly made new friends. We would make up a foursome with one of my training partners – a 'Brummie' or Birmingham exile – and his wife, another Patricia.

We'd go for a drink and on to dancing at the Regent Ballroom. There, Syd Dean and his Band played our type of music, sometimes featuring Jill Day as one of his singers. We had nights at the Devils Dyke Hotel noted for discos or a live band that emulated the latest Beatles hits, such as 'I Want to Hold Your Hand' or Chubby Checkers 'Twist and Shout' or Gerry and the Pacemakers with 'How Do You Do What You Do To Me,' to name a few. Yet again our taste in music was taking another turn, as was my dress code. Italian style mohair suits, with a four-button shorter jacket, Slim Jim tie and winkle-picker shoes were now the mode for men. Pat's style didn't change much though she went for the shorter hemlines of the mini and Mary Quant fashion.

Our first year in Brighton had gone quickly for Pat and me and we were about to experience our worst winter ever. With Brummie and his wife Pat, Dave Reed our gym's junior Mr Brighton and his girlfriend Helen, we had seen in the New Year at the Hove Bowl, noted for its ten-pin bowling. The MC stopped the music to announce a warning that heavy falls of snow were blocking most of the roads and that taxi and buses had stopped operating. We left the 'Bowl' wrapped up in our overcoats and hats as snow continued to fall, blanketing the town. Not wanting to be stranded we quickly said our farewells and passed on New Year wishes before trudging home in knee-deep snowdrifts.

The following morning the snow was up to the windowsills and I had to dig a path through three feet of snow to visit our only toilet in the back yard. Not a happy start to 1963, with the county in the grip of its worst snowfalls since 1947. Everything that could froze solid: water pipes, toilets and drains. The council had to install emergency standpipes with taps in the street so we had fresh water. As spring and Easter approached, the rubbish-filled snow that had been banked along the roadside was melting fast and ran in streams in the roadside gutters.

I had a letter from my sister Brenda telling me that our mother was over the worst of her illness. The doctor said there was no need for more hospital radiotherapy so she was back to her usual self, shopping on Corporation Road. After discussing it with Pat, I insisted that Mam and Dad come and stay with us for a week in the summer thinking the change of air would do them both good.

After the Easter holiday I passed my car-driving test, sold my motorcycle and took out a small bank loan to buy Adrian Heryet's 1961 Ford Anglia. This was the deluxe model, primrose yellow with a white roof, pale blue seats and whitewall tyres –

even a radio! Though, as Pat said, "It's a dream but paying back the bank loan is not!"

Unable to afford to go and fetch my parents, I met them at Brighton Railway Station, noting how exhausted they were after the eight-hour journey. It was only two months after Mam had been given the all clear after undergoing treatment for breast cancer. When I hugged her, I could feel the bones under her coat and I had never seen her so thin. Her once chubby, healthy face was pale and sunken and she had dark rings under her eyes. It had been months since I laid eyes on them both, and I was shocked. As I took the suitcase from Dad, thoughts came flooding back to the day Mam took me with her to meet him at the Grimsby railway station.

The familiar aroma of Old Holborn tobacco still lingered, but not the familiar smile. He was older, skinnier than I remembered, his face drawn. He wore a cloth cap instead of his trademark trilby.

"Are you all right, Pete? And where is Pat?"

"Yes, we're fine, Dad. You both look well," I lied. "I have a car now so I'll drive you and Mam to our place where Pat's getting our tea ready."

Although Mam had lost so much weight, I was surprised at how chirpy she was. Then again, my mother was never one to complain. Pat and I could only afford one week's holiday so we had days out in our car. Pat had already booked tickets for Max Bygraves at the Brighton Hippodrome as we knew Mam liked him.

We were lucky and as the weather was sunny, we visited the Royal Pavilion and gardens, where my mother was overawed by its splendour. I drove Dad to Shoreham Docks to see which ships were in dock. There were two discharging coal for the power station. Dad said he'd been there a few times. We had a pint of beer in a pub near the toll bridge that pleased Dad, as he loved his pint of bitter.

"Not as good as Hewitt's, though, Pete," he commented as he rolled another fag. "Bloody Southerners can't make good ale."

"Mam and I can't understand why you left Grimsby to live down here, I hope things are right with you and Pat. Your mother worries about you and she's still not well."

"There's no need to, Dad, I promise you..."

"Irene and the others can't think why you have to be here when there's plenty of work coming off. As Mam says, you're never settled since that shenanigans with that other woman and what has this bodybuilding lark done for you? You married a beautiful girl in Pat. No other would have had you back. When are you going to settle down and have a family like the rest of your sisters and brothers?"

Dad stood up and drained the last of his beer, wiped his mouth with his handkerchief and lit another cigarette with a shaky hand. Was it anger? We had never ever talked like this - man to man.

Their week soon passed and it was a sad parting to put them on the train so soon. I felt embarrassed not being able to drive them back to Grimsby, but I couldn't afford taking either the time off work or the cost of petrol.

Two weeks later I received a telegram from my sister Brenda telling me that Dad had had a severe stroke and was admitted in Grimsby Hospital, where he was being well-cared for. She never mentioned how my mother was or how it was affecting her.

We drove down to Grimsby the following day. Dad looked older than his 72 years as he lay unshaven and gaunt without his teeth in. He was unable to speak and unable to walk or use his arm and I realised he was paralysed down his entire right side.

Unable to do anything and knowing mother was coping with the help of my sisters, we returned to Brighton. Three weeks later, my poor mother had a relapse. The doctors said the shock of finding Dad on the bedroom floor might have brought mother's cancer back. The last time I saw my mother alive she was in the Grimsby District Hospital and looked barely human. My Mother died the following week on 3rd August, just six weeks after only staying with us in Brighton.

With that dreadful month done with, I tried to enjoy what was left of summer. Summers in Brighton seemed to transport one into a different world where, as in Cliff Richard's film 'Summer Holiday' everyone was happy. It was a great feeling to be near a seaside again and better still with Pat by my side.

My training partners, Al Maggs, Dave Reid, Adrian Heryet, Derek and Dick, were all part-time lifeguards. Patricia and I would often visit their 'patch' between the Milk Maid Café and West Pier on Saturdays and Sundays where we also took in some serious sunbathing. That autumn I won the 1963 Mr Brighton followed by the Mr South Britain held in Southampton. At last I had achieved one of my goals as winning the Mr South Britain title entitled me to enter the 1964 Mr Britain in April. I was also eligible to enter the Mr Universe the following September.

In the *Daily Telegraph*'s situation was an advert: 'Immigrants wanted for South Africa.' There was a long list of trades ranging from boilermakers, fitters and electricians topping the list of their priorities. After some serious discussion with Patricia, she agreed it wouldn't do any harm to write for more information.

"The grass is greener there, is it, Pete?" she quipped.

Two weeks later, we were opening two bulky A4, brown envelopes stuffed with forms and literature and beautiful coloured maps of South Africa. One showed its many tribal areas and game parks. Filling out the forms was an overwhelming exercise as immigration required total information including the far end of a fart! Mostly what they wanted were things we didn't have and had never thought we'd need: passports, birth certificates, marriage certificates, our medical history and work references from past and present employers, proof of work experience and our and educational qualifications. It took us eight weeks to gather everything together and send them back to South Africa House in London. The waiting was traumatic resulting in sleepless nights.

In November our applications were accepted and all we needed next were our medical examinations to travel to South Africa the following February. Derek Manthorpe suggested we put this off until we first asked our landlady about the remaining four months on our lease.

As a matter of urgency, we both arranged to see Mrs Hall at London's Knightsbridge Hotel where she worked as the housekeeper. We never thought that she would make us stay the full term but she did as the contract was binding. From then our relationship with her cooled.

I wrote to Samorgan, the South African Immigration Agency who were dealing with our applications. I told them why we couldn't go until the April and they were very obliging and assured me that our details would be kept on file.

In the meantime, we had a welcome surprise, a letter from Colin and Gwenda Bush. Colin and I trained together in the Grimsby Health Studio for several years. They had decided to move to Brighton after we had told them what it was like there. They both found jobs: Gwenda in a jewellers and Colin, a highly skilled Marconi radar engineer, with a local company servicing private yachts, boats and ships. It was like old times dancing at the Regency Ballroom, on a pub crawl or day trips along the coast to Arundel. After several months and realising that Pat and I were still thinking of emigrating, I think it came as a bit of a disappointment for them that life in Brighton would not be the same without us. They moved back to Grimsby just before Patricia and I finally emigrated.

The following February I contacted Samorgan again to let them know that we were free to immigrate any time after April 30th. In the meantime I had passed an interview with Baker Perkins in Peterborough who offered me a boilermaker's position in their Johannesburg works with free accommodation. The following week Samorgan the South African Immigration Agency sent me another bulky brown envelope with more forms to complete. They wanted them returned within two weeks together with our new medical certificates to verify our health. Had we ever had malaria, smallpox, polio, heart problems or venereal diseases? Other questions were endless and sometimes baffling.

While the doctor carried out our routine health tests, he asked me where we were emigrating and I told him South Africa.

"Lucky you," he chirped. "Wish I'd gone years ago when I had the chance. Anyway, good luck to you both."

While he was examining Pat, he noticed she was limping and saw the verruca on the sole of her right foot. He advised removal, offered to do it but said it would be painful for a few weeks. It was, too, as I sensed when she was hobbling around trying to do her housework. After two weeks, she managed to return her job at Graphic Arts. We then had to have chest X-rays, blood tests, injections against, cholera, yellow fever, typhoid, polio and smallpox. The doctor did advise we take some form of malaria preventative three weeks before we were due to arrive in Africa. For the following few days, we felt the effects from the injections.

142

We received a letter of acceptance from Samorgan and a firm date to travel. On the 4th May 1964 we had to be at Southend airport for the Channel Airways flight to Basle in Switzerland and then by Swissair to Johannesburg.

Our Brighton friends thought we were mad and thought we might change our minds after seeing what Stanley Baker and Michael Caine went through in the film *Zulu*. The film had just made its appearance on the British screens and it fuelled my desire to go Africa even more, in fulfilment of a boyhood dream.

From that moment on everything moved ahead rapidly. We had buyers for our furniture, car and anything we were unable to ship abroad or did not want. The things we did ship went in an old steamer trunk we had bought from a second-hand shop. It proved ideal along with another wooden crate for our meagre but invaluable possessions.

Ten days before leaving I entered the 1964 Mr Britain held at London's Scala Theatre London. I didn't expect to be placed anywhere as those last few months I had hardly trained with the same zest. Nevertheless, I had earned the privilege to be there. It was the last time we would see our Brighton friends: Derek and Louise, Dick, Adrian and many other gym members who turned up. After the show outside the Scala Theatre, I didn't realise until we had the photograph developed that they had all stood in front of a Beatles poster. All my Manorbe Gym mates stood with Pat and she looked amazing in what is still one of my favourite photographs to this day.

Afterwards we travelled by train to Grimsby to spend our last week with Patricia's sister Renée. That way we were central to visit Pat's mother Minnie and her other sister Joyce and her brothers and my own four sisters, who were all married with young children and living in Grimsby.

I had a strange feeling as I visited my father that this might be the last time I would see him and I wondered if he felt the same about me. He was staying with my eldest sister Irene, her husband Jim, and my four young nephews. It was a relief for me knowing that Dad was being well-cared for with such a wonderful family. On the other hand it was the saddest moment of my life seeing Dad sitting in sun on that final day of April. Something told me to take his photograph and I am so pleased I did.

Two days later on 4th May 1964, both aged 27, Patricia and I left Grimsby bound for Africa. As we sat together on the train bound for London and the plane to whisk us to a new world. I had only one question in mind.

What will be at the end of this road from Grimsby?

Part Two:
A Step in the Sun

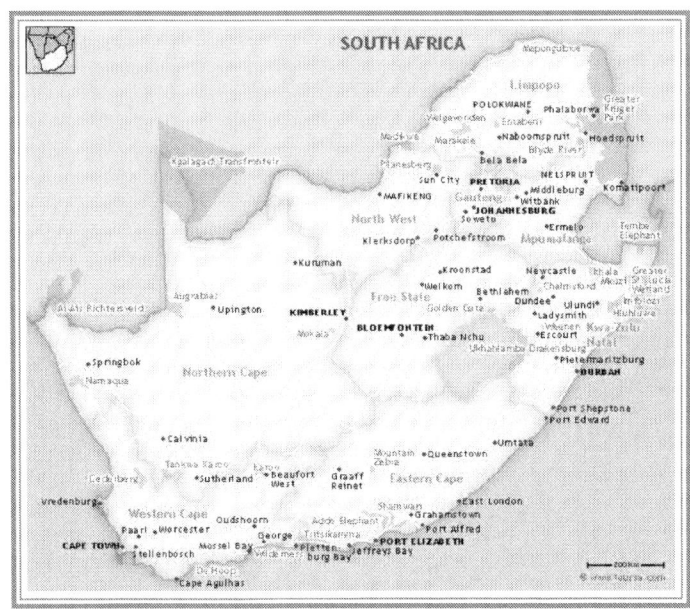

Maps by kind permission of Tour SA Travel Pty Ltd.
(2015)

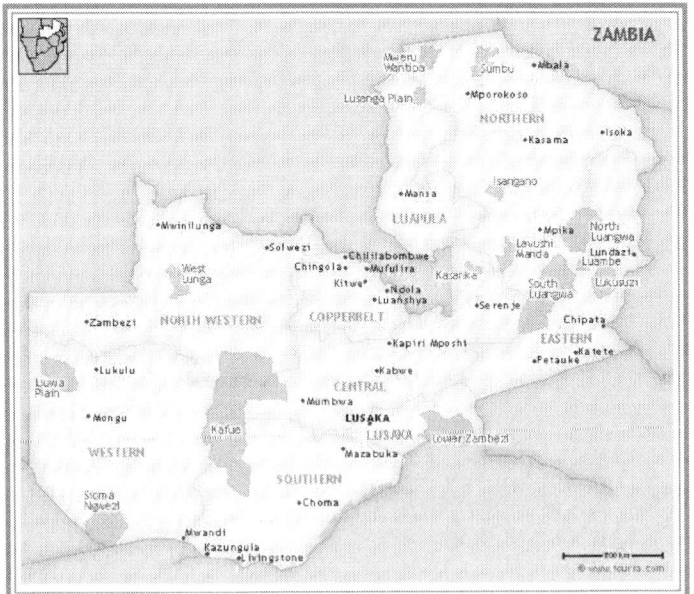

-13-
A Passage to Africa

On May 4th 1964, both aged 27 and the month before our seventh wedding anniversary, Patricia and I left England bound for South Africa. We had said our goodbyes to our families and friends who, amid all the tears, wished us every happiness and success.

Arriving at Southend Airport after four hours travelling by bus and train from Grimsby, we joined other immigrants leaving their homeland to settle in South Africa. The flight across the English Channel to Basel in Switzerland was the first leg of the journey, and this was the first time either of I or Patricia had been on an aeroplane.

I gazed around the aeroplane and wondered how what was basically a huge metal box could possibly hold safely some eighty or so passengers and a mountain of luggage. The Channel Airways plane was old, by all accounts, and didn't look to be in good fettle, according to a nearby adjacent passenger. My tummy squirmed. Was my first ever flight going be as exciting as I imagined it might be?

Settled in our allotted seats we strapped ourselves in as the flight attendant continued with his pre-flight safety demonstration. 'If we lose air pressure, oxygen masks like these will drop down, hold it over your mouth and breathe normally.' What concerned me most was his instruction concerning the inflatable lifejacket under our seats. What good is that if you're tumbling to earth? My neighbour across the aisle was fidgeting with his rosary beads as the flight attendant lifted the lifejacket over his head and secured the tapes around his waist. Then he pretended to pull a cord that would automatically inflate the lifejacket and indicated the light and whistle for signalling your whereabouts.

"Whatever you do," he advised, "don't panic or inflate the lifejacket until you're out of the aircraft."

Another flight attendant was handing out boiled sweets.

"Suck one to help relieve the pressure on your eardrums. At cruising height it also helps to swallow several times, pinch your nose and blow. Don't panic if your ears pop; it's a normal reaction."

Don't panic? I already was.

The plane slowly taxied to the far end of the runway and paused as if to take aim. Then the engines revved at an alarming rate and the plane vibrated and shook like a dog shaking water off its back. Another bout of panic. What was I doing here?

Before I could answer we hurtled down the runway and, like a stone hurled from a catapult, were airborne. I braced my knees and, white-knuckled, gripped the armrests. Within minutes we had swiftly left behind England's green and pleasant land, patchwork fields, country lanes and quaint cottages. Below the grey English Channel glistened and swelled. There could be no turning back.

I gently squeezed Patricia's hand.

"A penny for your thoughts, love," I whispered.

"Oh, nothing really." She smiled, and squeezed back. "I'm just admiring the view."

But I'm sure that, like me, she was thinking of our families and friends.

No sooner had we landed at Basel in Switzerland than a delay was announced over the airport tannoy system, a delay that lasted a tiring and boring seven hours, especially hard on fellow passengers coping with young families. Eventually we boarded our plane to Johannesburg, South Africa. The aircraft was a DC4, a handsome craft with Swissair boldly painted along its fuselage. The red-painted tailfin sported the same white cross as on my Swiss penknife.

I asked the flight attendant if I could retrieve our hand luggage, which held our change of clothes and toiletries set aside for this journey.

"Sorry, sir. All luggage has been stowed in the hold until we reach South Africa."

"How long will that be?"

He shrugged. "I'm not sure, sir."

We boarded the plane and found our seats overlooking the port wing. Like the Channel Airways plane the Swissair seating wasn't designed either for the six-foot tall and I found them equally uncomfortable. The pilot's gravelly voice came over the plane's intercom.

"Welcome aboard Swissair to Johannesburg South Africa. First I would like to extend my apologies for the delay and any inconvenience caused. After crossing the Mediterranean Sea our first refuelling stop will be in Libya on the North African Coast. I hope you all enjoy a pleasant flight."

My brother James was stationed at that time with RAF in Tripoli. Knowing we were to land there he had wanted to meet us at Tripoli International Air Terminal. He explained why he couldn't in a letter to me later. At the time South Africa-bound planes were not allowed to land at Tripoli International Airport due to their apartheid policies, nor was he allowed to visit the refuelling airstrip.

Instead we landed at mid-day at what appeared to be a desert airfield with only military aircraft there. The heat struck me as if through an open furnace door as we walked across the runway to a converted World War 2 corrugated iron Nissan hut. Inside it was even more oppressive without the luxury of any air-conditioning. The only furniture was a disorderly scattering of grubby metal tables and chairs. We formed a queue with our fellow passengers and were served refreshments by three bearded and scrawny old Arabs dressed in long white robes with white skullcaps and sandals. All they could offer was tepid orange Fanta, Coca-Cola and hot sweet tea and biscuits. At the entrance armed militia kept us company as if to prevent us from escaping. This scenario with its background of wailing Arabic music brought home the fact that I was indeed in a foreign land.

We were glad to be back in the scented coolness of the plane's air-conditioning. We endured four hours of turbulent flight over the Sahara desert and mountains, as air pockets sucked the plane into emptiness. Besides my own private fears, I had to listen to the cries of, "Oh, my God! What's happening?" or the excited screams of silly teenagers as if they were riding a big dipper.

Apologetically our captain warned us to remain seated with seat belts fastened. Occasionally he updated us on air speed altitude and outside temperatures. I wasn't sure how many of the passengers wanted to know.

We had been travelling twenty-six hours since leaving England when the plane landed at Kano International Airport in Nigeria. A tropical rainstorm was in progress, and silver streaks of lightning slashed across the night sky. A substantial dinner in the airport's restaurant laid on by Swiss Air was my first real meal since leaving England.

Pat was suffering badly from airsickness and like many other passengers could not be bothered to get off the plane. I was worried, as she lay up under a blanket, which was not like her at all.

After three hours in Kano, we took off for Brazzaville in the Belgian Congo, our final refuelling call before Johannesburg South Africa. By then Pat looked better and was eager to disembark.

"Good morning, everyone. I hope you all had a good night's sleep. We shall soon be over the west coast of Africa and landing shortly at Brazzaville. Please stay seated with your seat belts fastened until the aircraft stops. For your own safety the cabin crew will guide you to the terminal building."

As we lost altitude I saw through a break in the darkness a glistening silver ribbon, which an air steward informed me was the River Congo. We landed in the pink hue of dawn and I descended from the plane in a deathly quiet. The air was languid and humid with a low-lying mist swirling across the airfield as we traipsed to the terminal building. My first thoughts were of Joseph Conrad's *Heart of Darkness* that a friend lent me when he knew I was going to Africa. I shared in Marlow's thoughts: "No sounds, bird, animals or drums, chants or howls."

At Brazzaville's airport, as in Tripoli, heavily-armed guards dressed in army fatigues showed not a glimmer of welcome at our presence. Their faces were expressionless and their eyes missed nothing. The Congo was not the best of countries to be in during this period of coup d'état - a disorder spreading through Africa that Britain's Prime Minister Harold Macmillan once famously called "the winds of change."

The airport building seemed deserted except for the solders. The cafeteria in the transit lounge was closed and, as far as I was concerned, it could stay shut forever. Annoying and persistent flies droned in the air and insolent amber-coloured cockroaches scuttled along counters and floors. Now I realised why we had had to undergo a multitude of inoculations: typhoid, hepatitis B, tetanus, polio and yellow fever.

After a brief stop to refuel we flew swiftly out of Conrad's 'dark and unearthly Congolese forest.' Minutes later the blood-red orb of the rising sun spread its fire over the Southern African horizon. My fellow passengers came to life as its brilliance filtered through cabin windows. Not long after the 'Fasten Your Seat Belt' sign lit up as the plane made a slow banking curve. The engine changed tune abruptly followed by the familiar whirr of hydraulics and the final clunk as the undercarriage dropped. With a screech of the plane's wheels we came smoothly to ground.

Whatever doubts had been creeping in about this bold venture of ours were dispelled as I glanced up at Jan Smuts International Airport, Johannesburg. After a gruelling 35 hours: by bus, train and plane across 6,000 miles we had finally arrived in South Africa. What began as an idea had become a burning obsession, something that finally we had to do. Our £10 passage to Africa had come to an exhausting but truly successful conclusion.

We went through the formality of immigration control and baggage collection. Mrs Van Reardon introduced herself as the Samorgan representative and welcomed us all to South Africa, checking our names before we boarded the coach to Johannesburg. I glanced up at the clear blue sky and around the airport buildings, enhanced by the perfume from blossoming gardens where jacaranda trees, scarlet hibiscus and flourishing bougainvillea stretched up from the rich ochre soil. This first glance of South Africa was exactly as I had imagined it to be: colourful, bright and sunny.

Once clear of the airport the landscape changed dramatically to a red-brown open landscape, or veldt in Afrikaans. Sprawling farm dwellings and corrugated iron-roofed bungalows. This was a different scene from the verdant quilted fields of England. Groups of natives queued to board overloaded buses and barefoot children played football with a bundle of rags by the dusty roadside. They waved joyously as we sped by engulfing them in a cloud of red dust.

Young women in ankle-length dresses moved as gracefully as fashion models with bundles balanced on their heads. Others of all shapes and sizes carried babies across their backs wrapped hammock-style in shawls. Around their arms, ankles and necks were colourfully beaded necklaces and bangles. My limited travelling experience was around England, Scotland and Wales. Nothing had prepared me for scenes only previously known from films and picture books.

Mrs Van Reardon saw the interest we took in our first glimpse of the real Africa.

"Most African women carry their infants like that," she told us. "I was brought up with a nanny who carried me like that as she did my mother's housework."

Little did I realise then that one day our own child would be carried in this manner by her nanny Elizabeth of the Xhosa tribe. Africa had finally become a reality.

As the coach approached the city suburbs, houses were grander in style with red-tiled roofs, manicured lawns, exotic palms, rhododendrons and rampant white and crimson bougainvillea. To remind us this is South Africa those upmarket dwellings were fenced in with two-metre high railings.

Our first glimpse of Johannesburg was its mountainous backdrop of sand-yellow mine dumps, an unkindly landscape for such a modern city. The mine dumps, Mrs Van Reardon explained, were formed by the product waste after gold was extracted that was known as 'tailings.' She shared other facts about South Africa, its history and currency, the rand.

"May is the start of our winter and Johannesburg at 6,000ft 1753 metres elevation is known as the Highveld. Our winters here can be extremely cold, with temperatures falling below freezing.

Jo'burg as most people call it is the largest populated city in South Africa and relatively young. Less than a hundred years old, the city grew with the discovery of gold in 1886 by the Australian geologist George Harrison. In fact, this very street we are driving down now is named after him."

Johannesburg was modern in its architecture, unlike London's claustrophobic dark buildings and narrow grey streets. The roads and pavements were designed to be wide enough for ox wagons to turn around in and the street names were unfamiliar: Louis Botha, Bree, Jeppe, Bok, and Eloff and Harrison Street. Traffic lights are called robots throughout South Africa.

Our coach stopped outside the Welgelegen Hotel in Primrose Terrace in the city's hilly suburb Berea. Our room was clean and tidy and smelled heavily of DDT and floor polish. In one corner was a small washbasin and the only window was permanently locked with fancy scroll steel 'burglar bars,' something we learned to live with in South Africa. Taking up most of the floor space were two metal-framed single beds with neatly folded blankets, pillows and towels. On the floor were two rattan scatter rugs and the only other furniture was a single wardrobe and matching dressing table. It was all so different from what we had left behind in England. Travel worn, neither of us was in any mood to criticise these humble surroundings. Although it was mid-afternoon, all we wanted was a hot cup of tea, a bath and a good sleep.

We both surfaced the next day at 7am hungry and ready for a good breakfast. The hotel was almost empty, as the other immigrants had left for their allotted locations: the gold mines or steelworks at Vereeniging and Vanderbijlpark, South Africa's massive steel-making complexes around Johannesburg.

Knowing I had a job, I was eager to explore Johannesburg. First, I adjusted my Swiss Omega, which was still on British time. That brought thoughts of my father.

"It's the best watch I've ever had, Pete, but you'll have to keep a check on it as these days it loses four minutes a week."

Dad gave it to me for my 21st birthday before he went on his last sea voyage before he retired. Fifty odd years have gone by and I still have the Omega although it isn't working now. Yet I didn't have the heart to throw it away; the watch is the only thing I have left of my father's.

For Patricia and I this was a new beginning, and in a foreign country - so-called 'darkest Africa.' At first sight, Johannesburg was an over-powering city forest of tall glass buildings. Surprisingly, few black Africans were to be seen except for those cleaning the streets, digging trenches or laying cables while a white man supervised them in his bakkie (or pick-up truck.)

The clear morning air was cool, warming up as we stepped out of the shadows of the high-rise marble and glass buildings owned by De Beers, the Anglo American or Rand and Reef Mining's head offices. By lunchtime it was warmer than an English summer's day as we strolled hand in hand through the city streets, browsing in shop windows. I found a bank to exchange our traveller's cheques for South African currency. The twenty and ten rand notes and coins bore the image of Jan Van Riebeeck, deemed the founding father of their nation by the majority of the Afrikaner population. I was to find his image on postage stamps as well as currency and 6th April is Van Riebeeck's Day, a public holiday.

Eventually I splashed out, daring to order tea and cream cakes from a pavement café. I paid the bill with a R5 note and got in return a pocketful of coins. Fifteen minutes after leaving the cafe we had to retrace our steps as Pat had left her handbag there. The smiling Greek owner handed it back to her, untouched. That was fortunate as it contained all our money, our passports and many other personal and valuable items. I could hardly imagine such honesty in the UK.

The pain in my ears from flying had almost gone, but my throat was dry, swollen and sore. This resulted in a sleepless night. The following morning I was due at Baker Perkins to let them know I had arrived safely. As I could hardly make myself heard, I headed for the nearest drugstore. The pharmacist poked a spatula down my throat, inspected my ears and felt the glands on both sides of my neck.

"It certainly looks like you have laryngitis," he said, "and that could be due to the altitude."

He suggested I gargle with salt water frequently and gave me a dozen capsules to take three times a day, and off I set for the workplace.

Before we emigrated, Baker Perkins in Peterborough, England had offered me a job with guaranteed accommodation in Johannesburg. Now Mr Du Pree, Baker Perkins Johannesburg's general manager, told me something different in his guttural Afrikaans English.

"We had to let your accommodation go as we thought you weren't coming. It is most unfortunate, meneer (Mister) Pratt that you have arrived a week later than originally planned."

"What about this letter from your head office in England stating that you will provide accommodation along with the job?"

"The job is still yours, but now you will have to find your own accommodation, I am very sorry; we have none available at present."

Realising I was let-down I was furious, and in a husky but strong Grimsby style told him what he could with his f*****g job.

I returned to the Welgelegen Hotel and explained my plight to the manager, who let me use his phone to contact Samorgan, our immigration agent. We took a taxi to their office where Mrs Van Reardon, who remembered me and read up on my work qualifications. After a phone call she fixed me up with a job with Benoni Engineering.

"You will like Benoni," she said. "Many of the people there originated from Britain – the town hall was even built by an Englishman. Besides, you will find the town is a much better place to settle in. I grew up there and still live nearby. I will arrange for our driver to take you to Benoni in the morning. Until your company accommodation is ready, you will be staying at the Benoni Hotel at the company's expense."

Mrs Van Reardon gave me two letters of introduction, one for Mr Jubert, the manager of Benoni Engineering for Monday morning and the other for the manager of the Benoni Hotel.

Afterwards we sat in Joubert Park amid the beautiful city gardens. Our first noticeable sign of apartheid had been at the bus stops, now it was seats and toilets labelled in Afrikaans Slegs Blankes (Europeans Only.) As it was late afternoon we took Mrs Van Reardon's advice not to walk the city during darkness. We had an early dinner in an Italian restaurant near our hotel and spent the evening afterwards writing post cards to our family.

-14-
Benoni

The following morning, Saturday 9th May, our third day in South Africa, we checked in at the Benoni Hotel. I gave the receptionist the letter from Samorgan.

"Goeimore, meneer."

(*Afrikaans – 'Good morning, sir.'*)

He read the note and showed us to a room on the first floor that overlooked Voortrekker Street, one of Benoni's main shopping streets. Our accommodation was a spacious and comfortable bed-sitting room with a double bed, wardrobe and dressing table, with adjoining bathroom. By the window was a brocade armchair, a table and two chairs. This all seemed too good to be true and we'd been told we could stay here until the company flat was available. Whatever lay ahead, both Patricia and I were pleased to be out of Johannesburg, too big and overpowering. I stood at the window and wondered what was in store for us in Benoni.

While at the hotel we were allowed to eat all or meals there at the company's expense though not any form of alcoholic beverage. That first evening, and with me still recovering from our journey out and a sore throat, we ate in the hotel's restaurant, intending another early night. The headwaiter, a smartly-dressed Indian, greeted us and showed us to our table. There were no signs of any black Africans; the waiters and hotel staff were mostly Indian except for the manager and the reception staff, who were white South Africans. It was a pleasure to sit down at a table with crisp white tablecloths and silver cutlery. I ordered a Castle lager and a glass of wine for Pat. Our meal was sirloin steaks, potato fries and salad followed by fresh fruit and ice cream and coffees.

The restaurant walls displayed pictures dating back to Benoni's early settler days when gold was discovered in 1887 on farmland called Benoni. Another picture showed Benoni Town Hall built in the 1930s, a box style building, modern for its time, and with a tall clock tower.

The hotel's floors were parquet, wax-polished throughout, and with no caustic hint of DDT like the Welgelegen. The following day, Sunday morning, on my way to breakfast I watched with amusement as two young black youths with a duster strapped on each foot skated over the floors, singing happily as they polished them to a high gloss.

The restaurant waiters were dressed smartly in crisp white jackets. That first morning we were greeted with a warm smile and handed the menu. "

"Goiemore, mevrou, meneer."

"Good morning," I replied in my finest Grimsby dialect.

From then on it was 'Good morning sir and madam' in English with a pleasant singing lilt.

Soon after breakfast we explored Princes Street, the town's main shopping area. Most of the town's buildings were single-storey with a wide overhanging canopy. We noticed there were not many people about – white or black, probably as it was a Sunday and all the shops were closed. The only exception was the black African newspaper boys who hopped on and off the road selling papers to passing motorists. As in Johannesburg, there were any numbers of old-style 1950s American automobiles: Fords, Chryslers, Chevrolets more often seen in movies and television films such as 77 Sunset Strip.

A ten-minute stroll and we were out of the shopping area. Princess Avenue continued, but with trimmed grass verges and stubby palm trees, pineapple about three metre high, their curving fronds resembled wide-spreading umbrellas. During hot sunny days, they were a pleasure to walk under, forming shade from the sun and endless clear sky. Road junction signs pointed to other towns - Boksburg, Germiston, Springs and Brakpan - that were later to become so familiar to us.

The Town Hall was more impressive in reality than in the hotel's old photograph, as did St Dunstan's Church. Little did we both realise then, that one day our daughter Tracey Renée would be christened there.

On either side of the road were attractive red-tiled brick bungalows surrounded by spacious, well-groomed gardens. All the windows had some form of steel burglar bars like those we had seen in Johannesburg. The only sign of real life was in the gardens, where black men crouched among flowerbeds or cutting the grass with a long-bladed knife in a monotonous to and fro swinging motion. We learned later that in South Africa the male house servants were called 'boy' and the women 'girl,' - no matter what age they were!

Furthermore we were soon to find out that all natives and non-Europeans had to carry a passbook to enable them to work in white-designated areas. This showed all the holder's details and was signed by their employer every month. If they could not produce the passbook, they were arrested with no ifs or buts. This was part-and-parcel of the country's stringent segregation system.

Benoni had numerous shops catering for all tastes and Pat soon found that most food items were much cheaper than in England, especially meat. Clothing was more expensive and South Africa was well behind the latest fashions. There were the usual high street banks, building societies and a Woolworth's, not like the UK store but similar in style to Marks and Spencer's. There was also a quality furniture store, a Standard Bank and a wide-fronted store called OK Bazaars that looked as if it sold everything including the kitchen sink. The post office, I noted, had two doors, one for Blacks the other for Europeans. I found it comical because, once inside, blacks and whites converged in the same queuing area. 'Slegs Vir Blankes' sounded cruder than the English 'For Whites Only'.

On our arrival in South Africa window-shopping was a pleasure, but unheard of after dark. Mrs Van Reardon had told us that no one with any regard to their own safety would risk walking the streets after dusk unless escorted. In doorways dark forms huddled, wrapped in blankets and wearing balaclava or hats with earflaps. I asked Jan, the young hotel receptionist, who they were and if they were homeless.

'Ach, meneer, they are Bantu security guards," he said in his stilted English, "That is why they carry the Kerrie."

"A Kerrie - what is that?"

"A fighting stick. The knobkerrie has a hard wooden ball at one end, and it was a lekker (good) weapon of the Zulu, now banned. Now they carry a stick, especially the older watchmen."

Jan's description brought back memories of the film Zulu that we had seen in Brighton only three months previously, when our friends told us we were crazy going to Africa.

Over dinner I asked Pat about Benoni.

"What do you think, love, is this what we are looking for, do you think?"

"It certainly seems pleasant enough," said Pat, "but let's not count our chickens too early."

Thinking ahead, I had brought with me two pairs of overalls and my working boots in a holdall, along with my marking tools. The following morning, I reported for work at Benoni Engineering

Works. The manager was much taller than my own six feet and heavily built with a trim moustache and sandy hair neatly slicked back. He read the letter from Samorgan and past employment references and told me I would start on R1.00 an hour - ten English shillings - more or less what I was earning in England.

On such a sharp cold morning fire braziers glowed, illuminating shadowy figures in the dark corner, who at sight of the manager, dispersed rapidly into the smoke-fumed haze of the workshop. He strode over, shouting abuse after the retreating figures.

"Whet you bleddy kaffirs doing, hey? Get beck to bleddy work."

This was the kind of talk I would hear daily.

Without any hesitation, he continued his tirade, switching from Afrikaans to Fanagalo.

Fanagalo a pidgin language primarily based on the Zulu, English and Dutch Afrikaans languages. The gold mining companies formulated it in the early 1900s, so that the whites and blacks of different tribes could understand one another. Later this lingua franca spread to households and everyday use and became crudely known as 'kitchen kaffir,' according to Bill, my Scots work colleague.

As we continued through the workshops, the all-too-familiar staccato flashes from welders reflected across the factory. The usual fabrication machines and lathes, drills, and boring machines were used for work that was equally familiar. European and native labour worked side by side in groups of two or four, but never shared the same washroom and canteen. It was evident that 'Slegs Vir Blankes' existed here too!

The workshop was archaic, dismal with noise and dirt, but similar in size to those I had left behind in England. The manager shouted above the racket as he introduced me to Henne, his works foreman. Henne was nothing like his boss, who was built like a rugby prop. With the darting hooded eyes of a vulture, Henne preyed on any black and sometimes white workers whom he thought were not pulling their weight. It was here that in all innocence I added the word 'kaffir' to the growing list of words in my notebook. I soon learned through my work friend Bill this was an insulting term aimed at the native population.

I was given an African labourer to assist me in my work. Stephen Mbeki was smaller than I had imagined a Zulu to be. He came dressed in ragged blue overalls, worn over a worsted wool jacket and with a knitted wool balaclava or hat, like most Africans. Inserted in each earlobe was a brightly-decorated 50mm wooden disc. Around his neck and wrists were several strings of multi-coloured beads and an assortment of silver or copper wire and beaded bracelets. He had extremely full lips and sagging dark eyes and high on both cheeks were tribal scars. He could have been anything from fifty to seventy years old. Each morning he greeted me in Afrikaans, 'Goeimore, baas.' Not being a natural linguist I had great difficulty at first in understanding him. Somehow, during those first few days, weeks and months we managed until we got to know each other better. I picked up a little Afrikaans and Fanagalo and Stephen bettered his English somewhat.

During lunch break a welder, Bill Morrow, introduced himself. He had emigrated from Glasgow the year before, along with his wife Ellen and 16-year-old son. Bill was in his late forties and had worked in the shipyards. I asked him why the native labour sat in separate groups during the lunch breaks.

"The tribes never mix," he chuckled. "A wee bit like us Brits."

I suppose he was referring to the English, Irish, Scots and Welsh.

"Here there are Zulu, Shangaan, Ndebele, Basotho and the Cape Coloureds (half-castes). You'll get used to it after a couple of weeks, Pete."

It was Bill who suggested I keep up my Boilermakers Union Card and joined the South African Union.

We had been in South Africa 26 days and celebrated our seventh wedding anniversary in the hotel restaurant. It would have been a lonely affair except that I had asked another young couple we had said hello to the night before if they wanted to join us. John and Anne Smith were much younger than we were and this was their first time in a foreign land. John had recently graduated in engineering and was in his first real employment with the British Crane Company. They left after a few weeks as John was transferred to Port Elizabeth.

During our first weeks in South Africa, the daily newspaper headlines were full of Nelson Mandela, on trial for treason and later imprisoned for life on Robben Island. At the time neither of us realised how important a figure in the fight against apartheid Mandela would become.

I was too concerned with my own immediate affairs, such as work and accommodation to be bothered with politics.

The most important question was would we like it enough in South African to settle down here?

-15-
South African Winter

At 6am in the last week of June it was dark outside and the street was covered in a thick carpet of snow as unexpected as it was amazing. I thought my mind was playing tricks and woke Pat.

"Come and see the snow."

She thought I was joking and was as surprised as I was.

"I thought we got rid of this weather last winter in Brighton," she said.

I stood on the hotel steps watching the snowflakes fall before trotting off to work.

"Is this a rare event?" I asked the hotel manager as he stood beside me.

"Ach, not like this, meneer. This is something lekker (nice.) You will be used to this, hey?"

I was getting used to walking to and from work with a clear sky above me, in the glow of the rising sun and with the aroma wood-smoke in the air. I was definitely not prepared for snow half-way to my knees. Luckily, I had my work boots on and had brought an overcoat and cloth cap with me from England.

I watched with amusement as cars slewed left and right, making it obvious that South African drivers were unaccustomed to such conditions. It took some sinking in this was South Africa, as I glanced around me at natives wrapped in blankets and woolly hats. Africans on bicycles with friends perched on the crossbars tried riding in the car tracks. When the wheels skidded, off they'd come, rolling into the snow and laughing, ignoring the yelps and jeers of whites in passing cars. That morning I arrived to work like a snowman, and as wet and cold. I was half an hour late, earning that vulture look from Henne the foreman.

During the course of the morning snow continued to fall in flakes bigger than I could remember seeing before. In the afternoon intermittent streaks of blue sky appeared in the breaks between the cumulus clouds. During that first day of snow I was repeatedly asked, "What kind of snow is this?"

By mid-morning the flakes had changed from the earlier and heavier falls and as the day progressed, the breeze grew stronger, whipping powdery snow through every nick and crevice in the workshop. The average South African had not experienced snow on this scale on the Reef before and was as fascinated by it all as I was.

Cars drove around with a miniature snowmen perched on the roof bringing laughter to the passers-by. That afternoon as I trudged back to the hotel after work there were snowball fights along the streets between blacks and whites, a pleasing moment of respite from the rigor mortis of apartheid. Alas, it was an illusion, lasting only as long as the snow.

Stephen, my Zulu labourer, like most of our African workforce, came to work wrapped heavily in blankets. The snow had come suddenly and disappeared as suddenly after three days. The rest of July and early August remained dry and sunny, though temperatures sometimes dropped below freezing point during the night.

It was several weeks before I got used to the white South Africans who were my fellow-workers - and perhaps them to me! In their company, especially during tea and lunch breaks, the Afrikaners (Boers) showed an attitude of ignorance, especially towards the English. They would talk in Afrikaans knowing I didn't understand the language though I did pick up a smattering. The 'English-speaking' South Africans were less standoffish;

although they, too, could converse in Afrikaans they did not in my presence. To me it seemed tribal divisions ran as deep among the white population as amongst the native tribes.

Billy McVey, one of our machine fitters, noticing I ran to work offered to give me a lift each day. Billy lived in Veneto City, a block of flats nearer the town and better-looking than our company accommodation. I asked Billy to let me know if any became available and soon after Patricia and I moved from the hotel into the company flat. This was sparse and basic, with the double bed taking up 75% percent of the floor space in our bedroom. We had a small bathroom and kitchen, and the lounge was furnished by the company with a settee, dining table and four chairs. We could put up with this until something better came along of our own choosing.

Pat busied herself shopping for the basics: towels, bed linen, kitchen utensils and crockery, enough to get us by until our own household goods arrived from England.

Although the company flat was only ten minutes away from work for me, it was almost an hour's walk into town for Pat. Also, it was too near the industrial estate and the noise from trundling wagons and railway traffic at all times of day and night was disturbing. We had been three weeks in the company flat and before I could open the door, Pat greeted me.

"Guess what, love? I've got a job in town at Record Printers and start tomorrow. It's a family-run business at the back of Benoni's main shopping street."

She was that excited she almost forgot to tell me about the bicycle she had bought at the second-hand shop, with a number stamped on the frame in case it was stolen, NP 5018133.

"There's another British girl called Betty from Ireland who works there. She's about the same age as me and has been out here a year. Then there's Lynette, who's a South African and an older woman, very friendly, called Vera Allen, who is the forewoman. I think I'll like it there as it's small like the place I worked in back home."

At the finish of her first week, Pat bought a second-hand Grundig radiogram with a box of Readers Digest records. We were beginning to settle in, though we both knew this flat was only temporary until we found somewhere better.

With the worst of the wintery weather over the August mornings remained chilly, but dry and sunny, though it was still bitterly cold at night. Pat enjoyed cycling to work.

"It's just like old times in Cleethorpes. I get some strange stares from the local white women, though, and cars hoot as I cycle past with my shopping bags on the handlebars."

Cycling was how Pat had got about in the UK as most of us did. In South Africa it was mostly students or the Africans who rode bicycles here; never a white, especially a woman. Everyone seemed to own a car; cars were cheaper than in England and so was petrol, but that was still out of our reach. Our first few weeks were passing quickly.

I jogged and walked to training sessions at the gym, regarding this as my warm-up. Still in reasonable condition after my last competition in the 1964 Mr Britain last April, I was encouraged by another gym member, Corrie Wasserman, to enter the forthcoming Mr Benoni Physique competition. With something definite to aim for I started training three evenings a week.

Pat didn't mind, keeping herself occupied on a second-hand Singer sewing machine that she'd bought along with the bike. Always practical, my wife was in her element making curtains and cushion covers for the flat.

It wasn't long before I was introduced to Bert, Betty's husband, after Pat invited her work colleague and partner to dinner. They had been in South Africa for twelve months, migrating from

Belfast in Northern Ireland. Bert was a maintenance electrician at the local Colgate-Palmolive Soap Factory in Boksburg. Like us, they had no children. Betty was a tall pretty woman, with shoulder-length, light-brown hair, with a pale smooth complexion. The spectacles she generally wore gave her a secretarial look.

The four of us were all about the same age and got on as well together as if we'd been friends for years, with parallel taste in music, sports and films. Bert was as much into coarse fishing as myself, and we'd take any opportunity as the weather warmed to fish the lakes around Benoni and Brakpan. Once on the Vaal River near Villiers we had a strange experience, fishing on the wrong side of the river on a Sunday!

We set up and had been fishing (with no luck) for two hours when a police car stopped and a uniformed officer came over adjusting his Sam Brown gun holster.

He first addressed us in Afrikaans, then realised we were new in the country and unaware that by law no sports can take place in the Orange Free State on the Sabbath he told us to fish on the other side. We apologised, swiftly packed our gear and crossed back into the Transvaal. We stopped at the Villiers filling station for cold drinks and sticks of biltong before setting up again on the opposite bank where, in the first hour, we caught a keep net full of yellow-mouth bream.

Bert was a chain-smoker, a man about five foot eight with wavy fair hair, and typically Irish in manner and speech. He had a quick temper and would have violent arguments with Betty over the most trivial things. She told us Bert had suffered with ulcers for the past few years and blamed that on their rows.

During a particularly cold spell one evening after work, Pat and I took the half hour train journey to Springs, a small town further east of Benoni. I had an interview for a part-time job as assistant manager and instructor in a weight-training gym. Pat and I boarded the train at Benoni sitting in the 'European Only' compartment. Hundreds of black South Africans further down the platform crowded the tail-end compartments allocated for Non-Whites.

I got the job and started to work three nights a week at the Boksburg Health Studio. Boksburg was a small town, or dorp as the Afrikaans say. I was supervising a mixed class of ladies and gents in the art of weight training in a well-equipped professional gym, bigger than any I'd been in before. During the last two hours I managed to fit in my own training routine. The hours were long from 6 to 11pm, but the extra money was welcome. I would go straight from work and arrive home just before midnight.

In August I won the 1964 Mr Benoni title and Corrie, who trained with me, won the junior title. Six weeks later I was placed fourth in the Mr Transvaal competition held in Johannesburg, which was my opportunity to enter the 1965 Mr South Africa to be held in Durban the following June. While in Johannesburg I called in to Reg Park's gym, but he was in London for the 1965 Professional Mr Universe event.

Before I took on the manager's job at the Boksburg Gym, I invested in a good second-hand car. Although it meant credit we needed our own transport and my part-time job would help with the running costs. The 1600cc Vauxhall Victor estate was roomy, with light blue bench seats, a bright red body with a white top and white-wall tyres; altogether a handsome vehicle. On the forecourt on display was another Victor, but it had hundreds of dents spattered all over the roof and bonnet.

"Look at that!"

Pat walked around the car, sliding her fingers over the dents.

"Surely they're not hoping anyone will buy that?" she said. "I wonder what caused it."

A salesman told us - a hail storm in Cape Town.

To get my South African driving licence I had to pass an eye test and a competence test on road signs. Reluctantly I handed over my British driving licence in exchange for the South African licence. Before I left the examiner told me every car had to be police-tested at their test bay for roadworthiness. This meant buyers knew they were getting a reliable vehicle. The following day I drove the Vauxhall over and obtained the road certificate.

One afternoon straight after work I said to Pat, "Today is your first driving lesson."

I hadn't told her earlier in case it put her off. On a nice light evening I took the car out of town to an open stretch of road with no traffic. We exchanged seats and Pat got in behind the steering wheel. I gave her instructions on where to position her feet, what each pedal was for, and what it will do when depressed or let go. The lesson came to a sudden end when we both lost our tempers and argued.

When we got home, Pat set to and made us a good dinner and all was forgiven and forgotten.

"We'll try again one weekend," I said. "We'll have more time."

We both admitted it was a bit of a rush after work.

So we had a quiet night by the wireless as South Africa had no television in those days. Apparently, Television was not to be introduced in South Africa because, the Minister of Posts and Telegraphs, had described it as a 'miniature bioscope over which parents would have no control.'

"South Africa," he said, "would have to import films showing race-mixing. Television was devil's own box, for disseminating communism and immorality".

Bert came round to ask if I was interested in getting a job in the mines. We knew that if you worked for the mines there was good accommodation, partly furnished and many other benefits such as free medical cover, paid holidays and a pension.

"They are looking for artisans at the Carletonville gold mine," Bert said.

I was not too keen to work down a mine, but took time to think it over. I was curious to find out more and took a day off work after Bert arranged for us to see a Mr Nel at the mine's labour office.

We set off early and pulled up outside the mine gate where a black security guard let us through when we asked to see Mr Nel. The office was clean and tidy and had pictures of the mines' underground workings and mine personnel. When Mr Nel addressed me in Afrikaans I had to tell him that I didn't speak that language; that I'd only been in South Africa three months.

He switched to English.

"Why do you want to work for the mines? We're looking for experienced underground staff, and you've never worked down a mine before."

He was right and as it turned out I was grateful I didn't get a job there. A few weeks later two houses and part of another disappeared down a massive 30-metre deep sinkhole at Carltonville with the tragic loss of a family of five and their servant.

-16-
The Road to Durban

Stephen, my Zulu labourer, asked me to bring him back a bottle of seawater. Four of us – Pat and me, along with Bert and Betty, were setting off for a trip to the seaside - to Durban!

"Is good muti (medicine), baas," he said, grinning.

I mentioned this to Henne, my foreman.

"Ja, it's the custom of the blacks to drink and wash in the water from the Great Ocean as they call it. They believe drinking the seawater makes them strong and to wash in it wards off evil spirits. When they go on leave to their homelands that is the first bleddy thing the kaffir do, man. Ach, they've been doing it for centuries, hey."

The night before I could hardly sleep thinking of our journey to Natal and how much I wanted to see the sea again. Bert had agreed to share the driving.

"Durban's 650 km and a tiring long haul especially if it's hot," Bert said. "In my 1,000cc Fiat it took me eight hours before. In your

1600cc Vauxhall, we could do it in six hours in more comfort, Pete."

We left Benoni at 5am bypassing Johannesburg and refuelled at Villiers, the last filling station for 160km. No sooner had we left Villiers than the N16 highway tarmac road disappeared into the veldt and a vicious 10km dirt-road detour took its place. After some, five minutes a peppery cloud of red dust had searched out every chink in the car, coating our hair and skin.

Bert seemed to be used to these kinds of roads and drove at breakneck pace, as if in a rally. Sensing my concern, he explained that speed allows the wheels to float above the corrugated surface, and this means both car and passengers can avoid being shaken to bits.

Back on the tarmac, the N16 highway made driving a joy again, to hang one's arm out the car window and experience the whoosh of cool air. The road through the Orange Free State was desolate with only the occasional farm vehicle trundling between fields. The farmhouses, corrugated iron-roofed bungalows, were all but hidden from sight, shaded under mimosa and shrouded with cascades of scarlet and white bougainvillea. The only movement came from black farm workers, dogs and geese or the windmill pump. Nothing much broke the monotony of the endless parched ochre-red veldt that stretched either side of the road, or the dried limp stalks from the end of harvest maize crops.

We seemed to be in the midst of nowhere, passing groups of barefooted black women and young children in colourful clothes, carrying bundles or branches as usual on their heads and with not a male in sight.

This journey would be a good test for my car as most of it lay along uninterrupted stretches of roads that were almost too tempting. I soon found I was doing 112km/h without even realising, but the thought of the heavy fine if I were caught speeding soon dampened any urge to be a Stirling Moss.

We refuelled before leaving Harrismith and after driving for almost three hours, I relished a pit stop to stretch my aching legs. Betty and Patricia went to find a toilet for a 'freshen up' and get rid of the dust from the road detour. Harrismith was a pretty town, with an abundance of rampaging bougainvillea, shading jacarandas, tall nodding hydrangeas and houses with neat manicured lawns. Harrismith is named after its former governor,

Sir Harry Smith, who played a major role during the Anglo-Boer War of 1899-1902.

Leaving Harrismith, we joined the N5 highway that climbed and wove through the Drakensburg Mountain range. To the Zulu they are 'The Barrier of Spears' and to the Dutch Voortrekkers 'The Dragon Mountains'. My intention was to stop and take photographs, but as we climbed higher a disappointing swirl of mist blocked any worthwhile view we might have had. From here on it was downhill as we drove further East and deeper into Natal. The scenery changed with every passing kilometre from craggy mountains to verdant woody rolling hills and farmlands. We passed waterfalls careering down, fed from the Tugela River that starts high in these ranges and empties into the Indian Ocean.

By the time we reached Ladysmith, I was beginning to realise the vastness, the contrasts, the heat and the breath-taking beauty of South Africa. Ladysmith owes its name to Juana, a Spanish woman who married Sir Harry Smith, the town's founder. Here in 1899 the Siege of Ladysmith took place, one of the fiercest battles during the Boer War that resulted in many years of bitter hatred against the British. Even then there was still a strong resentment towards the British - especially the English. 'Die Engelse Oorlog' (The English War or Boer War) is still recalled with rancour by many Afrikaners.

The Voortreckers founded Pietermaritzburg, the capital of Natal, in 1838 after the battle of Blood River against the Zulu. We arrived there in a sweltering 26C, crawling through the busy town centre with no advantage of any breeze at all through the car's open windows. Pietermaritzburg, like most big towns in South Africa, took pride in its floral beauty. Gazing around, however, what impressed me most was its colonial charm: pristine whitewashed houses, gabled Dutch architecture, churches and verdant parks with historical statues of the early Voortrekkers who founded the town. It would have been a bonus to stay for longer, but time wasn't on our side.

We entered Durban through Pinetown, a hilly and residential suburb with an abundance of rhododendron, frangipani and jacaranda. Once on Marine Parade, I was reminded of Brighton's white-painted seafront establishments, gardens and hotels by Durban's own sweeping seafront. It was refreshing to smell the salty air of the Indian Ocean and hear the tide wash onto the beach. We stopped to watch adventurous surfers riding atop rolling breakers of ocean to glide with great dexterity into the shallows, only to swiftly paddle out again. I found it exciting to see the sea again, as Pat and I had lived by the seaside most of our lives. The beach was already packed with sun worshippers and families beneath a mass of umbrellas, as colourful as a rainbow fallen from the sky.

We were lucky to find a parking place on a grassy spot under the shade of a mimosa tree. Nearby a large signboard in English and Afrikaans stated that this was a beach for Whites Only. We picked a perfect spot in full view of the sea, with only a short walk to the shops and hotels across Marine Parade. Betty and Pat organised lunch from our picnic hamper while Bert and I sampled a refreshing dip in the surf to wash away the sweat and dust after almost seven hours driving.

The 'rickshaw boys' as they were called were dressed as Zulu warriors; bedecked in the traditional leopard skins with horned headgear. Beads and ankle bells jangled as they loped up and down the sea front.

After our picnic, Pat suggested a walk so we threaded our way through the crowd of oiled-up sun devotees to paddle in the ocean. In the distance cargo ships sailed in and out of Durban Harbour. I imagine my Dad had been here many times; I know my brother James had during World War 2. His troopship, the

Dominion Monarch, called into Durban for emergency repairs before heading north to Suez.

"I could settle here, Pat," I confided to my wife. "I wonder if there's much work here. There should be with all these engineering works and a shipyard. We shall have to come back again. One day's not enough."

I had the same feeling as when I first saw Brighton.

"How do you feel about us moving here, love?"

She didn't answer me directly. She was smiling.

"Pete, looks like you're going to be a Dad. I think I'm pregnant."

I didn't know what to say or do next. We sat silently with our arms around each other, gazing out over the Indian Ocean. I kissed her before suggesting we wander over to Bert and Betty.

"Let's go and tell them the good news, love."

"Betty already knows."

"Ah! I thought there was something going on between you two. So it's definite then?"

"Looks like it, love."

I put my arm around her as we walked over to Bert and Betty and after many hugs and jokes we went to the Edward Hotel. No rooms available, but we booked a table in the restaurant. At reception I asked if we could use the hotel's toilets. I didn't let on we intended a full wash and brush-up.

That evening after a change of clothes we celebrated over grilled T-bone steaks with an abundance of salads and potato-fries, washed down with three bottles of the cheapest Cape Sauvignon Blanc and finishing with fruit. We spent the rest of the evening down in the hotel cellar where the disco thrashed out all the latest rock and roll hits for a writhing mass of sun-tanned bodies: Manfred Mann's Do Wah Diddy, the Beatles Let me Hold Your Hand and other heady tunes of the early sixties.

In the early hours of Sunday morning the four of us tottered, pleasantly inebriated, across Marine Parade to our car. Pat and Betty crawled into the back of the station wagon and huddled under blankets while Bert and I sat on the grass and guzzled the last of the dozen bottles of Castle Lager we had bought.

Wrapped up in a spare blanket, I stared at a black velvet sky studded with a million stars, wondering which might have been our baby and what it would be like to be a father. I woke partly from the cold but more from Bert's snoring, which competed with the roar of the incoming Indian Oceans rollers. I watched the surfboarders' antics with envy; how easy they made it look to glide in from the towering waves. At 7 am I nudged Bert awake who, bleary-eyed, suggested we go down for a dip. I was not a confident swimmer and was troubled by the memory of the sharks we had seen earlier in the aquarium, so I kept to the shallows. More than anything I needed to clear my head, not only from the booze but also from Pat's unexpected news. Now I had serious responsibilities realistically ahead of me.

Edging out of Marine Parades heavy traffic, I bumped the rear wing of a Mercedes, smashing a rear light and crunching my right front wing against its front wheel. We exchanged details for insurances then Bert and I did a quick repair job before we headed home.

On our return to Benoni, the car coughed and spluttered to a stop; we had run out of petrol. We were 20 km from Villiers just before the start of the gravel detour road. After standing by the roadside for almost an hour hoping someone would stop, the situation became grim as the light faded fast. I was most concerned for the girls' safety as either I or Bert would have to walk the distance to Villiers in the dark with no flashlight between us. South Africa had a notorious reputation for carjacking and armed robberies that ended in the victim's deaths.

178

I had just drawn the short straw to do the walk to a gas station when a bakkie (or pick-up truck) stopped and the driver offered me a lift. We shook hands and he introduced himself as Mannie. He was a typical Boer farmer by dress and manner, surprisingly friendly. "Voertsek kaspar," he instructed his ridgeback and the dog leapt out of the passenger seat and into the rear of the bakkie where his African labourer lay, wrapped in a blanket. After waiting half an hour at the Villiers fuel station hoping for someone to take me back with my can of fuel, Mannie said he would drive me back if need be.

"You have to be careful, meneer, in these parts after dark," he said, sucking on his pipe. "Most kaffirs will slit your throat for a tickie." (That was sixpence.)

A battered American 56 Ford Fairlane chugged into the filling station. Mannie walked over to the driver speaking in Afrikaans. Mannie assured me that I would be safe with these Cape kerels (fellows). I thanked Mannie again. Baie danke - thank you very much!

The driver of the Ford Fairlane had four other passengers with him and offered me a front seat as they were going to Durban anyway. I sat next to another well-dressed young man, a Cape Coloured not much younger than me. I shook hands with everyone, then sat back silently, gripping the petrol can with one hand and ready to swing into action should these fellows try anything.

The driver broke the silence by telling me he was a sports teacher in Pinetown, a Durban suburb.

"You must have been to a football match of some kind," I commented, "judging from your hats and scarves."

"Yeah. We've been to the friendly match between our national team, the Castle Knights, against Real Madrid at the Rand

Stadium in Jo'burg. Do you play soccer, sir, and what football team did you support in England?"

The questions came at me now from all quarters. They didn't know Grimsby Town but knew Tottenham Hotspur and reeled off familiar names - Jimmy Greaves, Danny Blanchflower and Dave Mackay. I didn't mind talking about my favourite sport as it lessened my earlier misgivings.

We finally arrived at my car. The windows were misted over and there was no sign of movement. I tapped three times on the driver's window as we'd arranged and Bert wound the window down, apprehensive but relieved to see me. He said afterwards that when he saw the big American car pull up he told Betty and Pat to duck out of sight under the car blanket. The .22 Beretta he had put in the glove compartment was in his hand as he hadn't realised it was me until I gave the signal.

My saviours even made a funnel from some cardboard to transfer the petrol into my tank. I offered them a ten-rand note, which they refused, and we all shook hands before they sped off in a cloud of dust and disappeared into the evening gloom. We refuelled at Villiers, glad to put that incident behind us and head home to Benoni.

- 17 -
Settling Down

A month after our trip to Durban, Bert and Betty helped us move into our new flat in Veneto City in an apartment block in Park Street. The following day our shipping-trunk arrived from the UK to be collected at the Benoni Railway Depot. Opening the packing cases and trunk was great fun as we found things we'd almost forgotten we had packed. I was especially pleased to discover my toolbox.

Veneto City was a spacious one-bedroom apartment on the second floor of a three-storey brick building, only a ten-minute walk into town and ideal for Patricia's workplace at Record Printers. No doubt and much to the satisfaction of the town's white women, Pat took her bicycle back to the second hand shop. In exchange she brought back another 12-box set of Readers Digest LPs of Mood Music for Listening and Relaxation.

The flat's entrance hall opened up to a spacious lounge 8m x 4m with a window at one end the width of the lounge overlooking Park Street and the front of the building. The walls were painted in emulsion in modern colours. Heating consisted of a two-bar electric fire set in a teak fireplace surround on the main lounge wall. The up-to-date kitchen boasted an electric stove, washing-machine, stainless steel sink unit and there was a tiled bathroom and a handy broom cupboard.

We bought a glass-topped cane coffee table to go with the bamboo cane three-piece-suite and Pat made scatter cushions in various colours to match the décor. In the dining area a bamboo cane bookshelf acted as a divider between the lounge and hall. It wasn't long before Pat had filled this with potted busy lizzie plants, photographs and ornaments as well as a varied collection of books and record albums for the Grundig radiogram kept nearby.

Pat's sewing box and Singer sewing machine were on hand, too, and she bought red twill to make full-drop lounge curtains to match the carpet. The curtains helped to keep out the hot daytime sun as our window and balcony faced east. Over the following weeks, Pat busied herself making up the curtains and settee cushions. I would watch her set out the materials on the lounge floor as she deftly marked out and measured, then pinned the pieces together before finally sewing them for me to help put up.

We bought a dining table and four metal framed chairs with polished hardwood seats. In the hall the springbok skin rug from Durban was spread-eagled on the floor as decoration. Pat added African style prints and copper plates and, as her final touch, she hung a large mirror over the fireplace. On the opposite wall an African tribal mask stared mysteriously at its own reflection.

A door from the lounge led to the veranda and to our bedroom with a king-size bed, cane chair and dressing table and fitted wardrobes.

On summers evenings we would sit taking in the last of the sun and watch with amazement at a gecko's antics as it darted around the ceilings, clinging upside down with splayed toes, and with a blink of an eye snatching at flies with its elastic tongue.

From our lounge window or while we sat on the veranda we would hear the chatter of Africans passing by in steady stream,

182

catching the train home to their townships after working in the town. Some barefoot in tribal dress linger in my memory. The Ndebele women wore silver-wire bangles around their arms and lower legs and a rolled or rounded collar of brightly-coloured beads around their necks. Draped around their shoulders were colourful woven blankets and they wore equally colourful hats. If they were hot in that garb they didn't show it.

Generally our evenings were quiet and after dinner, Pat and I would sit listening to Springbok radio. I recall the supernatural series The Creaking Door after the 7 pm evening news. Mostly we played vinyl 45rpm classic records on our Grundig radiogram, a godsend, as there were no television transmitters in South Africa or any other worthy radio programmes for that matter. For me there was nothing more peaceful than to hear the call of a nightjar and the cricket's song competing with the Bert Kaempfert Orchestra, Ray Conniff, James Last or Mantovani's Moon River. We both missed our dancing, the Gaiety Ballroom and the Cafe Dansant. Patricia would invariably rouse me from a half-slumber.

"Come on, love, it's eleven. Time for bed."

After our first four months of relatively dry weather, and some extreme cold and snow, October's spring dawn greeted us daily with a rosy pink sunrise. I never tired of waking up in the South African spring. Below our balcony the garden began to bloom with red-hot pokers, pink irises and trailing vines of jasmine. In the last throw of October we basked in wonderful warm sunny days, though our neighbour told us, "We'll be starting to smell the rain any day with November just around the corner."

Sometimes my thoughts strayed back to England where the kids would be throwing sticks up into the horse chestnut trees, collecting and threading their prizes on string ready to play conkers or building November bonfires. Although Patricia and I were getting ourselves acclimatised to the South African style of living, England was never far away from our thoughts due to letters from friends and relatives.

One evening I came home to hear Pat chatting.

"Who's a cheeky boy then? Give us a kiss!"

She had bought another budgie she named Charlie after our other bird in Brighton.

"I couldn't resist him. Isn't he like our old Charlie?"

"Perhaps. He has similar markings, although I wouldn't really know the difference."

"That's typical," she snorted. "You men never seem to notice anything unless it's a mini-skirt. Our Charlie in Brighton was yellow and black with a black collar."

I opened the cage and put my finger under the budgerigar's chest. Immediately he hopped on.

"His blue feathers attracted me first and he looked so lonely sat in the cage with all the other birds, who were yellow and green."

Pat gently stroked his head, while Ming, the next-door cat, who often sat on our veranda wall, stared at Charlie, mesmerised by this colourful new creature in his territory who spoke a foreign tongue.

Before going to bed, Pat covered Charlie's cage with a beach towel in case Ming got any bold ideas!

November's mid-day temperature climbed to 26C (70F) bringing frequent afternoon thunderstorms. I could almost set my clock by the first raindrops falling at 4pm or thereabouts before the leaden skies burst with a whoosh into a torrential downpour. Thundering across town, the storm drummed a startling staccato on house and car roofs and amazed me with the speed with which it filled the roadside's gullies. Driving in such conditions was difficult with wipers a no contest against the rain. The night sky lit up as blue-white lightning streaked angrily across the heavens to let us know the summer rains were here. Yes, even on Guy Fawkes Day, the infamous 5th November; even here in Africa a damp squib never fails to kill a joyous evening.

Our hot summer months finally arrived, bringing out the cicadas with their monotonous drone pulsing through the air. No African night would be the same without the little blighters. My South African work colleagues referred to the cicada as the Christmas beetle; a change of name did not change their tune. The rainy season also woke up hordes of colourful moths, flying ants and mosquitoes that whined mercilessly around you as you tried to sleep. Swatting them didn't work as they took revenge in sly bites that left behind red and itchy lumps. I could always tell an expat by the calamine dotted on face, legs and arms - the vulnerable parts of our anatomy.

A month before Christmas Pat was told that because she was pregnant she wasn't allowed to continue working. This came as a big shock as we were only just managing our finances above the waterline. Her friend Betty and the women Pat worked with and other friends arranged a surprise 'Stork Party'. Pat thought she was going to a Tupperware party as they were all the rage. I dropped her off and arranged to collect her three hours later. The number of gifts she came home with were unbelievable, from diapers to a baby bath. Our car was loaded from floor to roof.

We had a shopping spree in Johannesburg and I fitted myself out with tailored shorts, short-sleeved shirts, a safari suit with shorts and a pair of longs to match, along with high knee socks.

Pat bought cotton dresses, shorts and matching tops to match. For now she was wearing the UK summer clothes she'd brought with her, but her body was changing week by week and she had to buy something to accommodate our growing bump. She set to making cotton garments for herself- you can't keep a good girl down.

It was high summer and our first Christmas was imminent. At first it was hard to get into the spirit of things where the daily temperature often soared into the 90s, and we wore sunglasses, sandals and shorts. The town's department stores, Woolworths and Bazaar's, ignored all that and were decked out with tinsel, fake snow and colourful decorations as they played Jingle Bells and Bing Crosby's White Christmas.

On a visit to our friends, Bert told us he knew where we could get cheap Christmas trees. We stood in his flat on Windermere Drive overlooking Benoni Golf Course and the Laundry Dam. This narrow stretch of water got its name from the Africans who once washed clothes there. Now on most Sundays you could witness an African priest baptising his flock in its calm water. Bert pointed to the line of 3-4 metre high fir trees, across the narrow stretch of water from his flat.

'We could lop the tops off and nobody would know the difference," he said in his broad Northern Irish brogue and with a mischievous smile. "What do you think, mate?"

"I think it's a crazy idea, Bert, and we'd need a boat."

Bert pointed to an African-type dugout laid on the bank beside a wider rowing boat.

The following night we met at Bert's flat again. First he shoved a frosted bottle of Castle lager in my hand, and showed me the coil of rope, ladder and two hacksaws ready in the hall. Another friend Danny stood there like Edmund Hillary in woollen hat, with his trousers tucked into his socks, a knitted polo sweater and another coil of rope over his shoulder. I was beginning the think I'd joined the IRA.

Without further ado, we silently slid the rowing boat into the water and crossed. No mishaps and Bert had already strung a rope across the narrow 10m stretch of water with one end tied to the mooring stake where the rowing boat had been.

Danny was first ashore and placed the ladder against the nearest fir and was up it like a squirrel. Within seconds I heard sawing then a crack like a rifle shot. A six-foot top section tumbled down almost on top of me. As Danny jumped down I grabbed his saw and ladder over to the next tree. I heard the rasp as Bert sawed then another loud crack. Remembering that sound travels further at night, I glanced around, heart pounding in the pitch black darkness.

The sound of dogs barking put me in a panic. Flashlight beams approached and the yaps grew excited. After my tree crashed to the ground, Danny dragged it to the boat while I climbed down. In water up to my knees I pushed the boat out from the bank and jumped aboard while Danny paddled as fast as any Indian warrior. Bert was already on the far bank hauling on the rope attached to our boat. We left the trees in the boat at the water's edge and ran like the clappers to hide behind the walls of the apartment block.

I was wet with smelly dam water and sweat, my adrenalin peaking. On the far side water two dark shapes appeared at the water's edge. Africans, presumably night watchmen and both armed with sticks, jabbered excitedly in their native tongue. With the dog whining and tugging at the leash, they played their torches around the area then ambled back the way they'd come.

On inspection Patricia and Betty declared they were not the right kind of tree.

"The needles will dry and drop off before Christmas," said Pat.

I opened another cold beer and watched lightning blaze in the sky over the Reef. Within half an hour the heavens opened.

The following day I arrived home to find the tree whittled down to a third of its original size, stood in a bucket and festooned with the usual seasonal trimmings. I wasn't fully robbed of the triumph of my trophy, as she made use of the off-cuts to decorate the lounge.

Wherever we set up home, Pat always made an effort whatever the occasion. She wasn't too happy sweeping up pine needles daily as the tree dried out, but for all that we had a good Christmas, though we missed our families, and it felt strange celebrating Christmas in bright sunshine and temperatures of 30C.

What would the weather be like in the UK right now? I imagined the big stores and streets glittering with Christmas lights, and mums and dads wrapped up against the cold and kids with noses red and dripping singing Silent Night through letter boxes.

Patricia made a wonderful Christmas dinner for the four of us, a big roast chicken with walnut stuffing, fresh vegetables and a plum pudding aflame with brandy. Bert and Betty exclaimed at the Christmas cards from family and friends in England and we exchanged presents. I opened the bottle of Cape brandy they had brought me while the girls sipped wine and Irish coffee.

Patricia put on our new LP, Bert Kaempfert's Christmas Wonderland, and we sat there half-pissed until Patricia suggested Monopoly. That certainly broke the silence and monotony.

Yet again Betty and Bert bickered; he was unwell with his tummy again which was what triggered it off. Soon after Christmas the couple returned to Ireland so Bert could have surgery on his ulcers there. It was a sad farewell as they were such good friends, especially Betty for Patricia.

They sold up all their household goods and car and Bert's Irish friend Danny drove them to Johannesburg International Airport. Pat tried to keep in touch by letter with Betty, but her letters in return were rare and eventually we lost contact.

-18-
Tracey

We had been out in South Africa for six months and were getting used to its very different way of life, its people and its customs. Afrikaans was another matter; to me it sounded harsh, almost aggressive, though in later years I found our South African friends excessively proud of their language. Sadly, I was never good at learning any other language perhaps because I had not been in the upper stream at school, whose students were taught French.

Traffic lights were robots and bioscope a somewhat dated term for the cinema. Films and radio were strictly censored; for instance, they would not dare show black kissing white or even holding or shaking hands. The cinemas in the cities and towns were for Europeans only. Saturday nights at the movies were formal occasions with the women in cocktail dresses and the men in suits and a tie. Blacks and mixed races had their own cinemas in the townships.

Bert was your typical casual type, but for me and especially the girls it was a pleasant change to get dressed up. The first time we visited the cinema was in Benoni with Bert and Betty. Ian Fleming's Goldfinger was showing starring Sean Connery and Honor Blackman. When she introduced herself as Pussy Galore – ostensibly referring to her feline acrobatic skills – that brought a few giggles from the broad-minded, whereas others were probably aghast at what the pious censors had overlooked.

After Bert and Betty had departed for Northern Ireland, our old friends Bill and Helen Morrow introduced us to Archie and

Edie MacKay and Allen and Monica McMaster, newly arrived from Glasgow. Archie was a welder and Alan a fitter-turner; and both their wives were secretaries of some sort. Both couples were younger than we were and had no children.

"Only married a few months before we came out," Archie joked. "Emigrating was our honeymoon."

Like me, they saw no future in the British shipyard industry and thought this better than being on the dole. We soon got to know more Scots, and a Welsh couple, Howell and Linda Hewitt, who had two young children. During the Transvaal's long hot summer we would gather on Sundays at any nearby beauty spot that boasted a swimming pool and restrooms. Out of all the weekend retreats our favourites were the nearby Babsfontein Park that put on musical talent shows and Mimosa, a quieter venue.

In her advanced state of pregnancy, Pat welcomed a cool dip in the pool. Was that what encouraged our baby daughter to take to the water so early? Neither Pat nor I were great swimmers, but Tracy by three was a real water-babe.

On these family occasions everyone brought food of some kind; a good variety of meats, salads, fruits, breads, homemade cakes and soft drinks. Most retreats had a braai (barbecue) you could use if you brought your own charcoal. Cooking meats on an open fire was a different kind of picnicking for Pat and me, and probably for most expats.

We first visited the Pretoria Zoo and Snake Park with John and Ann Smith, and later introduced Archie and Edie to the sight of the zoo keeper 'milking' the snakes for anti-venom. He held the puff adder's head held over a glass tumbler with a paper lid, punctured by the snake's fangs and releasing enough venom enough to fill an eggcup.

Patricia was near her due date, so I gave up my part-time job at the Boksburg Health Studios and any idea of entering the Mr

South Africa competition. Archie probably understood we were struggling financially, without Pat's wages and with no chance of any overtime where I worked. Archie told me there was plenty of work at Wright Anderson where he was employed. He knew I had played some football in the past. He was on good terms with the works manager, who was football crazy. If I showed interest I would easily get a job. I told him to go ahead and arrange an interview.

I started at Wright Anderson the following week, working two hours overtime on Tuesday and Thursday and a Saturday half-day. I had volunteered to play in the works soccer team, and practice sessions filled the void weight-training had left.

I knew I'd enjoy this new job, where I got on well with my supervisor Joe Horn, a friendly, English-speaking South African. On my first day I was allocated a lock-up toolbox beneath a drawing (blueprint) table where plans could be laid out flat. Now I had my own marking-off tools and engineering reference books I had carried with me since apprentice days, I felt more confident. As I had forfeited my weight training sessions at the gym I worked all the overtime offered.

Again I had an African helper, Michael, a Shangaan who came from Northern Transvaal's Limpopo Province close to the South African Mozambique border. Taught by the missionaries, he spoke and understood English well enough, and turned out to a little too cocksure. He didn't need much telling what to do, as he had been here several years and had once worked with Joe, my shop-floor foreman.

The job entailed marking out designs from engineering drawings onto steel plates for others to cut to size, formed and shaped in the workshop; a good system. The company workshops were the biggest I had worked in, easily covering an area the size of several football pitches. Wright and Anderson were one of the biggest steel fabricators of its kind in South Africa and manufactured all manner of heavy engineering. With the expansion of the Sasolburg Oil Refinery and power stations and goldmines throughout South Africa our workload steadily increased. Another department fabricated man-cages for the mines; I never once thought that one day I too would ride in one of these contraptions down to the bowels of the earth!

Archie got us tickets for the African mine dance display held on Sunday mornings. These dance competitions were organised by the Chamber of Mines and had to be booked and paid for well in advance. Performances were held in a specially constructed amphitheatre on the mine compound that held an audience of about one thousand. The dance teams comprised teams of twelve or more black African mineworkers: Zulu, Xhosa, Shangaan, Logi and Basotho, as far as I recall.

The music came from homemade instruments: rattles, xylophones, concertinas, whistles and drums, supported with tribal songs and chants. The performers were extraordinarily energetic and spectacular in tribal costumes of coloured beads, feathers and animal furs. Each tribe had its own distinctive music and dance style and the finale was the famous gumboot dance. A dozen or so dancers dressed in full underground rig-out - hardhat, overalls and gumboots - stomped and jigged to the rhythm of feet stamping on the hard ground and a melodic sound made by slapping the sides of their gumboots.

(This slapping action was once a kind of Morse code that originated down the mines where black workers were not allowed to talk.)

Occasionally we went the Greyhound Drive-in cinema or bioscope; it was a novel sensation to watch films in the comfort of your car and free from cigarette smoke. Furthermore, by pressing a button on the microphone post next to your car you could order a toasted steak sandwich and fries or ice cream and a cold drink anytime during the show. We had seen such drive-ins in America movies, never imagining we'd be doing the same one day.

When I mentioned to Archie that Pat's birthday was coming up soon he suggested we try the Chinese restaurant in Bree Street, Johannesburg. Although I wasn't keen to go into the city after work, we all had a good night out and a meal such as we'd never been served with anywhere in the UK.

Easter was over and beside the inconvenience of her 'bump' Pat was suffering from foot pain. Before we'd left England she had an operation to remove an oversized verruca on the ball of her foot. She'd been off work for several weeks, her foot too painful to walk on, and with the extra weight of carrying our baby the verruca was back. The consultant assured Pat he could get rid of it forever, but only after the baby was born.

On June 13th 1965 our first child, Tracey, was born 8lb 6oz in the Boksburg Hospital, the most beautiful baby girl I had ever seen. In those first few weeks after her birth, our lifestyles changed dramatically and it took us a while to settle into the routines of parenthood. We bought a pram that folded down and detached in two sections: a chassis and carrycot to fit snugly in the car. It was a formidable 'chariot': midnight blue with 300mm white rubber wheels, well-sprung and with a parasol for added shade. Pat was proud to push Tracey in it around the streets of Benoni.

When the time came for her foot operation I took a week off work as I didn't want Pat struggling with the baby while she was hobbling about on one foot. In the early hours a few days after her operation, Tracey woke us up crying. Pat hopped out of bed to pick her up for a feed and slipped, spraining her wrist as she fell. What with her poorly foot and her arm in a sling, she was immobilised.

I tried to cope but a newborn baby was beyond me and I could not afford to take more time off work. Anne, our next-door neighbour, realised our predicament and came to the rescue by suggesting we employ a house-girl. The following day Anne introduced us to her own – Lizzie, a robust and cheerful Xhosa woman. Like most black house servants, she understood and spoke reasonable English. I agreed to pay her the going rate to work two hours mornings and afternoons Monday-Friday between her other tasks.

I also asked Joe, my works supervisor, if I could slip out during our lunch break. He agreed as long as I was back within the half hour. It was a tight schedule with no time for drinking tea and ate my sandwich as I drove to our flat. I could not work overtime either as that was when I did our main food shopping and helped prepare our evening meals under Pat's supervision.

With all our friends working, Patricia still had daily visits from Helen Morrow, who was like a big sister to her. Helen took Tracey out in her new pushchair and helped with the daily shopping and was good company for Pat while she recovered from the foot operation. Lizzie also proved an invaluable help as she did cleaning, washing, ironing and dusting and any other job Pat couldn't handle. If Tracey woke up while Lizzie was about she was first to bottle-feed her, humming some African lullaby. Often I arrived home from work to see a little white leg dangling from the shawl draped around Lizzie's back. Lizzie sang to her as she worked as if Tracey were one of her own.

After three weeks, Pat was back on her feet and recovering well. She decided to keep Lizzie in our employment. Pat wanted to work again and we did need the extra money.

Our favourite haunt in the winter evenings and a change from listening to the radio or records was a drive-in restaurant, The Fireplace. They played UK and USA TV films from 6pm to 9pm inside a room at the rear of the restaurant - 77 Sunset Strip, The Avengers and other popular series. This was a convenient venue after Tracey was born as she would sleep in her carrycot under our table while we ordered snacks and watched the films.

Going out as a family was a novel and welcome experience, something we would relish for many years to come.

Our daughter Tracey's christening: St Dunstan's Church, Benoni, SA
with godparents Monica McMaster & Edith & Archie Mackay, (1965)

With Archie and Edie at Babsfontein

Van Reenen's Pass, Drakensberg Mountains(1965)

Zulu dance display, Durban (1965)

Margate, SA (1965)

Tracey with nanny Lizzie (1966)

Patricia at Jan Smuts Airport (1965)

Kalambo Falls, Lake Tanganyika, Zambia (1966)

Kasaba Bay, Lake Tanganyika:
fishing for Nile perch & watching wild elephants at

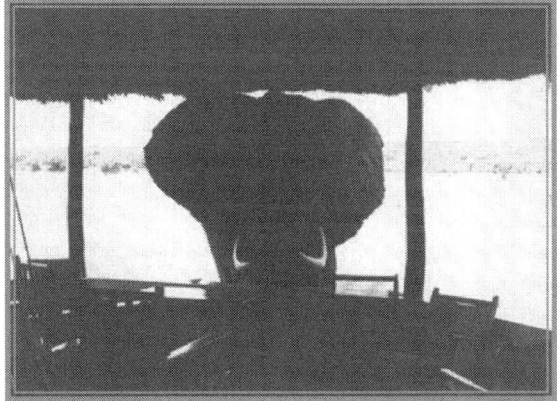

A daily visitor to the nsaka, an open sided building (1966)

-19-
A Christening and a Farewell

With a holiday weekend coming up Archie asked if we'd go down to Durban with him and Edie as they had an offer of an apartment for a week. As I was working hours of overtime and had holidays due, I decided the break would do us good. And this time I would not run out of petrol!

On the Saturday before Settlers Day on Monday 1st September we left Benoni before dawn. In her wisdom, Pat fed Tracey who then slept through most of our journey without a murmur. Re-fuelling at Villiers we drove non- stop to Harrismith without incident, where we stopped for a top up and a comfort break.

On this popular public holiday the town was too busy for us to want to stay longer, and so we pushed on. The N5 wound its way up through the Drakensburg range and when we reached Van Renan's Pass, I parked the car and took photos on a day with no mist. The scenic views were fantastic with miles of jagged cobalt peaks rising up above the thorn veldt, with a riot of green and yellow grasslands in between.

By all accounts, Dutch settlers had wiped out the San bushmen, the true dwellers of this region who had lived there for thousands of years. According to my Southern Africa touring atlas, our altitude was 7,500ft. Through my binoculars I picked out Cathedral Peak, and beyond were the higher mountains of Basutoland.

We stopped in Pietermaritzburg for a refuel only as we wanted to be in Durban before mid-afternoon. We stopped again briefly to give Tracey her noon feed by the falls in Howick, which plunged into the pool below in full flow.

We made Durban in good time and the Italian landlady opened up the apartment for us. The apartment was well-equipped for cooking with a refrigerator, kitchen utensils and plenty of towels and bed linen for the week. And we could hire the in-house babysitter for one rand a night if we wished, she told us.

The first two days we walked around the town and sunbathed on the beach. In spring Durban was hotter than the Transvaal. We strolled again down Marine Parade with Tracey in her fancy pushchair. Later, when we visited the aquarium, the pushchair attracted a pelican fascinated with the parasol, which it tried to bite. When Patricia screamed in panic, an attendant heard the ruckus and came running to shoo the bird away.

"It was only curious," he explained, as he led it back into its enclosure, "and there's not much strength in its beak."

That night we ate out in a seafront hotel with a disco in the basement. Herman's Hermits latest number was playing, "Can't you hear my heartbeat", which became one of our favourite songs.

After two days in Durban, I suggested we drive down the coast to Margate. The two hour journey on the N2 southern road offered occasional views of the Indian Ocean as it took us through the quaint seaside villages of Scottsburg and Port Shepstone. Dotted around the hillside were groups of beehive huts with the walls decorated in varying designs and colours. In between lay a vast expanse of rolling plantations of sugar cane and bananas. We stopped by a fruit stall where young African boys chewed sticks of sugar cane. They offered a sample, but I found it much too sweet and stringy, so instead we bought apples, oranges and bananas. Our hefty one rand tip left them whooping with glee.

Margate was a peaceful seaside resort, like a retirement town, surrounded by low sprawling red-tiled bungalows with well-kept gardens and trimmed lawns. In most shop doorways was a doggy bowl filled with water. The streets were immaculately clean and Margate had an English village friendliness about it. The beach nestled in a half-moon bay with high rocky buffs and grassy landscaped picnic areas surrounded by tall palms, tropical aloe plants, cannas, lilies and exotic flowering shrubs.

The surf rolled in between rocky buffs with a shark-net stretched across to protect the bathers. Archie was first in as usual and I followed, only to be caught by a backwash that sucked me under and spewed me in the middle of the bay. I surfaced, spluttering to find Archie at my side.

"Are you OK, Pete?"

I nodded and managed to make it back to the beach; I am not the best of swimmers, learning to swim long after leaving school and only the breaststroke.

On our last full day in Durban, the highlight of our visit was the Zulu war party performance. The tour guide fluent in Zulu brought events vividly to life and was a knowledgeable interpreter. We sat transfixed with an audience of a hundred or so under a covered terrace something like a football stand. A group of some fifty Zulu came over a hill silhouetted against a clear sky and impressive in full war garb of leopard and civet skins, feathered headdresses and beaded armbands. First they rattled their cowhide shields with assegai and knobkerries, then fell silent for a few moments, then roared out the humming cry of *Zuluuuuuuuu!* as they charged downhill towards us.

I was as excited as when I first saw the film Zulu starring Michael Caine and Stanley Baxter. The only sound missing was the Welsh soldiers singing 'Men of Harlech' in defiance to the Zulu horde. The audience were gripped by the drama, too. A few paces short of us the mass of glistening black Zulus halted to rattle shield again and stomp and jab in an imaginary battle. As the dust settled there was a signal from the chief upon the far hillock and the Zulu impi (warriors) turned and walked away with their shields above their heads in respect to their enemies' bravery.

Throughout the narrator continued his storytelling on the Anglo-Zulu War.

The show ended with tribal dancing from children and young Zulu females, half-naked except for beaded skirts. Archie came away happy with a miniature shield and a wooden assegai.

On our return home from Durban a stack of mail from England awaited us. Opening our letters from home was always a special event and we would sit on the veranda with a pot of tea to read them. I was eager to hear from my sister Irene with news on whether my father was improving after his stroke and how everyone was getting on. My sister Doreen was getting married to a Polish chap called Basil and Brenda and her husband John were moving into a new house. Pat's sister Renée kept us in touch with the Dowson family gossip. Minnie (Pats mother) was doing fine and still enjoyed her fags and riding her bike.

Pat wrote back to report that she and Tracey would be home next spring and asked if she could stay with them until I came home. Derek Manthorpe had let us know he'd be pleased to be Tracey's godfather, if only by proxy, and that a small gift was already in the post.

The November rains came in time for Guy Fawkes Night in such force that it seemed him up there held a grudge against us. Forked lightening played across the Reef and next day the newspapers were full of the havoc caused. Hailstones as big as chicken eggs were reported, breaking house windows, denting cars and damaging property. The streets were flooded as rainwater cascaded down drains and water gullies, filling them to the brim. This freak storm brought a swarm of flying insects in its wake. Summer had arrived. Thankfully, the weather settled back to its normal pattern, though during the rainy season you could guarantee umbrellas were out by four o'clock in the afternoon.

The 28th November was our special day when our six-month old baby girl was christened Tracey Renée (Renée after Pat's oldest sister) in St Dunstan's Church in Benoni. She wore our neighbour Anne's family heirloom christening dress that had been passed down through her family. Sadly Anne could never have children. The Reverend had no problems baptising our lively daughter who had already taken to water like a fish. Afterwards we took photos and returned home with all our friends to feast on the banquet Pat and Anne had prepared and to wet the baby's head.

The build-up to Tracey's first Christmas was as exciting for Pat and me, and first on our list of presents was a high chair with a row of counting beads in red, white and blue that made Tracey scream with delight as she watched them spin as she flicked them. She also had plenty of dolls and fluffy teddies that she kept for years afterwards. In the midst of spoiling our own child, we did not forget Lizzie's family, and she took home presents for her own children and herself.

After Christmas we faced the fact that without Patricia's wages we couldn't afford to live in this rented property and save enough to buy our own house. For us the streets of South Africa were certainly not paved with gold.

Pat had tried to return part-time to Record Printers, but they didn't need extra staff. With two of her friends, she enrolled for a comptometer course in Johannesburg, though working in an office was not her cup of tea. I sensed she was unhappy while training for a change of occupation. She came home from work worn out from studying this new technology and after two months gave up on the idea.

Once again, I started to scour the newspapers for another job, preferably with accommodation. After weeks of disappointment, an engineering company based in Zambia advertised for a boilermaker foreman. I sent my CV to the address in Springs, a town only 10km from where we now lived. Three weeks later I was interviewed by Eddie Reed, the managing director, a slightly built man of medium height some years older than myself. He spoke briefly and to the point in the typical South African accent, rolling the Rs. His pleasant manner hid a shrewd businessman, who in the years to follow I came to admire. He told me he'd be in touch and a week later I came home to find him waiting for me at home with his wife Marie, who was holding baby Tracey when I walked through the door. We shook hands on his offer of the job as foreman boilermaker in his Bancroft works on the Zambian Copperbelt.

We had already decided that Pat and Tracey would return to England even if I got the job in Zambia. Then it would be up to me to determine whether it would be worth our while to bring them back to Africa. Mr Reed was disappointed and told me not to believe the stories in the newspapers about Zambia's political problems since its independence from Great Britain in 1964.

Our friends were equally disappointed and showed it, they all were. The closest of them, Archie and Edie and Monica and Alan, knew I'd been looking for work in Southern Rhodesia, but after so many rejections, thought I had given up. My immediate problem now was what to do after we sold up and where we would stay. Allen and Monica came to our rescue, offering us accommodation until we left South Africa. Our house girl Lizzie could still come and take care of Tracey up until we were leaving.

I sold all our furnishings and the car to pay for Pat and Tracey's airfare, with enough left over to keep them going for a month or so. I did not know what was in store for me regarding sending money to the UK though the salary offered in Zambia was more than enough for Patricia and me to live on until my return to England. We worked it out that if I stayed six months in Zambia I should have sufficient savings to apply for a mortgage on a house back in Grimsby, the town of my birth. That was going by the cost of houses two years ago.

So our time in South Africa came to an abrupt end after two exciting and eventful years. A sad occasion to be saying farewell again to good friends and it came hard to me that Patricia and Tracey would be going home without me. Our last few days together were long with many sleepless nights. My one comforting thought was that they would be staying with Renée, Pat's oldest sister and her husband Arthur, who had two young daughters. Her brother Alec was to meet them at London Heathrow and drive them north to Grimsby.

-20-
North of the Zambesi

The Central African Airways plane whirred into life, and then settled down on its steady course north. Johannesburg was left behind and presently the plane crossed the Limpopo, a river dividing South Africa and Southern Rhodesia (Zimbabwe.) Further, north we crossed the Zambesi, the mighty river separating Southern Rhodesia (Zimbabwe) and Zambia.

As I read earlier in my Southern Africa AA Road Atlas, the Copperbelt of Northern Rhodesia, now Zambia, is one of the richest copper-producing regions in the world. Ndola being the commercial and administrative centre with a huge copper refinery. From Ndola, the Copperbelt area stretches 70 miles north towards the Congolese border and is 20 miles wide. Besides Ndola, Kitwe is the biggest town in the Copperbelt; other mining townships, Luanshya (Roan Antelope), Mufulira, Kalulushi (Chibuluma), Chingola (Nchanga) and Bancroft, only five miles from the Congo border.

As the seatbelt sign went off, passengers around me unfastened their seatbelts and stretched their legs. As I settled back in my seat, my thoughts drifted to Pat and our daughter Tracey, who had left three days previous by South African Airways to London. We gave each other a final wave as they gazed back at the airport lounge window where I stood.

This was my second experience of flying and I hoped it was not going to be as traumatic as my first. Thirty-five hours would put the most seasoned traveller off.

I unbuckled my seat belt and checked my inside jacket pocket bulging with my passport and a note about the man I was to meet at Ndola - Les Merrifield, a name that would suit an old colonial British diplomat.

The seat across the aisle groaned as it took the weight of a fellow passenger. I knew immediately when he spoke that he was South African, with the unmistakable guttural tone of the Afrikaner.

"Where are you heading for?" he asked.

"Ndola. I have someone meeting me to take me to Chingola."

We were half an hour into our flight and the cabin crew served complimentary drinks and nuts, followed later by sandwiches and coffee on cardboard trays.

"My name's Peter Pratt," I added as we shook hands.

"Ach, sure, and mine's Jan Le Roux. I get off at Lusaka."

We both ordered beers. Jan poured two miniature bottles of brandy into the plastic cup and opened up his can of Lion Lager. He saw me looking.

"Ja, I like to have a chaser after a beer, meneer," he chuckled. "It's an old habit-but a good one, hey?"

Jan obviously knew the co-pilot.

"When do we get in, Barry?"

"Landing in an hour, Jan. We're pretty well on time, hey?"

The two and half hour flight took a bus stop call at Lusaka, the Zambian capital, before continuing to Ndola a 45-minutes flight. I said farewell to Jan as we shook hands.

"Good luck, meneer." His round face creased into a smile. "You may need some, hey?"

I remember reading the headlines in the *Johannesburg Daily Star* back when Zambia celebrated independence from Great Britain in 1964 and Kenneth Kaunda took over as President. Before then, while staying in the Benoni Hotel, Pat and I had met a young couple a little older than us and first heard of Zambia! John and Ann had come down from Lusaka the capitol where they had lived most of their life. There was no future for them in Zambia as South African passport-holders, they said, and many besides them were leaving.

The Viscount turned westwards on a slow banking curve, preparing for its run-in to Ndola as I pondered what I had let myself in for. I handed my passport to the uniformed black immigration official at passport control. He said nothing as he scanned first it and then me with heavy-lidded eyes. He stamped my passport and gave it back to me without a word.

I collected my suitcase and went to the concourse. A smallish chap walked up to me.

"Are you Peter Pratt?"

"Yes. Are you Les Merrifield?"

We shook hands as Livingstone and Stanley had done in Tanzania in 1871.

"Did you have a good flight?"

"Not too bad. Not much to eat though."

"We'll fix you up with something later," he promised.

Les Merrifield was not as I had pictured him; he was shorter than me by a head, slightly built with light-brown hair and a round and friendly face. Unlike his boss Mr Reed, his attire was informal, a short-sleeved shirt with an open packet of cigarettes in his top pocket. His dark grey slacks were so creased and crumpled, shiny of seat and baggy at the knees – something any self-reflecting steam iron would run from. His brown suede shoes were scuffed and dotted with cigarette ash. He was definitely not your old colonial type.

Les drove an Austin Cambridge, bristling with chrome, with leather seats and a walnut dashboard and all the refinements of a luxury, British-built car. Inside it smelt of stale booze and tobacco, this due to its overflowing ashtray spiked with butt-ends that spilled onto the carpeted floor.

"It's an hour's drive to Chingola."

Les lit another cigarette and offered the packet.

"No, thanks I don't smoke."

By now, it was 10pm. The roads were quiet and not well marked or lit, with no such luxury as cats' eyes. Les drove on full beam, his headlights picking up the countryside, mainly dense bush, as we negotiated long sweeping curves. The roads, as in South Africa mostly ran dead straight for mile upon mile. We had been driving almost an hour when the car sped past an industrial complex that Les was able to identify as the Kitwe Nkana copper-smelter. Tall chimneystacks belching black smoke were lit up in the evening gloom by the orange glow from molten slag tipped down slagheaps like lava from a volcano.

Half an hour later a Welcome to Chingola sign appeared in the glow of our headlights. This copper mining town has one of the world's largest open cast mines.

"Drop your bags in here, Peter."

Les opened the door to a small room with only a single bed and chair.

"Let's go meet the gang, hey?" He smiled boyishly. "We'll have a nightcap; it's just across the road."

I checked my watch again. Had I mistaken the time? No, it was definitely half an hour to midnight. Les closed the door behind us and strode across the road towards a church outlined against a clear and starlit sky. If it were not for the street lamps, it would have been pitch black.

I followed Les down concrete steps that led into a long, smoke-filled room at the back of the church.

The place was heaving with folk laughing and singing, and the air was so thick with cigarette smoke you could have cut it with a bread-knife. Sat on top of the bar was a grey-haired, bespectacled chap playing an accordion and singing his heart out. He turned out to be the diminutive local Catholic priest, Father Claude, and this was the Catholic bar. Les introduced me and someone thrust a glass of ice-cold Lion Lager thrust into my hand as my initiation to the Copperbelt.

-21-

The Copper Mine

I could not remember how I got back to my room until a knock on the door woke me and a young woman popped her head in.

"Good morning, Peter. I have a mug of coffee for you." I recognised the pleasant South African lilt and sat-up squinting at my wristwatch. 7.30 a.m.

"I put one sugar in your coffee, is that OK? I'm Judy, Steve's wife. We saw you last night with Les in the Catholic bar. You can use our bathroom upstairs and breakfast is in fifteen minutes - number four.

Les and Steve were sitting over breakfast of a cigarette and a cup of coffee. Judy put a plate of eggs, bacon, tomatoes, beans and toast and another steaming coffee in front of me.

"You lot had a skin-full last night," she said. "Hey, Pete, did you sleep OK?"

"Yes, thanks."

I got on with the serious business of cleaning my plate and within fifteen minutes, I was back in Les's car again en route to Bancroft, which he said was a 15-mile drive north of Chingola. Les said he had to go into work anyway and had decided to give me a rapid tour underground at No. 1 shaft.

"Have you worked in a mine before, Peter'?

"No. This will be my first time."

He smiled. "It'll be an experience for you then, hey."

It was a clear sunny morning, warmer than winter in South Africa this time of year. The sun hanging just above the treetops gave the bush a glow like burnished copper. The landscape was dense bush, very different to the South African Transvaal's wide-open veldt. Like miniature pyramids, ant mounds 3-5 metres high and twice that at their base dotted the bush. Les said the road-bridge we were about to cross over was the Hippo-Pool on the Kafue River. As Les slowed a baboon as big as a full-grown Labrador leapt on top of a concrete pillar. He glared balefully down at us, ever watchful as we slowly passed.

"He's been there every morning for the past couple of days," said Les. "There'll be a troupe of them in the bush."

"Ah. I thought I was seeing things. I've only seen them in zoos."

"They were regular at one time; not so much these days. Too much traffic and since a few have been run over, I think they have learnt a lesson. The local Africans don't like them because they damage their maize crops."

Les drew up in front of 6ft double gates near a signboard for E.W. Reed Electrical and Mechanical Engineering Co. He sounded the horn and an elderly African came loping out with a pack of mongrel dogs yapping at his heels.

He opened the gates and took off his woollen hat, a sign of respect.

"Bwana Les."

Les spoke to him in the *lingua franca* or pidgin language similar to Fanagalo used in the mines of South Africa and told me his name was Phiri. The man smiled, showing pegs of yellowed teeth.

Les waved a hand at me.

"Bwana Peter."

Phiri closed the gates and trotted after us followed by the barking dogs.

"Phiri's our watchman, gateman and labour foreman."

The workshops were smaller than I expected, but equipped with all the usual machines for small fabrications and machining.

Les took me into the offices whose windows gave a good view of the works yard and workshops. The desk was stacked with engineering drawings.

"That lot's for you sort out tomorrow as Eddie is away."

By Eddie, he meant my employer, Mr Reed.

Hung on the wall behind the desk hung a framed picture of the Zambian President Kenneth David Kaunda.

"We have to catch the last cage down in fifteen minutes."

Les threw me a white hard-hat and a pair of white overalls and invited me to help myself to gumboots. I found a size 10 in the row of a dozen or so, a size bigger than I normally wore and sloppy, too, as my socks were the type worn with shoes.

A short drive from the workshops we came to the mine's entrance and a sign for Bancroft Mines Konkola No 1 Shaft. A black gateman opened up the barrier, briefly acknowledging us.

"There are three shafts," Les told me, "numbers 1, 2 and 3, but number 2 is way down the road and mostly flooded." He smiled. "You're about to go down the wettest mine in the world."

Since independence two years ago, racial discrimination had become a serious offence in Zambia. Some of the whites practised it, but less so than in South Africa. The newly independent Zambian was not yet used to the freedom bestowed upon him, especially the older natives. Here, there were no racist notices as seen in South Africa, such as 'Slegs Vir Blankes,' Whites Only. On the shaft bank was a crowd of fifty or so miners, the Europeans kitted out in white overalls with yellow waterproofs, and most of the Africans in navy blue boiler suits and blue hard-hats.

Les showed me into the lamp-room where we had to sign for our cap-lamps and battery, a mandatory safety precaution. The shaft headgear towered a hundred feet above us, with its massive wheels turning at an amazing speed. A constant humming came from the thousands of feet of steel cables that wound their way into the hoist house. I had seen similar structures from a distance on coalmines in England and Wales.

I followed Les into the cage; not knowing what to expect. I remembered that day when Bert and I went seeking work at Carletonville gold mine in South Africa, how only weeks later a sinkhole swallowed up three houses

The man cage could take a load capacity of 120 workers, half in the upper and half in the lower level. Once inside we formed a compact body of men, shoulder-to-shoulder and back to back. With a metallic clang, the banks-man closed the steel gates and then the cage doors. A sharp bell rang once... twice ... The floor dropped beneath me as the cage descended. After a few seconds, my belly came up to press against my ribs and we continued downwards in a long continuous rush into the dank darkness. The lights of the stations at the different levels flashed by in the blur of speed and the cage lurched and clunked, not unlike a train.

Except that, we were going down, not horizontal, and going faster.

The air smelled musty and earthy and the atmosphere was almost sticky. Heavy droplets of water dripped and ran constantly from the rock-walls. Konkola was living up to its reputation as one of the wettest mines in the world. Les had told me the de-watering system was working 24/7 to pump out many thousands of gallons of water a day.

I braced my knees and still they buckled as the cage braked and yo-yoed, as steel ropes stretched under the full weight of cage and thousands of feet of 50.5mm steel rope. In less than three minutes, I was standing on terra firma at the 3,400ft (1036m) level. The shaft station brightly lit by overhead fluorescent strip-lights surprised me with rocky walls partly concreted and whitewashed.

Signs gave directions or instructions on the do's and don'ts of mine safety. Three cavernous openings - haulages - almost the size of a railway tunnel curved gently away somewhere into middle earth where every sound and step echoed. A continuous string of dim light bulbs lined the haulage roof. Set in the floor railway lines disappeared into the gloom seemingly guided by the overhead lights. Water flowed continuously in the gully like a natural stream. Racks of electric cables, compressed air pipes and large diameter ventilation ducts, hung from 40mm diameter steel eyebolts driven and wedged into the rock walls along the haulages. Every single item of equipment was dependent on those eyebolts.

I was beginning to learn mining terms as I followed Les along the haulage. Crosscuts linked other haulages with railway lines. He unerringly took the left haulage on some signal as yet unheard by me, warning me to be careful of diesel engines in motion. Several noisily trundled by as he spoke, towing a string of coco-pans loaded with rocks – copper-bearing ore being transported to skips to be hauled to the surface.

We had switched on our hat-lamps as soon as we came out of the cage, a mandatory safety regulation. From the illuminated shaft station, we now entered a claustrophobic and dimly lit tunnel, with only our own hat-lamps and a single string of overhead electric bulbs to guide us. The craggy rock walls wept water from fissures, water that flowed continuously into the eighteen-inch open gullies. I could pick out half-clad figures, glistening with sweat as they shovelled loose rocks into ore-pans, the beams of their hat-lamp dancing as they bobbed up and down. I was cautious to the point of turning back, but forced myself to remember I was here on a mission.

Les broke into our silent plod.

"My men are down here, Peter; it's only a short walk now," he shouted above the echoing rat-tat-tat of air-machine drillers. "You'll find it easier to walk between the rails, on the sleepers."

216

Sweating cobs in the claustrophobic and humid atmosphere, I stumbled on, unaccustomed to this terrain and to the non-stop hiss of compressed air escaping. Les found walking easier than I did; my legs, being that much longer, missed every other sleeper. We had been tramping through the mine non-stop for twenty minutes; my feet were burning hot. Somewhere deep down inside the steel-toed gumboots, my socks had fallen asleep, as we say; just like they did when I was a boy fishing or playing in the snow in my older brother's wellies.

We came to a signpost indicating a 60-degree incline shaft that led us down to another level. I dumbly followed Les down a steep flight of robust, well-trodden timber stairs, grateful for the handrail. Alongside us lay two sets of rail lines, where steel cables hauled ore skips, grunting as they ascended, and passing empty skips returning for a refill.

The water dripped monotonously on, but not heavily enough for us to don our yellow waterproofs, though some miners had. The lighting got dimmer, and I noticed some of the bulbs that lined the roof were broken. By now, my legs were like rubber, as much from a lack of sleep as from the unaccustomed exercise. I was still a bit tipsy from the night before extended drinking session. I counted steps trying to forget my aching head, but gave up at a hundred and twenty. At every step, I brought up a nauseating burp. At last, we reached the bottom of the incline shaft, where I sicked up my breakfast and felt better for it.

"Ach, there's no sound of work going on," whispered Les. "The bleddy *muntus* (Africans) think I'm not coming down, hey?"

He stepped out from the haulage. Six native workers were sitting by a coco pan (ore-carrier) surrounded by shovels picks and lengths of familiar steel sections: channels and angle irons, a welding set, toolboxes and drums of electric cable. Two appeared to be sleeping while the others smoked and chatted. All of them froze into rigidity as Les played his cap-light beam on them, black faces gleaming with perspiration from the thick stagnant air. We were greeted with beaming smiles displaying lines of white teeth. Bwana Makuba (Big Boss!) I smelt the sweet pungent drift of homegrown dagga, the African equivalent of marijuana, an aroma first encountered in South Africa.

Les rattled off a reprimand in what I thought was Fanagalo to his boss boy. Later I learned this was Chikabanga, the Zambian equivalent, influenced by Bemba Zambia's main tribal language.

By two o'clock Les and I had finished our tour underground and were in the cage, resurfacing. The cage braked as it slowly returned to ground level and I followed Les out into bright sunshine with not a cloud in the sky. Clean air flooded into my lungs, a satisfaction I would never fail to appreciate. We returned our cap-lamp and battery to the lamp-room and crossed our names off the register, a security check to indicate we are out of the mine.

"How did you find underground, Peter?"

"Frightening at first, Les, but OK once I was out of the cage with my feet on firm ground."

I had felt better as the morning and things got more interesting.

'Starting to-morrow, Eddie has work for you in the workshop. "You'll get to know the men better and the things we do."

"And when will I go underground again?"

"You're not allowed to work underground before your medical. Today was classed as a visit. Tomorrow I will get you booked in for your medical and chest X-ray in Kitwe. There will be four of you going. The others are John Stewart, Peter Hauptman and Jan Fourie."

After we had dropped off our underground gear at the office, Les took me to the Nchanga Mine Club in Chingola where the usual Sunday Rugby match was in progress.

Around the generously sized Mine Club bar native bartenders were serving already inebriated, and boisterous, customers clustered in groups sharing jokes laughter and banter. Most were casually dressed in what I now regarded as almost regulation wear here: shorts with short-sleeved shirts worn with knee-length socks or the ubiquitous safari suit.

The bar and lounge was spacious enough to easily seat a hundred or more people and not a black person in sight apart from the servants. Next door was the club's restaurant with windows overlooking the rugby field and cricket ground Drawn by the smell of cooking, we wandered out into the sun around the rear of the building.

Men, who with a long fork in one hand and a bottle of Castle beer in the other, expertly poked and turned the fare on offer, mostly managed the braai. As the meat and sausages sizzled, they sprinkled beer over to 'bring out the flavour.' I am not sure if I got drunk eating the meat or drinking the beer. I found them a friendly lot, mainly Rhodesians and South Africans with a few British expats. Nearly all worked in mining of one kind or another.

Les introduced me to Peter and Ted Hageman, both of whom I thought to be Rhodesians, and who were employed by E W Reed. Ted was Eddie Reed's second-in-command and a highly respected electrical engineer. His brother Peter was workshop supervisor at our Chingola workshops with Johnny Sweet, who also supervised our mobile cranes.

Both Peter and Johnny lived in OK Flats with their wives and children, as did several other families. Ted and his wife Estelle had a bungalow in Chingola, as did Eddie Reed.

My flat-mates were Peter Hauptman, a tall fair-haired German electrician and John Stewart a sheet-metal worker from Liverpool and two South Africans, both electricians, whom I only remember as Bill and William. Out of the five of us, I was the oldest and the only one working in Bancroft; the others worked in Chingola at the Nchanga Mine. The five of us were all newcomers to Zambia.

As I took in the mood around me, life here on the Copperbelt seemed friendlier and relaxed compared with South Africa. I had only been here one night, but already I had met numerous co-workers, open and friendly. I really missed Pat and Tracey as I watched children with their mums playing freely in the sun. It occurred to me that I had better write a letter to Pat with my new address, letting her know I had arrived safely in Zambia. It would be another two weeks before I would get news from her. None of our family in Grimsby had the luxury of a telephone.

"You look lost."

I turned to find Judy Oelefson, Steve's wife, at my shoulder.

"No. I was thinking I must write home and it has been a long twenty-four hours for me. These days I'm not used to burning the candle at both ends."

Judy laughed.

"You'll get used to it, why didn't you bring your wife with you? Steve told me you were both in South Africa."

"It's a long story. We were unsure about settling there; that's why I took this job, to find out more about Rhodesia and Zambia. We found it difficult to fit in with South Africa's lifestyle and the strict apartheid system. Anyway, our folks back in England wanted to see Tracey, our baby daughter, who was born in Benoni last June."

"'I'm going back to OK Flats now if you want a lift. You can collect your things then and settled in your room. The other four have left already."

Judy had fair hair, cornflower-blue eyes and a surprisingly pale complexion. She held Noel, her newborn son in her arms, and her four-year old daughter Christine, who obviously wanted to go home. We drove back in her American Ford Galaxy with leather bench seats and ample room for six passengers.

My first impression of the OK Flats and our single quarters was of an army barracks. The exterior was dull grey pebbledash with the usual fancy burglar bars at every window, strong enough to repel any would-be thieves. She rang the bell on the singles flat that was across the passage from her own.

The door was opened by a sleepy-eyed and shirtless individual with a mop of uncombed black hair and beard. Without saying a word, he turned and slumped back bare-footed on the settee in front of the TV – the first I had seen in two years. Both he and his companion Bill were South African and the floor littered with empty beer bottles. No wonder both seemed somewhat inebriated.

"I'll leave you to it then," said Judy. "Give us a shout if you need anything. Steve said he'll see you later this evening if you fancy a drink in the Catholic bar, or he'll pick you up in the morning for work."

"What time does he go?"

"6.30, in the green panel van outside."

"Thanks. Tell Steve I will be there. I am getting my head down now. Thanks, Judy, and good night."

"Good night Peter."

I went down stairs to the room I had slept in earlier and collected my suitcase. John Stewart, whom I had met at the mine club, was waiting for me as he shared a room next to mine. I had a room to myself and was glad of it. Tired as I was, I sat and wrote to Pat as Judy had promised to post my letters in the morning.

OK Flats in Chingola belonged to Eddie Reed, mostly to house his married employees and their children. The workers included

Johnny Sweet, Harry Hunkin, Les and Norman Merrifield, Peter Hageman and the McMasters. I shared the bachelor flat with four others: John Stewart, the only other Englishman then working for Reed, the German Peter Hauptman, and Bill Gardener and Willie Swanepoel, both from South Africa.

Soon I was in my bed and sleeping soundly.

-22-
Bancroft

The town was named after Dr J. Austin Bancroft, the consulting geologist who directed the exploration programme after copper was discovered in 1924.

Monday was my first official work day at E. W. Reeds Bancroft workshops, though I had had a brief look-through the two open-sided workshops the day before. As Eddie Reed wasn't there Les, the electrical foreman, showed me around and introduced me to my fellow-workers.

We had expat workers from South Africa, from Germany, Italy, Holland and England. Boilermakers: fabricators, welders and pipe fitters, mechanical fitters, the largest contingent of tradesmen was among the electricians. The only black Zambians then were mostly labourers, although over time some trained as sand-blasters, spray painters, welders, drillers and lathe machinists.

The workshops were the smallest I had ever worked in, but as Eddie Reed pointed out during my interview, I would be joining a growing company in steel fabrication. The engineering workshop had a radial drill, pedestal drill, lathe, besides the usual fabrication shop machinery: hole-punch and angle bar cropper, plate-shearing machine and welding machines, steel workbenches with metal toolboxes underneath.

Fifty metres across the compacted gravel yard was another similarly sized workshop, 80 metres long x 40 metres wide and a good-concreted floor. There was a 2m plate roll, workbenches, welding sets and a horizontal boring machine. The stockyard had a good selection of steel plates, girders, angle irons, and channels, pipes of all diameters and drums of electric cables. All materials from the stockyard were brought into the workshops using our native workforce besides for off-loading deliveries and loading finished items.

My boss Eddie Reed was fond of his dogs, and as our lunch break drew near, Robson Ngwani, our one-eyed storeman would begin to panic. It was his task daily to fetch Les Merrifield's 2kg of rump steak and his newspaper, *The Northern News*, for when he returned from underground. He also fetched bones for the dogs from Copperfield butchers: Pluto, a tall sandy ridgeback and Ladybird, the mother of the three other mongrels. Robson a Bemba had worked for the company many years, spoke English well, was always polite and respected his place among the white man. He had a younger brother who was high up in UNIP (United Independent Party) and Government.

One Saturday morning during a rabies scare all pandemonium broke out as a young jet-black Labrador plodded into the works yard. Our dogs, tied to the workshop posts, yelped and howled and all work came to a halt. Eddie dashed out of his office to see what the commotion was. A puppy perhaps six-months old, scruffy and muddy, was drinking water from one of the dog's bowls. Without further ado, Eddie got Robson the store-man to wash, dry and feed the animal and tie him to a spare post. Eddie brought him a collar and as it was a Saturday the day the pup strayed into the yard he named him 'Overtime". He grew into a fine dog, followed Eddie everywhere, and in Eddie's absence would lie outside his office.

During a rabies scare, the streets became littered with the dead animals as the police shot all stray dogs on sight from their Land Rovers as they patrolled the town. The dead dogs where collected by the local refuse company. After the all clear, we had a laugh the first morning the dogs were let loose and Ladybird, in her excitement, grabbed Des Pienaar's trouser leg and pulled him off his Vespa scooter.

The first few weeks after my medical I was working alternately between underground and our fabrication workshop, more so to get to know the different areas of work. Sometimes there were new installations or maintenance work carried out on the mines surface process plants; or installing pipelines to the tailings (sometimes) referred as the slimes dam. These tailings are the sandy waste product from the separated copper ore and dumped three kilometres away from the mine area.

Les Merrifield showed me around the mine surface production sheds. Here a maze of massive conveyors transported the raw ore brought to the surface and passed under huge electro-magnets. The magnets picked up any foreign metal among the copper ore missed by careless underground workers and brought up to the surface in skips. This might include pieces of wire rope, shackles, welding-rods and sometimes hammers, spanners, nuts, washers, bolts and pick heads that could do untold damage to the ore crusher jaws.

Though I had worked in similar factories in England, here I was working in the two functions of mining, first underground and now surface operations, all within my first two weeks. As Les took me around the operating plants, he explained the basics of what happens once the copper ore is brought to the surface. The ore goes through a series of cone-crushers, vibrating screens and huge rotating drums loaded with steel balls and water to pummel the ore to a fine watery paste. Finally he took me into the flotation shed where the paste is channelled into 'launders' (vats), mixed with a soapy chemical and agitated to create black bubbles. Les dipped his finger in.

"That's copper, Pete," he said. "Only the copper sticks to the froth. The rest sinks to the bottom and is piped out to the slimes dam." He smiled. "Try it."

I collected some in my hand; it was warm and finely gritty.

He led me into the filter house where rotating drums skimmed the paste off for the drying process. At this stage, the product resembled nothing so much as a fine charcoal-coloured talcum powder. The final phase would be transporting it for smelting at Nkana Kitwe.

As the months passed and the company took on more workload, Eddie employed other European tradesmen, especially electricians, as electrical engineering was then the company's main function.

During those first few weeks underground, I worked alongside Steve Oelefson and George Sammons, our apprentice electrician. As a team, we built electrical sub-stations, platforms and conveyors, and fabricated and installed hundreds of metres of electric cable racking. Although it was hot, damp and sometimes claustrophobic, I enjoyed this new challenge. The company employed a further twenty or so native Zambian labourers, mainly for pulling cables, digging trenches and other menial jobs, and it was fascinating to hear Steve and George speaking to them in Chikabanga, the lingua-franca used in the mines.

After my first three months as a working supervisor, my boss Eddie Reed took me around the Bancroft Mine surface engineering departments introducing me as his new man. Our main contacts were Jack Sammons, Bancroft Mine's divisional maintenance engineer and Johnny Munro, the mechanical engineer, both close friends with Eddie. Together we visited the mine's drawing office and engineering workshops so I could be introduced to supervisors I might be dealing with. The mine boiler shop was most beneficial, and run by foreman Bernie Lloyd, a pleasant, easy-going Welshman.

Back in his office after the tour with Eddie, my head was swimming. I was not used to the ins and outs of contracting and had not expected to take on so much responsibility so soon. As Les told me, "You'll get used to Eddie's way of working Peter."

As I became familiar with the Mine's different engineering departments and the people running them, I began to enjoy my new role. Over the following months, I shared the responsibility with Eddie of dealing with mechanical contracts, buying in materials, planning, estimating and submitting tenders. There would be site visits to attend along with our competitors in Bancroft and from Chingola. Besides my new tasks, I still had to oversee the fabrication workshop and muck in on site work underground and with surface installations. My working day was mornings underground and afternoon are workshop supervision and preparing estimates. A 10-12 hour shift was not out of the ordinary five days a week and sometimes on the weekends.

This was the first time I had been paid monthly and sometimes my wage packet exceeded £300 pounds, a small fortune compared to what I had earned in South Africa and the UK. I opened a Barclays Bank account in Bancroft and transferred most of my salary to Pat in England. This was, after all, why I had made the sacrifice to work here - to enable us to buy our own house in Grimsby or Cleethorpes.

Knowing I was a keen bodybuilder, Judy's husband Steve told me his brother Eric knew of a gym in the Chingola Mine library. It seemed an unusual location for a gym where one of our Chingola employees trained. Adam was Greek, several years younger than I was, and spoke good English. He had a good physique and was an enthusiastic bodybuilder. I began to spend two or three nights a week there, not only to keep in shape, but also to stay off the booze.

Staying in Chingola, I never had much spare time to wander around Bancroft, unless hopping between the Cricket Club bar and Vega Bar after work. I began to see why it is the garden town of the Copperbelt. It was a pleasure to drive along its main thoroughfare Kamenza Way under pale lilac jacarandas and scarlet and yellow-flowered flame trees. (These grew at intervals, each with a trunk painted white to deter termites.)

The street names intrigued me the most - Francolin, Spurwing, Ibis, Impala, Hartebeest, Sable, and Kudue to name a few. Most gardens had manicured lawns fringed with tall orange or yellow cannas, azaleas, hibiscus, magnolia and poinsettia. Centrally located were the Mine Club and a great expanse of playing fields - rugby, cricket, and football, with indoor and outdoor courts for tennis, badminton and squash, the velvety pitch for lawn bowls, a swimming pool and the arts theatre and bar.

Due to our increasing workload, my weight-training sessions came to an abrupt end and I was back on the pub-crawl soon after leaving work. We were a boisterous crowd as the beer flowed, with our boss Eddie buying the first round and sometimes-laying several pounds on the bar to cover the next round before he left for Chingola. Les, Jan, Steve Oelefsen, George Sammons and I became good friends. Each afternoon after work, we made our ritual to visit the various bars in Bancroft taking on all-comers at darts in the Cricket Club, Vega Bar or Mine Club.

The Vega Bar, sited in the shopping area, was a typical frontier bar. One night with Eddie and our crowd a ragged old African stumbled into the Vega Bar, dragging behind a beheaded 12ft python for sale. After some heated discussion in Chikabanga, Eddie threw him a few coins to get rid of him and the snake. It was the longest snake I had ever seen and as thick as a 4-inch drainpipe. The skin would have made quite a few women's handbags.

On July 30th, I had been in Zambia for ten weeks and the 1966 World Cup football final between England and Germany was underway. The Zambian television announcer promised full coverage. If there were no breakdowns, it would be a miracle and a feather in the cap for the Zambian TV broadcasting history. On the night of the big match, our lounge was a multi nation gathering: English, South African, German, and Greek.

England proved the critics around me wrong and won 4-2 after two extra time goals to seal the victory. I had the feeling John Stewart and I were in the wrong camp, all smiles as we toasted victory while everyone had wanted Germany to win.

It was music to my ears as the BBC commentator, Kenneth Wolstenholme, shouted out, "Some people are on the pitch, they thought it was all over until Geoff Hurst scores again...it is now!" The English fans swamped the pitch.

The rest of 1966 flew by and on my weekends off - and there were not many - John and I would go fishing on the Kafue River for bream and catfish, with tiger-fish as the most sought-after specimen. On one such trip to the River Kafue with Peter Hageman towing his boat, I called in at one of the roadside stores, Indian-owned, for cool drinks. Headlines in the *Zambia Times* newspaper told of a tragedy in the UK. George Thomas, the Minister of State for Wales, was commenting and said of the disaster, "A coal tip has buried a generation, and children have been wiped out."

In the Welsh mining village of Aberfan, a giant slag-tip became an avalanche of black slag that engulfed and demolished a local school, killing 116 children and 28 adults. I had not a clue where

Aberfan was, but could not help being sorry for the victims and their families.

After four months beneath the Zambian dry season's almost cloudless skies, I would watch fascinated as dust devils swirled around our works yard and along the paths picking up leaves and debris before sinking down into the yellow dry grass. October is suicide month, especially among the natives, because of the almost unbearable heat. After five dry and dusty months, the smell of the first rains was as sweet as any Parisian perfume.

The evenings grumbled with thunder and the cracking staccato of silver-blue streaks among rolling dark clouds. Then, a deafening drumbeat as raindrops splattered down on pavements, through branches, and on tin roofs and cars. The rainy season started as Judy Oelefsen had foretold: "It always rains on Guy Fawkes Night." Once the bonfire lit and the firework display started, the night sky rumbled into confirmation of her words. We found shelter inside the Mine Club and sat nursing our beers.

As we drove to Bancroft in our rattling Morris panel van, the roads were often awash after the night rains. The River Kafue swelled to a monstrous torrent as it gushed over boulders and flowed under the Hippo Pool road bridge. Likewise, Chingola and Bancroft's storm drains were choc-a-bloc with the dry-season's debris, drains barely coping with the sudden deluge. The red earth of once sun-hardened bush paths was rutted and swampy. The rains were a signal for the flying ants – termites - that had been nesting dormant and they took flight in their millions. The windscreen wipers were helpless against the onslaught, even driving a car through this phenomenon. There were frequent stops to wipe the glass clean.

The termites were now easy prey for the birds – bulbul, wood dove and dusky flycatcher. When the flying ants shed their wings and fall to the ground like raindrops the natives scramble to collect these nutritious and wingless bodies. I would watch fascinated as birds, African women, and young children busily gathered up their breakfast.

Eddie Reed made a big thing of Christmas by putting on a party for our native labour. Besides his weekly pay, each worker got a hefty food hamper, with everything needed to tide him and his family over the two weeks of the Christmas holiday. On the last day, Eddie had us set up braais for the occasion. Eddie took great pride in dishing out steaks, boerewores (Afrikaans for long sausages) and dollops of mealie pap, the native porridge. In addition, each man got a carton of Chibuku, a popular African beer made from a mix of water sorghum and maize and extremely potent.

We Europeans benefited, too, with an abundance of food and bottles of Lion and Castle lagers, Dimple whiskey, Smirnoff vodka, Cape brandy and Bacardi rum. Over the week, Eddie had gifted all the mining engineers that we dealt with throughout the year. He did everyone proud.

As the company would shut down for two weeks over Christmas, John Stewart asked me if I fancied going on a ten day fishing trip to Kasaba Bay. I jumped at the chance, although I hadn't a clue where that was until John picked it out on the map.

Once again, my *AA Road Atlas and Touring Guide of Southern Africa* proved invaluable, indicating that Kasaba Bay was located on the south-west shore of Lake Tanganyika. The lake's immense depth (almost a mile deep) is 4,000 feet above sea level in the Great Rift Valley. At 500ml long and 75ml, wide Lake Tanganyika is the second largest lake in Africa.

Nile perch are common there, tiger fish at 12lbs and giant catfish, some weighing over 200lbs known locally as vundu. With this information, we borrowed some heavy fishing tackle and lures from Johnny Sweet and Peter Hageman, who had once fished the lake. We had Zambesi spoons 4in long, fashioned from metal and with barbed hooks; wood warblers with bright eyes, 10in long and hinged so they wriggle when trolling and others with feathered gills. We also took 150lb of breaking strain lines on two reels. On arrival, we were told fishing equipment could be hired along with a small boat with out-board motor.

With everyone gone away for Christmas, OK Flats were deserted and not to be outdone we took two dozen beers and a bottle of Dimple whisky and Bacardi knowing we would be spending Christmas in Ndola. John had booked us into the Savoy Hotel for two nights but informed that, as the entire kitchen staff is away no meals served on Christmas Eve and Christmas Day. Luckily, around the corner a Greek cafe was glad to serve us meals any time. We spent the two days in the hotel lounge watching TV while polishing off our beers and spirits to drown our sorrows.

On the morning of Boxing Day, we left for Ndola Airport.

-23-
Lake Tanganyika

Our flight from Ndola took off without incident and we landed two hours later at Abercorn (now Mbala.) At the Grasshopper Inn, our host Peter Parton introduced us to fellow-guests bound for Kasaba Bay. Abercorn is Zambia's most northern town, sitting at an altitude of 5,500ft (1676m) in the North Eastern sector of Zambia where it borders Tanzania and the Great Rift Valley.

That afternoon we followed our guide along a narrow trail on the crest of the sheer cliffs of the gorge separating Zambia and Tanganyika. Below in the lower gorge was the cacophony of hundreds of marabou storks. I was in awe at my first sight of the falls, a silver ribbon that plunged down unhindered to disappear into the hidden gorge pool below. The falls are among the highest in Africa, a 726-foot (222m) drop, and although not in full flow still an amazing spectacle.

On our return to the vehicle, I had my first glimpse of Lake Tanganyika over 1,000ft (305m) below and shimmering in the fading light. Peter Parton had warned us we had to be back at the inn before dark for our dinner (and because leopards still roamed the area!)

The Grasshopper Inn built in typical African style, a veranda furnished with cane tables and chairs. From the interior walls big game trophies stared blankly down at us with unseeing eyes: eland, waterbuck and duiker to name but a few. Above the entrance was an enormous set of buffalo horns protruding from a bleached white skull. Scattered around the polished parquet floors were skins - zebra, lion, waterbuck and leopard, all complete with gaping jaws. The bar would make any 'Brit' feel at home with the plaques of several English county cricket teams, and football and rugby photographs.

We had a quick shower, downed a few beers and gobbled up an excellent dinner of fresh trout followed by venison with all trimmings, tempting us to stay longer. We ended our evening on the veranda watching the sun go down with a few beers, toasting the days ahead in traditional sundowner style with a nightcap. Most of our fellow guests were from Rhodesia, some of British pioneering stock. One, a farmer, told us a yarn about the baboons that often raided his maize plantation.

"The blighters would pick one cob, take a bite then tuck it under an arm, pick another cob and take a bite and tuck that under his arm. Meanwhile the first cob has already dropped to the floor. They would pick another and another, decimating the maize field in troops of a hundred or more. Until all that is left, is an acre of half-eaten cobs while they run off with only one. Baboons are destructive buggers."

After a hearty breakfast, we travelled by Land Rover twenty-five miles down to Mpulungu, a fishing village on the southern shore of Lake Tanganyika. At the water's edge, fishing craft lurched on the crest of the waves, dirty but substantial vessels, low-set with a good beam. Nearby was an Arabian dhow, a handsome craft with three Arabs aboard dressed in belted robes, each bearing a curved dagger? The stench of the fish aroused memories of my birth town, Grimsby.

Young native women were laying out kapenta by the bucketful to dry. Kapenta-fish is in most rivers and lakes in Zambia and is important to the native diet. Not much bigger than the size of my little finger yet extremely nutritious, and served with nshima, an African traditional dish throughout Southern Africa made from maize corn flour. The girls stared at us with big round eyes as we walked towards our boat, one standing in a cloud of flies holding a kapenta by its tail

"You want, Bwana Mkubwa?"

"Ikona – no."

I laughed and walked on to catch up with our group. I was hoping to catch something bigger.

Mpulungu became an important port for the British during World War1 when Germany ruled East Africa and the lake with the aid of the steam ship Graf von Götzen. Before the conflict ended, the Germans scuttled the vessel. The British helped to refloat it and repaired renamed the MV Liemba in 1927. The vessel was still ferrying up to 500 passengers and cargo from one end of the lake to the other.

At 8am, I boarded Peter Parton's catamaran, a fair size vessel with a powerful diesel engine and canvas sails. Peter greeted us as we went aboard as skipper of the vessel. There were plenty of seats around for the fifteen or so passengers and, thankfully, adequate shade under a canvas awning. We took off at a steady pace with the scent of fresh coffee brewing in the galley.

After about an hour's sailing the vessel slowed to a halt, riding the troughs. Peter shouted, "Anyone for a swim?" Most needed no further prompting and were already in the water by the time I plucked up courage. Not being too good, a swimmer I used the steps located aft and breast-stroked for a few yards, keeping the vessel within easy reach. The water was ice-cold, refreshingly so, as the temperature gauge showed 30C.

"We are about ½ mile (1km) from the shore," said our skipper. "How deep do you think it is here?"

After a few wild guesses from the swimmers he laughed.

"It's more than a 1000ft deep (305m.)"

I considered the dark blue depths beneath me and decided to get out for a cold beer!

It was late afternoon when we arrived at the south side of Kasaba Bay and waved goodbye to Peter and his crew before the vessel returned to Mpulungu.

Jack Curtis, the Kasaba Bay manager welcomed us ashore and took us by Land Rover to the camp, a 20-minute ride through woodland scrub and rocky out crops. The camp had twelve separate dwellings, each sleeping two or four. After our 4-hour lake journey, I was hot, sticky, and ready for a shower. Jack told everyone to meet in the main building he had also pointed out on our arrival.

Our accommodation, built in African style with a thatched roof, looked straight out onto the open lake. Fifty metres from our door the expanse of sandy beach stretched a kilometre either way. Our accommodation had a toilet, shower and hand basin, and in the main area, two single beds with crisp white sheets. Above the beds was a canopy of mosquito netting. I spent my nights sleeping under a single sheet knowing the 'mozzies' would be kept at bay.

On the first night, it was hard to sleep for the first hour because of the night sounds, mainly crickets and toads until about 3am when we heard the whoop-whoop of hyenas scavenging around the kitchens. Next day Jack Curtis pointed out a hyena dropping, the size and shape of an ice-cream cone and resembling a lump of chalk. Over the week, we had nightly visits from hippos 'mowing' the grass around the while emitting a series of grunts and farts.

Inside the main camp building, the bar and restaurant was decorated with tinsel and a 2-metre high Christmas tree. The tables were set out for our first dinner complete with Christmas crackers and paper hats. Jack introduced his wife Mary and the staff who would be attending to our needs during our week's stay. For our own safety, he told us the dos and don'ts to follow around the camp and beyond. We were smack bang in the middle of big game territory on shore and in the water. The camp built on an elephant trail; they continued to roam at will at all times of the day. This was Jacks main concern and he emphasised that elephants were wild and dangerous. If elephants were about, he would light the lamp outside the Nsaka (open rest hut) to warn us not to leave our chalets.

The Nsaka is an open-sided thatched roof building, encircled by a one-metre high wall built around an enormous 18m high winter-thorn tree. Here we discussed and exchanged fishing tips and techniques, reviewed the day's events and took refreshment. Because it was extremely hot, fishing mostly took place from first light to mid-morning and then mid-afternoon. Lunch packs were provided if ordered the night before and cold drinks for the early risers. Boats had to be back by 5pm.

Sometimes, elephants strolled soundlessly upto the open-sided Nsaka intent on exploration, with trunks out-stretched like a vacuum hose. We would move swiftly and quietly to the opposite side or cross to the main building to get out of harm's way. Jack Curtis would come out to feed those he trusted, though cautiously at arm's length with a bun or potato on a stick. There was one female he named (for obvious reasons) 'Broken Tusk' who came daily around mid-morning in the hope of a snack and would hang around stubbornly until Jack fed her. The Curtis's had known these particular elephants for years, but were still wary of them.

John and I fished every morning and late afternoon, watching the sunset over the lake as we drew in and tied the boat to the jetty. On our early morning trip we set off before first light with our packed breakfast and as relative amateurs, we followed the keen and experienced anglers quietly padding down to the boat quay in the early dawn. Tembo, the boatman, made sure we had enough fuel and drinking water aboard, with a reminder to be back before noon.

The first two days we took the southern route about half a kilometre offshore trolling for tiger fish. The silver and red Zambesi spoon, a spinner lure 100mm long was the most favoured for this fish and proved its worth when John's reel screamed for mercy as he wrestled with a 12kg beauty - a fearsome specimen. There were plenty of Nile perch (though no heavyweights), bream and a 4kg lake salmon that was cooked for our dinner. Daily we saw the majestic fish eagle perched on lakeside trees, herons and gulls followed our wake back to camp as if we were a returning trawler - they were most disappointed.

Along the lakeshore small herds of elephant played to an audience of hippo, who watched half-submerged while the elephants hosed each other down. I had often dreamed as a boy about wildest Africa, not gold or copper but the tribes and animals. As we motored back to base, we had to dodge pods of hippo blocking our usual route as they wallowed in the shallows. John spotted others in the deeper waters. My heart was thumping as only their ears and eyes where above water. Like an iceberg, the other two tonnes of hippo meat was beneath the water.

Hippopotamus and crocodile are known to be the biggest killer of humans in Africa. On the sandbanks, crocodiles 4-5 metres long lay sunning themselves, hideous mouths gaping wide so their personal dentists, the white egret birds, could clean their teeth. Sensing our presence, they would slide their prehistoric forms silently into the water and float submerged except for eyes and nostrils.

On our last but one day, our group was escorted through the bush to Pebble Beach for a swim in a crystal-clear lagoon. Two armed African game rangers escorted us, as besides crocs and elephants, this was also leopard and lion country. Along the way, we disturbed impala, bushbuck and waterbuck all too quick for a camera shot; all I saw was their white bull's-eye butts. Most

238

species of gazelle reside in this area, Jack Curtis had told us, along with reedbuck, bushbuck, puku and warthog frequented lakeside.

The lagoon was as peaceful as any Cornish beach, but 50 metres long with fine sand and pebbles. The mangroves and bush spread to the lakeside in places, so we had to beware of crocs, though Jack Curtis reassured us there had been no sightings there. We saw no bird life either except for the fish eagle. One of our groups was an avid 'butterfly nut' – John's name for him – and ran around with his net billowing out behind like a windsock. After an hour's swim and after long trek we returned after too short a time to camp for lunch.

After we had eaten, although it was baking hot at 36c (96f), John and I decided to try our luck fishing from the end of the boat jetty. We sat quietly nursing a Castle lager, and I thought of my planned flight home to England. John noticed a movement along the jetty and nudged me.

"Don't panic, Pete," he whispered, "but there's an elephant nearby. Get in the boat."

Broken Tusk was padding silently towards us. We grabbed our fishing rods, made quietly for the nearest boat, and paddled away from the jetty. It was a shame neither of us had a camera, as she would have made a great subject as she stood there watching us with her trunk sniffing the air. She trumpeted and flapped her ears and five metres away we felt the draught.

On our last day, I earned the fishing certificate that named me as a member of the Golden Perch Club. I was the only one among us to catch a Nile perch, and before we left camp the certificate was mine confirming it as the best 29lb single catch of the week.

The last night after a farewell dinner a group of us sat at the end of the boat jetty enjoying our usual sundowner. With beers in hand, we watched the sun dip below the great lake's horizon. Within an hour, it was pitch black and we were able to view another of Africa's wonders, the Southern Hemisphere stars and the Milky Way.

The following day we said our farewells at the Grasshopper Inn in Abercorn and flew back to Ndola with Alf Peterson and his family, who lived in Kitwe.

Working six-days a week over the next three months, my last days in Africa passed quickly. When I had said farewell to all my friends in Bancroft and Chingola, Eddie Reed asked for my address in England. He tried to convince me again to think things over saying that if I should decide to return, he would pay all our airfares and any expenses. Peter and Ted Hageman, Jan Fourie, Steve Oelofsen, and Johnny Sweet and their wives were the last I said goodbye to at a grand farewell braai.

Jan Fourie shook my hand.

"Now, meneer, we South Africans have a saying. Once you've tasted the waters of Africa, you will return."

I left with those parting words ringing in my ears.

At Ndola, I shook hands with Les Merrifield; it seemed much less than nine months since he had first welcomed me to Zambia. The Alitalia Air DC8 was an altogether different aeroplane from the cramped Swissair on first flight into Africa three years ago. After the plane took off, I remembered the envelope Eddie gave me as we shook hands. I opened it soon after leaving Ndola to find £200 in English five-pound notes inside with a simple note: 'Think about what I said, Peter – Eddie.'

-24-
Oh, to be in England

April in London was cold and uninviting under a leaden sky - a sharp contrast to the Africa I had left. As I descended the aircrafts steps, I pulled up my overcoat collar against the chill. I remembered Jan Fourie's farewell, "You will come back, meneer."

At Heathrow's hotel reservations desk I booked into the Avon Hotel near Russell Square, a short taxi ride away from Kings Cross railway station where Pat and Tracey were due to arrive the following day from Grimsby. It was hard to imagine that in a few days I would be back working in England again.

The English maritime weather never changes. Showery April with its biting winds brings out the dullness in its population, with black umbrellas and rainwear between the gloomy buildings. What a sudden change from the azure African skies, the lavender-blue jacaranda trees, the omnipresent bougainvillea and its colourful races. I arrived at the Avon Hotel wrapped in the same overcoat I had originally taken to Africa. It didn't seem three years ago and had never seen the light of day after that first winter in Benoni.

I arrived early at Kings Cross with time to buy Tracey a present. In the toyshop, I saw the very thing: a cuddly monkey, almost lifelike with its glassy brown eyes and cheeky grin. I spotted Patricia weaving through the crowd of passengers alighting from the train, pushing Tracey in the baby stroller before her. After we hugged, I lifted Tracey into my arms. She had grown into a bright and beautiful little girl, her curly blonde hair neatly tied with red ribbon. She studied me intently, possibly wondering who I was, and then her dimpled hand touched my bearded face. I was pleased to find that the monkey had taken second place to Daddy

We arrived back at the Avon Hotel and to the hotel door attendant's wink of approval. He was resplendent in his gold-braided get up and we had already had a brief conversation when he found out I had arrived from Zambia. He had served in the RAF after the war had ended in 1945 and briefly posted near Salisbury in Southern Rhodesia. He was a firm admirer of Ian Smith whom he had once met.

"I'm all for (UDI) Unilateral Declaration of Independence," he asserted, "and I hope that buffoon Wilson will see sense and accept Smith's terms."

Talks were still going on between Smith, then Rhodesia's Prime Minister and Harold Wilson, the British Prime Minister, who ironically first met on HMS Tiger in early December 1966. While we were fishing for tiger fish and Nile perch on Lake Tanganyika, the Rhodesians among us seemed optimistic that it would 'blow over' within the year. History shows that it did not.

After two days, we left London's wet and windswept streets and caught the train to Brighton to visit our friends Derek and Louise Manthorpe, who were Tracey's godparents. Before we immigrated to South Africa, the Manthorpes had helped Pat and me to settle in Brighton when times were difficult in our marriage, a kind of seven-year itch.

Derek took us back to their apartment where we had stayed before departing for Africa. Louise hugged us and made a particular fuss of Tracey as she did with all children, having none of her own. After the superb dinner, she had prepared and with Tracey tucked into bed we talked of the old days over a glass or two of wine. Derek had not altered and still called Lou by her nickname of 'Slobby.' He was as enthusiastic as ever about his business. His two fitness gyms were still going strong and I returned to the room where I had once trained under the guidance of Derek; and found nothing had changed in the three years I had been away. One could still hear the metallic clang of steel weights and the musty smell of sweating bodies and the dampness from the ice-rink above. As I opened the gym door, I heard the familiar "Aye up!" Derek's usual greeting who too soon tabbed me as a Northerner. To a Southerner anyone born north of London is a Northerner.

"What's your plan now, Peter? Are you going to settle down here for good?"

"I haven't made up my mind yet, Derek. Pat and I will talk about that once we are back in Grimsby. Though I shouldn't think we could afford Brighton again unless I won the football pools!"

"Well, you're always welcome here, you know that. And tomorrow, if you like, we can visit the stables where my horse is kept."

Two days later, we were on a train and hurtling through the southern counties to Lincolnshire. I can never tire of travelling by train; there is always so much more to see. The Lincolnshire countryside was unmistakable, flat as a pancake and beautifully green. The winding country lanes led to squat farm cottages and newborn lambs gambolled in the paddocks or herds of cows munched pastures. It seemed hardly any time at all since we had taken this same route to go to Africa.

We stayed with Pat's sister Renée and her husband Arthur in Heneage Road in Grimsby. He was a shipwright by trade, an old-fashioned, bespectacled, braces and pipe man and good at entertaining children as they had two young daughters of their own. We had spent many an hour while courting in this comfortable Victorian terrace, a typical Northern three up and three down with a long back yard and small front garden. Take three strides from the front door and you would be run over by a passing motor vehicle or bicycle. Here Patricia and Tracey had stayed after two years in South Africa whilst I took the job in Zambia.

On arriving home my first thoughts had been of my father, who resided staying with my eldest sister Irene in Brigg, a village some fifteen miles from Grimsby. He was still hardly able to walk unaided, speak a word or write. A severe stroke at 77 had not made life easier for him or for my sister, who also had to bring up four boys. At some stage, Dad moved into an old folk's home in Cleethorpes. I visited him as often as I could, but transport was the problem, as we had no car.

My first few days back in Grimsby I was busy juggling our finances. I had hoped we would save enough to buy a house in Cleethorpes without taking on a mortgage, but as usual, inflation beat us. Property had more than doubled in price since the two years we had been away. We only had enough cash to lay down the minimum amount to get a loan on the house we wanted. The remainder went on furniture and the other bits and pieces that make a house a home.

Within a week, I was offered a job where my Uncle Jim worked, Robinson's Ships Engineers. I didn't want to go back into ship repair work, but I had no choice. From being responsible to running an engineering workshop with all that entailed. I had slid down the ladder and chances were slim being offered a foreman's position. Not having the money to buy a car, I bought a second-hand bicycle so as not to be dependent on buses.

Three, months later in the middle of our first English summer in three years we moved into the kind of house Pat had always wanted, a 3-bedroom semi-detached in Camden Crescent, Cleethorpes, near to Brereton Avenue were Pat was brought up and where we had started married life together.

It did not take Pat long to make our house comfortable as she has always done with much careful planning of our resources and expert hands on the sewing machine. We re-decorated and had carpets fitted in the lounge. Pat already had a bike with a baby seat at the back for Tracey and they visited her sisters and her mother Minnie most days or went grocery shopping.

I had another job offer with Starco Engineering in Immingham. Although it meant travelling 15ml (24km) there by bus, the work was more to my liking and better paid, with overtime. I also knew the foreman, Jack Ramage, from my apprenticeship days.

I came home after work one night to find our old friends Pat and Roger Woodliffe there. They said that they were hoping to immigrate to Tasmania. Where was that? I asked. Roger had brought the information to show us, as they were not sure how to make the application. As we were old hands at emigrating, they thought we could help! I was fascinated as I flipped through the brochures. Tasmania was in Australia and they had copper mines there.

Flippantly I remarked that under our present circumstances I felt like making an application myself. Pat gave me a certain look I have seen before.

"I suppose there's no obligation, is there?" she said, and then turned to check on Tracey, playing happily in a garden almost hidden with snow. I stood and put my arms around Patricia.

"Penny for your thoughts, love?" I said.

"I have the same feeling I had four-years ago in Brighton," she said, smiling.

Three weeks later, I had a letter with a bundle of forms to fill in from the Australian Immigration in London. The following month a letter said we that we have been accepted and to go ahead with the medical examinations. We were experiencing the same excitement we had felt when applying for South Africa. We all had medicals with a doctor in Grimsby and chest X-rays.

A week after that I had a telegram from my old boss Eddie Reed in Zambia urging me to ring him and reverse the charges. I did so the same night after work. We had a long discussion and he made me an offer hard to refuse a partly furnished bungalow, use of a company vehicle and paid holidays every three years to the UK. The salary he offered was four times more than I was presently getting in England and, as I quickly calculated, what I could expect in Tasmania. I broke out in a sweat as I listened to Eddie's enthusiastic outline of his plans and prospects for expanding the fabrication business in his company in Bancroft.

Before he rang off, he said that airline tickets for the three of us has been arranged, together with my 3-year work permit and would be forwarded as soon as I agreed to return to Zambia. My mind was in turmoil, though in my heart I knew I wanted to go back to Africa. I had a long talk with Pat, who finally said, "Do what you think best, love."

To which I responded, "Better the devil you know."

I phoned Eddie back, forgetting to reverse the charges in my excitement.

When I broke the news to Roger Woodliffe, he was surprised.

"I never thought you'd venture back to Africa, Pete, with all the trouble with Rhodesia and this UDI thing, whatever that means. Our Pat will be disappointed, but we wish you both luck."

We found out years later that our friends Pat and Roger Woodliffe did not go to Australia after all, due to some medical defects his son had.

I told Dad myself, going to the nursing home in Cleethorpes. I sat with Pat and Tracey by his bedside, perhaps for the last time. He was propped-up with pillows, a bewildered expression on his face as he mouthed words that did not come out right. He had to point out words his brain wanted to say from a little book my brother James had put together for him. Dad managed to open it at Zambia with his left hand flicking its pages. Saying goodbye was a wrench, both of us knowing this was almost certainly the last farewell.

We put our house up for sale together with all the furnishings, and within two weeks had a firm buyer. We only had the house seven months and made only £50 profit after paying back the mortgage.

The big day arrived and again we had said our goodbyes to families and friends. The taxi driving us to the Grimsby railway station passed the Grimsby Docks and the Dock Tower. For the second time we were leaving Grimsby, this time with our young daughter Tracey a few weeks before her third birthday. I often wonder what goes through a child's mind at these times.

Part Three:
Shadows under the Sun

Photo: Courtesy of Chris Mackay
The Flame Trees of Kamenza Way, Chililabombwe

-25-
Home of the Croaking Frog

We were all travel weary after the six-hour train journey from Grimsby to London Heathrow Airport for our twelve-hour flight to Zambia. Negative thoughts crept in. Was I doing the right thing by dragging my family back to Africa? Inwardly, however, I was excited to be returning to the country and the company that had so much to offer. I held Pat's hand as the South African Boeing's engines changed their tune before landing at Ndola International Airport.

The Zambian immigration officer thumbed through our passports, glanced at me then Pat and without any sign of welcome, waved us on without a word. After my year's absence, it seemed nothing had changed.

At the time of our arrival in Ndola, I recognised Peter Hageman with his friendly smile waiting in the crowded arrivals area. After his typical Rhodesian greeting of 'Howzit, Peter!' we shook hands and I introduced him to Pat and Tracey, who was shyly hiding behind her mother.

'What's your name, beautiful?" Peter smiled in a fatherly manner.

Peter Hageman was Eddie Reed's foreman in the Chingola Sheet Metal Workshop. I had half-expected Jan Fourie to be here, just to rub in his parting words, spoken in his husky Afrikaans accent.

"You'll be back, Meneer."

During our drive to Bancroft Peter filled me in on the comings and goings at Reed's.

"The company has expanded both workshops at Chingola and Bancroft and employ more staff. Remember my brother Ted, Peter? He now manages all Eddie's electrical contracts in Chingola and Bancroft. We are not Bancroft anymore but Chililabombwe, an African phrase that means the "home of the croaking frog."

"The big issue is the Zambian pound, now the kwacha."

Peter grimaced.

"All hell broke loose on our first payday using the new decimal currency. Even us whites were convinced we'd been swindled. Instead of getting 12 pence an hour, the Africans get 10 ngwee. I tell you, times are changing rapidly."

We passed through the familiar Copperbelt larger mining towns, Kitwe and Chingola, and crossed the Kafue River at the Hippo Pool a couple of miles from Bancroft. The town had not changed much from what I recall, but I preferred its birth name Bancroft to the tongue-twisting Chililabombwe.

Memories abounded as we drove down Kamenza Way, the town's main artery, through the white residential area of the town. Either side of the road were lilac, jacaranda and flamboyant scarlet trees and sprawling avenues of lush green lawns. Street names like Duiker, Bushbuck, Impala, Francolin, and Spurwing romantically reminded the house dwellers they were in Africa. The mineworkers who lived here fondly called this area the 'Zoo'.

I had already told Pat a little about this town. The mine workers' houses were built around the mine club, the hub of the community with its outdoor swimming pool, arts theatre and the Bongo Bar. There were recreational fields for cricket, rugby, squash, lawn tennis, lawn-bowls, most with a member's clubhouse with bar. Nightly these were packed with beer-swilling golfers, cricketers and rugger-mad expats.

About three kilometres outside the township was the Bancroft 'Hippo' Golf Club, the Shooting Club, the Gymkhana Club, the Flying Club and the Mine Farm. In its early days before independence, these facilities were clearly for whites only and whites still predominated, though since independence black Africans could become members - if they could afford to.

Kamenza Hill, overlooking the township at the time, was the residential area of the mine's general manager and other senior mine employees. At the highest point sat the observatory building where the Bancroft Masonic Society Lodge 7549 held their meetings. Generally, the majority of the other mining residences were sprawling redbrick bungalows, with corrugated tin-roofs and a carport. Their gardens back and front, besides an abundance of tropical flowers, were planted with exotic fruit trees, the most common being banana, paw-paw, lemon, avocado and peach. Windows generally had fancy scrolled wrought-iron burglar bars and fly screens, and most owned a dog or two - and not only as pets.

It was late afternoon as Peter parked outside Copperfield Flats on what is termed the government side of town. The shopping area separated the homes of the white mine employees from the government residencies. I recognised the flats as if it were only yesterday and not a year ago that I was drinking across the road in the Vega Bar with my old work colleagues at E. W. Reed Engineering.

Copperfield Flats were in a block of three duplex dwellings with two bedrooms upstairs and a bathroom. The kitchen and lounge downstairs overlooked both front and back garden with the usual sub-tropical flora and fauna one expects in Africa.

Peter introduced us to Des and Marie Pienaar, our immediate neighbours in the middle flat, No. 2. I thanked Peter before he left. He lived in Eddie Reed's OK Flats, Chingola, and must have been weary after driving the two hours to and back again from Ndola.

I remembered Des from the previous year I spent here. He worked at E.W. Reeds as a welder and was a devout Jehovah's Witness. He lived at Number 2 with his wife and two daughters. Des handed me the keys for Number 1, handily located across the road from the town's shops.

We were not impressed to say the least; the furnishings came as a shock. In the dining area was a makeshift dining suite, the table once a rough timber workbench covered with an oilcloth to hide the oil stains, and three metal chairs with plastic seats. In the lounge was an old settee and two armchairs; as a lad I had seen better furniture thrown onto Guy Fawkes bonfires. We went upstairs to find a metal double bed in one room and a single bed in the smaller bedroom with a bundle of bed linen.

All the rooms had bare concrete floors, painted red as is most favoured in Africa. Windows were fitted with the usual metal burglar bars and, thankfully, fly-screens too.

Des and his wife welcomed us into their flat next door for tea and something substantial to eat, realising that we had had a long and tiring journey. As it was almost dark, they said we'd be welcome for breakfast the following day. Then Des went on to tell us of the deteriorating situation in Zambia, which was hardly encouraging and certainly upset Pat to tears. Before he could go on any more, I stood up and thanked the Pienaars for their hospitality. We needed an early night.

Once back in our flat the tears welled up in Patricia's eyes as she sat down, holding Tracey on her knee. Soon she was crying hard, and I put my arms around her.

"I promise I will put things right the minute I set foot in Eddie Reed's office tomorrow."

Sleep didn't come easy for either of us that first night, what with the disappointment and, outside, the whistle of crickets and the constant croak of frogs.

Eddie apologised for not checking the flat himself and asked Steve Oelofsen if he knew of any furniture for sale. Steve took us to his house to ask his wife Judy to take Pat and me to Chingola where an OK Flats residents was selling up and later Judy telephoned Reed's office for someone to collect the furniture for us. From then onwards Judy and Pat became good friends. Judy took Pat and Tracey shopping in her Studebaker Lark and suggested Pat should learn to drive.

Judy also took Pat onto the African compound to the Lubengele Butchery where they even had hippo meat on sale. Pat said it was a revelation shopping there among the African shanties, but that the meat was cheaper and better than the town's.

The first few weeks were difficult for Pat as I was working ten hours a day and we only saw each other for a full day at the weekend. We introduced ourselves to Bill and Margaret Wynn in the end flat. Bill, who originally came from Yorkshire, was manager of Copperfield Butchers in the town and another on the African compound. His wife Margaret came round with a freshly made pork pie, one of Bill's creations for which he was noted in the town.

Tracey played happily in her own little world as children do and made friends with Roy, one of Bill's border collies. The Wynn's left Zambia some years later for Rhodesia, and I heard that Bill had started a Kennel Club there and trained collies, so obviously an enduring passion.

Copperfield Flat was handy for the town's amenities besides its churches and its primary and junior schools. The shops opposite our flat demonstrated that the town, though small, had a good variety, including the Vega Café, Vega Bar and Vega Cinema; a ladies' hairdressers, Bancroft Trading Company, Barclays and Standard Banks, a chemist, jewellers, bottle store, Bata Shoes, cycle, clothing outfitters, food store and petrol station. The Boma was the council and administration offices. Adjacent was the Post Office with post collection boxes – there were no such luxury as home delivery of mail.

The town's biggest shop by far was Smartwear and Grocery Department Store, a family-owned emporium that sold everything from a tin of baked beans to material to make your own clothes.

"Good morning, sir. Good morning, madam."

Mr Patel's greeting was always followed by a pleasant little nod or two.

"You are most welcome to browse. Would you like a nice cold drink or sweets for your little girl?"

The first thing customers noticed behind the pay counter was the portrait of Kenneth Kaunda, Zambia's first President. Rolls of materials in all colours and textures filled the shelves or were spread along counters. Children's clothes were neatly hung or piled in a heap as if in a jumble sale. Drawers housed hundreds of cotton bobbins of all colours and multitudes of buttons. There were stacks of loose linens, blankets and bed sheets. In fact, they stocked almost everything and, if they didn't have what you wanted, then it was no trouble to get it for you.

As you browsed the store's aisles, you would find shelves with all manner of tins, packets, jars and bottles of foodstuffs neatly arrayed. The air was scented with the exotic aroma of herbs and spices: nutmeg, cinnamon, fennel and other such spices. There was baby food, breakfast cereals, powdered milk, flour and sugar, boxes of tea and coffee, Milk of Magnesia, Eno's

Liver Salts, Beecham Pills, razors, cigarettes and a selection of pipe and cigarette tobaccos.

The efficient Mr Patel stocked most of our daily requirements.

The town's shops were built in a quadrangle with, in the centre, a lively open-air market with a daily abundance of fresh vegetables and fruit on offer: cabbages, pumpkins, squash, sweet potatoes and carrots, bananas, paw-paw, lemons, grapefruit, pineapples and melons. Stallholders tried to force you to buy, thrusting produce into your hands, shouting, laughing and name calling as they bartered.

The town centre was compact enough to walk around the shopping area in fifteen minutes. In Chililabombwe everyone knew who was in town by their car and when strangers were visiting.

We arrived before the close of the rainy season so everything was still verdant and colourful. From June until the end of August it's the dry season, when leaves and grasses turn yellow or tawny. Tall paw-paw trees with rugby ball-sized fruit and heavily laden avocado trees were common sights. Bill Wynn, our neighbour in the far end flat, No. 3, had a typical neat English garden and vegetable patch where he grew all manner of vegetables. The outer leaves of his cauliflowers were bunched over to protect the white crown from the sun. Rows of green beans were supported on 7ft canes like wigwam posts, their scarlet flowers a contrast to the lush green foliage.

Tracey bent and pointed to a lizard, a blueskop (in Afrikaans) or blue-headed lizard. Almost like a miniature prehistoric dinosaur, with an upright comb from head to tail.

"They can grow up to twelve inches long," said Bill. He warned us, "They move quickly and if cornered can be vicious and give you a nasty bite."

The town had a friendly atmosphere and everyone spoke English. The expats were mainly from South Africa, Rhodesia, England, Scotland, Wales and Ireland with a minority of Italians, Greeks and Germans. In its early days the town was made up mostly of South African and Rhodesian mine workers, but since Zambia's independence in 1964 most of the town founders had left for their homeland, to be replaced by young Brits or other European nationals.

Known to be new to the town, you could expect a friendly welcome. Overall, the town consisted of around 300 residential mine workers bungalows, mainly for the white employees. Most expatriate workers were on three-year contracts, with a lucrative copper bonus if production met targets, paid leave with return flights, help with private schooling and a pension. Generally, but not always, wives enjoyed a life of constant leisure and could languish by the pool with their young children and bask in the warm sub-tropical sun. Some women had jobs such as schoolteachers, shop assistants, or clerks in banks or offices that African women were mainly not yet qualified for. There was no other industry in towns like Chililabombwe apart from mining and ancillary industries. For work, some of the white woman might need to travel to the bigger towns of Chingola or Kitwe.

Because we were employed by a private contractor, we lived on what was termed the government side of the town. We were a rare mix of expats: teachers, shopkeepers, engineers, businessmen, clergymen and government personnel, all qualified in our respective field. Our detached dwellings were of the same quality as those of the mine employees. The dwellings had large fenced gardens with a tropical style to them. With the exception of the subtropical flora and fauna, the town resembled a close-knit English village community, where everyone knew everyone.

When we arrived there were few black Africans, if any, living in the town, as they had their own township a mile or so away, unless they were in some upper management employment. The difference between housing for blacks and whites in Zambia was as staggering as in Rhodesia and South Africa. The black African houses were mainly two or three rooms crudely built, with a corrugated iron roof, often housing families of four to six or more.

The African planted their gardens with banana, paw-paw, sweet corn, cassava, sweet potato and other vegetables for their own consumption and mainly did their cooking outdoors. Usually they had a few chickens and a dog not trained as a favoured pet who would bark day and night from hunger or lack of love.

At first sight, African townships seem never to change from one African country to another and can be a shock to the system. Roads and pathways are uneven with red-ochre rutted earth paths interlinking the houses. Children play in the dry dusty streets and gardens with homemade toys, some of wire ingeniously shaped into a motorcar or bicycle complete with a rider with moving legs. In the often-lush gardens or infant schools there'd be a paradise of climbing frames, swings, slides and swimming pools to keep the children happily occupied.

During our first year Patricia coped well with the help of Judy and made our home more comfortable, buying better pieces of furniture from families who were leaving. The mine had a constant flow of workers on attractive three-year contracts, better overall than ours as privately employed contractors. Yet though we might not have guaranteed paid holidays to our homeland or bonuses, we were well-paid - well above the norm in England and South Africa. It was up to individuals to save for those rainy days or for a future back home.

We had come to Zambia when some of the South Africans and Rhodesians could not tolerate the changes that were taking place. Zambia before its independence, had been the land of milk and honey, or so it was said.

"This was a white man's paradise," I was told, "We were well paid, topped up with lucrative copper bonuses and the bwana was the boss."

They found it hard to accept the changes in this ex-colonial, free and independent Zambia.

-26-
Settling In

After three months, our packing crates arrived from the U.K. Opening them was as if Christmas had come early. We had clothes that we had not been able to bring with us and Pat's collection of her favourite ornaments. She was delighted to see her Kenwood mixer and assortment of kitchen utensils among other things that she had favoured over the years. They had been around a bit, from Grimsby to South Africa and back and now Zambia, as had my box of tools and engineering books.

Our favoured records, 75rpm vinyls, were unpacked: Ray Conniff, James Last, Engelbert Humperdinck's number one hits Release Me and The Last Waltz; Andy Williams and a number of others we had collected over the years. Those Reader's Digest record albums had saved us from endless boring nights during our two years in South Africa. We lifted out our photograph album and treasured AA Southern Africa Road Atlas. Tracey, excited, helped her mother unwrap the packaging and jumped with joy to find her dolls.

During those first weeks in Copperfield Flats Bill Wynne, helped me cultivate a vegetable plot. Bill gave me young scarlet runner beans and broad beans, together with six-foot canes for them to climb up. We planted carrots, onion, cabbage, cauliflower, tomatoes and gem squash that became Pat's favourite, a tasty vegetable only the size of a tennis ball. As there were no facilities for weight training, gardening gave me a good workout.

Now my family was here, propping up the cricket club bar held no further interest. I had gone there in boredom when I was by myself. Those gardening workouts gave me the idea that one day I would start a weight training gym and get back into shape.

One evening, Bill Wynne suggested we go for manure from a friend with a chicken farm near Mufulira. He hitched his khaki shorts up a notch as he straightened his back from digging, then stood with hands on hips surveying the garden. Bob, his faithful collie, sat at his heels if waiting for instructions. Both could have come straight from the Yorkshire moors. Bill had a younger collie, Roy, whom Tracey had taken a fancy to who would sit in the shade of Bill's paw-paw and mango trees. Often the dog was tied there, as occasionally he would run off, as he was not yet fully trained.

"It will teach the little bugger a lesson."

Bill still spoke with a Yorkshire accent.

The following Sunday we took out the seats in Bill's Volkswagen Kombi to make room for the manure. Bob sat on top of the pile of hessian sacks as we set off for Mufulira, a journey just over an hour. Two miles before Mufulira, another major mining town, Bill left the tarmac to follow a stretch of rutted, ochre-red dirt road through thick bush veldt.

Arriving at a set of 6ft high padlocked steel wire gates, Bill honked his horn several times. An old African loped towards us and seeing Bill, he grinned, taking off his hat in respect for the bwana.

"Open the gates, Benjamin. We have come for chicken manure. Is bwana Frederick home?"

"Bwana Frederick, he gone town, bwana Bill."

Bill drove through the gates and up the track towards several rickety lap-wood sheds built on brick pillars three feet off the ground. To get at the manure we had to crawl under the chicken sheds wary of any snakes that might be present. Bob sat calmly with Benjamin's ridgeback who, he claimed, would alert us of their presence.

I donned an old pair of overalls buttoned up to the neck and slid elastic bands around the cuffs, tucking the legs of the overalls inside my Wellington boots. To protect my eyes I wore plastic grinding goggles. Bill had told me chicken shit has a high volume of ammonia, but my thoughts were mainly of encountering a spitting cobra.

As I was the fittest, I crawled under the sheds and started scraping up chicken droppings with the help of Benjamin who had a long rake. At the first touch a black cloud of flies rose from the heap of manure. Feathers floated down as I disturbed the frightened birds from their Sunday morning slumber. The noise was horrendous for the first few minutes. It was hot work and the little black flies in their millions did not help matters. They crawled all over me and in my ears and nose. The atmosphere was toxic with ammonia.

"It's good stuff that, if you have a cold," Bill said, grinning, as we filled the twelve hessian sacks. Before leaving the farm, Bill gave Benjamin a packet of cigarettes and a crate of Coca-Cola and sweets for his children. Bill sternly warned Benjamin to be extra careful with the cardboard box and not to open it as it was for the bwana Fredrick. Inside was a bottle of Oude Meester brandy, and Bill's own made boerwors (Afrikaaner sausages), with sticks of biltong and two carefully packed pork pies.

It took us three hours to get back to Chililabombwe as we had a puncture before we reached Chingola. We had to unload half the load to enable me to get the jack under the chassis. Again, the flies were disturbed and surrounded us once more with their frenzied buzzing as Bob snapped at them. Two hours later than planned we eventually pulled up at the back of Copperfield Flats and by dusk had the twelve sacks unloaded. Tracey and Pat were with Bill's wife.

"We were worried about why you were so long and were about to send a search party to look for you," she told him.

Pat came to inspect our cargo.

"Oh, my god, what is that awful smell? And the flies!"

Each afternoon after work I dug in the manure before it got dark, which it did suddenly. There was no lingering dusk as in England.

"Although there is no shortage of fresh vegetables, Pete, it is still worth the sweat to grow your own stuff," Bill said, as he poked and raked the soil.

After our first four months, my boss Eddie asked me if I wanted to move into a three-bedroom bungalow - I could not refuse such an offer after living in a poky flat. Eddie helped me with a loan to purchase a car and better furniture more to our liking.

Number 41 was one of many red-brick, semi-detached dwellings along President Drive. Typical of this part of Africa the house had burglar bars at every window along with fine mesh fly-screen, a corrugated iron roof, open veranda and a long gravel drive that led to the carport. A four-foot wire fence, hidden by rampant purple and white bougainvillaea, surrounded the property. The front garden was much better kept than the back garden with its over grown lawn.

Hidden by banana and paw-paw trees a brick built kaia (hut) with a toilet and hand basin for the servants stood at the back. The back garden's dominant feature was the mango tree that stood as high as the house, resembling a giant umbrella and weighted down by succulent fruit. Tracey immediately used this to play under as it provided good shade from the burning sun.

Nevertheless, I was ever fearful should snakes also want a little shade, and shared my thoughts with her mother.

Now we had a bigger place, Pat employed a houseboy called Stephen Sangwapoa. He lived on the African compound. Luckily, Steve and Judy Oelofsen lived next door with their two children: Noel, who was a year younger than Tracey and Christine, two years older. Pat was already friends with Judy and found her a great help. Judy spoke Chikabanga and, being South African, conversing with the Africans was second nature. Stephen could speak and understand a little English and was pleased to work for us. We paid him K20 (kwacha) a month (about £10.00) and he got free meals daily. He started at 7am and worked until 5pm, with Sundays off. Stephen did all the cleaning, washing, ironing and polishing of floors throughout the house.

I came home from work one afternoon to see that Patricia had acquired an Alsatian called Jesse, a good-natured six years old who turned out to be good company for our other dog, Sally. The owner was leaving and wanted him to go to a good home and Tracey begged her mother to keep him. Jesse took to Tracey and followed her everywhere like a shadow.

Tracey started at Bancroft Infant's School, a short walk from our house. As Judy was taking Noel and Christine they all went together. Jesse followed them each day and lay in the shade of the nearest trees until Tracey came out.

Once again I started a garden, digging over the old vegetable plot that previous tenants had started and abandoned. It was hard work, but after several weeks I had soil ready to sow bean, cabbage, carrot and lettuce seeds. I used banana plant leaves to cover them from the sun as Bill Wynn had showed me when I was in Copperfield Flats. When bringing most of my young plants from Copperfield Flats, Bill also dropped off a few sacks of the chicken manure.

I settled back into my work as if the past year in England had never existed. The mine was still as wet, said to be pumping out 600,000 gallons of water for every ton of copper produced. I had to go the Pneumoconiosis Medical Centre in Kitwe, a procedure I remembered from before. The annual X-ray and physical check-up is mandatory for everyone working underground.

My responsibility doubled as the company grew and employed more expatriate tradesmen. One hailed from Newcastle, England, where they're better known as Geordies. Tom was a competent fitter and turner and a pleasant enough chap who had not lost his hometown accent. Before coming to Zambia, Tom had worked in South Africa; and before that in Australia, on the Snowy Mountain Hydro-Electric Scheme.

Often my work schedule consisted of a ten to twelve hour day, split up by six hours underground and the rest in the workshops or office depending on our workload. I was beginning to enjoy my work, soaking up the responsibilities attached. On my arrival back at the workshops, I would have a stack of blueprints to tender on. Eddie was a demanding boss, wanting everything yesterday. I would go home with my head spinning with pipes, steel girders and machinery.

As it was now the dry season every afternoon after work, I kept up the ritual of watering the garden before lounging on the stoep to watch the sun go down. Patricia would bring me a cool lager and together we would watch Tracey play with the dogs. There were times I would hear Judy from next door talking to Pat over the fence in her pleasant melodious South African dialect.

"Yees, we go that way sometimes, its lekker (sweet), you know." Then her giggle or that phrase, "Shame, hey?"

I knew Judy from the first time I had set foot in Zambia 1966, when I was by myself, the nine months I spent without Pat. I wish I could turn back the clock. I should never have let Pat and baby Tracey go back to England; better to have taken Eddie's advice to bring them over with me.

Judy by now was giving Pat daily driving lessons and within a week, Pat mastered the clutch and gear changing and could drive reasonably well. After three weeks Judy let her drive the fifteen miles to Chingola, a bigger town than Chililabombwe with more shops and more variety. The main store was CBC, with Stubbs Chemist, Princess Bakery, a good butchery and several other shops owned by Indians - Solanki's for fine furniture and electrical goods, Lentin Jewellers, a deli and café, the usual banks and post office and the Nchanga Hotel. The Bernina shop caught Pat's eye and she came home all smiles with a new sewing machine.

"It has everything for dressmaking! Much better than the old Singer I had in South Africa."

Chingola had wider streets than Chililabombwe, one set of robots (traffic lights) but neither roundabouts nor hills. The streets had no names only numbers as far as I recall; 1st Street, 2nd Street and so on. Steve Oelofsen's parents and brother lived there.

After two months as a learner-driver Pat had passed her driving test in Chingola with flying colours and drove our Volkswagen 411 with utmost confidence. Now she could go shopping in Chingola for the items she could not buy in Chililabombwe, but only accompanied, I stressed. Although Pat was adapting well to life in the Copperbelt, Judy would always go with her on shopping trips in and out of town. Not many women, especially those with young children, travelled alone between towns, day or night. Breakdowns on these lonely roads with dense bush either side so near to the Congolese border could be fatal.

Steve suggested we have a night out at the Hotel Edinburgh in Kitwe, as cabaret nights were staged every Saturday. Another English couple occasionally joined us, Bernard and Betty Harris, who had an eight-year old son Paul. Bernard worked as an electrician for the mine. We would all pile in Steve's Studebaker Lark V8 as it had bench seats and could take the six of us. The Hotel Edinburgh was upmarket, something I never thought existed here, with a good dance floor and swing-band.

Pat was thrilled to be able to wear her long evening or cocktail gowns again. Smart or formal dress was required and tables had to be reserved weeks in advance. Over the following years, we had some great nights there. The only problem was that it was a good hour's drive from Chililabombwe. Driving back in the early hours was chancing fate on a road well-known for hold-ups by robbers from across the Congo-Zairian border.

As our first summer drew nearer, clouds like clumps of sheep's wool gathered on the horizon. Sometimes you could smell the rain; you acquire that instinct after several months of the dry season. When rain did arrive, the sound of it falling was like a hammer beating on the car and house roofs. Down it came in torrents, a curtain of silver shards. Trees and lawns glistened as the heavy droplets hit them. Storm gullies flowed like rivers and house drainpipes gurgled, while street sumps belched and street manhole covers were lifted by a mushroom of water.

In Zambia October is known as the suicide month with temperatures reaching over 36^C. The rains bring out all manner of flying insects, including moths with wings the size of a sparrow and a kind of transparent roundel at the tip of each wing that reminded me of a toy Spitfire I had had as a boy. There were incredible four-inch long stick-beetles, the colour of cinnamon or the thumb-size stag beetles with pincer-like mandibles.

Of all the insects to watch the most fascinating is the furry brown and black centipede that glides endlessly along. Mopane flies swarmed from under windowsills and around door jambs, their nests a transparent tube something like a drinking straw. Ants appeared out of nowhere by the thousands, sometimes marching in formation to an even, synchronized rhythm, a red mobile mass that devoured anything in its path. The black Matabele ant, as fierce as the warriors for whom they are named, carried a deterrent gas that should you stand on them would emit a pungent acrid smell.

No matter what spray you used, irritating mosquitoes would manage to slip through the net. It almost seemed as if these insistently aggressive little devils had a battle plan. You'd hear their demonic buzz as you were trying to get a good night's sleep until finally you stagger out of bed and organise a hunt. As soon as you turn off the light again, your tormenter's friend is waiting for you and, in kamikaze fashion spirals down until he settles on you unnoticed before you make it under the bedcovers.

Pat and I often thought about our folks back home and wrote home regularly. We had been in Zambia three months. I would write to my sister Irene, with whom my father stayed; she reported no improvement from his stroke. A sad ending for a man who had travelled the world in many different ships for over fifty years and who enjoyed his life so much. The other letters we received didn't tell us much, although Renee, Pat's older sister, would go into detail on goings-on in their family, down to her brother-in-law's new image.

"Our Bob's got a wig, you know, and looks three inches taller than his five foot five. Arthur said it's the quiff that doesn't look real."

Pat killed herself laughing. Bob was bald as a billiard ball all the time we knew him. Renee would also let Pat know about the latest pop idols or who was sleeping with whom in Coronation Street.

With adjusting to Zambia, making a home and meeting new friends we had no time to feel homesick – a different kettle of fish to South Africa. At least we had Zambian Television, albeit the best programmes by far were the children's, especially Sesame Street and the Magic Roundabout. Our Sundays mornings were spent at church and afterwards relaxing on the veranda after lunch. Africans constantly arrived trying to sell wood curios and malachite figurines or ornaments, shaped and polished to resemble eggs; sometimes as ashtrays. These street hawkers mostly came across from the Congo–Zaire borderlines, sometimes trying to sell diamonds that would turn out to be the industrial kind.

The summer in 1968 was our first Christmas in Zambia and Tracey was dressed as an angel for the school's nativity play. We gave Stephen his Christmas present, a white long-sleeved shirt and a T-shirt. He didn't know what to say. I think it must have been his first Christmas present.

"Thank you, bwana. Thank you, madam."

We also gave him a food hamper for his family and told him that he could have a week off on pay.

We invited Tom Phipps, my fitter and turner, over for Christmas dinner, as he would be on his own in OK Flats. We pulled our crackers and wore the fancy paper hats for dinner as we would have done back home. Tracey was disappointed with Father Christmas for not bringing her the brown doll she had seen in Solanki's store in Chingola. The Zambian Government had banned this toy, considering it demeaning. To European eyes this was an illogical decision: surely little brown girls would cherish a little brown doll? Also condemned, was the world famous Robertson's jam gollywog character, which later on many other nations deemed to be racist.

Christmas is not the same when it is sweltering hot but, as always, Pat created an English festival. She decorated the house with trimmings, bought crackers and a fine Christmas tree, albeit artificial, from Solanki's festooned with toys and ornaments she had kept over the years. The tree was different from that Bert and I cut down in South Africa and were chased for by knobkerrie-wielding Africans. We sat down to traditional Christmas fare, a steaming hot roast chicken, pork, roast potatoes, sprouts, carrots and cauliflower, followed by homemade plum pudding and brandy sauce.

After dinner, we sat on the veranda in the orange glow of the late afternoon sun. Tom had brought me a cigar and a bottle of Cape brandy, a Dior perfume for Pat and colouring books and a multitude of pencil crayons for Tracey. It was then that Tom told us that he was moving on, this time to Canada. I think he must have been working his way around the world.

True to his word he kept in touch with letters of interesting value that made my travelling juices flow. He kept in touch with us for two years and even got me into thinking about seeking work in Canada. Tom sent me some details of a mine in Lynn Falls in Manitoba. He said they were looking for tradesmen experienced in copper mining. On the map it was far north and the photos he sent were of a cold environment. So I forgot about that, to Pat's relief.

-27-

The Bungalow on President Drive

After we brought the New Year in at the Theatre Club in January 1969, we moved into 39 President's Drive, another property that Eddie Reed rented for his employees. Number 39 was a good-sized bungalow, nicely decorated with a spacious lounge and modern kitchen. The gardens and drive had been better tended and housed the usual servants' kaia. Since Les Merrifield, our electrical foreman and his wife Pat had moved back into OK Flats, Chingola, we were able to take over.

I was surprised when Steve left Eddie Reed to take up employment with our competitor Bodwin Engineering. It was a shame because we were getting to know each other, especially Pat and Judy, and our children played well together. Soon after Judy and Steve moved out of number 41, Alan and Iona Goddard and their two-year-old daughter Candice moved in. Alan worked as a fitter and turner in our Bancroft workshops taking over from Tom Phipps. I believe Alan had served his engineering apprenticeship with Bancroft Mines. He soon proved himself in supervising our machine and fitting workshop contracts. Standing six foot four and over sixteen-stone, he was a gentle giant and the perfect gentleman in the company of women.

Not long after they moved next door Alan offered me a slice of paw-paw and, grinning, asked, "What do you think, Peter?"

"It tastes different. What have put on it?"

"I injected it with a shot of Bacardi about three weeks ago before plucking it off one of my trees."

A great friendship began with nights out at the theatre club, the golf club and occasionally to the Edinburgh Hotel in Kitwe. Sometimes we gathered in their house to sample Alan's cocktails and Iona's cuisine.

As we settled down with more confidence in finding our Shangri-la, I bought six laying hens and a cock from a friend of Bill Wynn's, who promised me that when fully grown the hens would lay eggs every day. They did, and Tracey as she got older enjoyed collecting the eggs.

"The garden's much too big for you to be working at after working all day," Pat said.

So she waved her magic wand again and employed a garden boy called Tembo Boniface who, like Stephen, lived on the African compound. As in our last garden two houses away, tropical flora abounded, with bougainvillaea, paw-paw and banana trees. I dug the back garden over this time with the help of Boniface and together we planted vegetables. One thing about the soil in Africa, everything you plant flourishes, even if you don't have green fingers.

Once again, at the back of our garden stood a single room servant's building with toilet and a corrugated iron roof. Inside was a single steel bed, a chair and table. Outside wash basin near the garden's water tap. As at number 41, the building stood at the far end of the garden almost hidden by banana trees. Sometimes we let Boniface sleep there if he wanted to especially if it was raining heavily, as it was a good hour's walk to the African township.

Boniface seemed a pleasant young man, content that he had a job and with looking after the garden. He would sing as he cut the grass with a one-handed swinging movement any golfer would be proud to acquire. With each stroke, he skimmed the panga blade across the lawn, leaving behind a half- inch of grass and no divots! Boniface, his round face as black as polished ebony, was courteous with a pleasant personality. He never seemed to resent what we whites had, as did other young African around the towns; Boniface always seemed happy with his lot.

Stephen was content washing and ironing all our clothes and polished the parquet floors to deter white ants from nesting between the cracks and joints. Stephen was a quiet young man, tall and slim, the opposite to Boniface in build. Stephen was from the Lozi tribe whereas Boniface was a Bemba so naturally they didn't have much in common - almost like the Welsh and the English. They were both twenty years old, but Stephen seemed to be the more grown-up and intelligent of the two.

As we settled down, we let Stephens's older sister babysit for us whenever we went out at night, but I had to take her back to the compound. It was unsafe for anyone to walk those streets in the townships after dark: even when driving a vehicle you stopped for no one. For protection, I had a pickaxe handle by my car seat.

As time went on Boniface proved that he had gardening skills. Tomatoes were among his favourites. By the time six weeks was up, we had a good-sized vegetable and salads garden and a new bougainvillaea hedge. One morning as I was going out to work I saw Boniface walking towards me, carrying a sack over his shoulder full of 12-inch cuttings, cut from another bougainvillaea hedge. By the time I came home after work, he had planted these new cuttings in a criss-cross fashion along the length of the chain-link fence. Within a few weeks, to my amazement, they began to sprout new leaves and after a year, we had a 3-foot hedge.

Boniface gave Tracey a chameleon he had found in the garden. Tracey at first was apprehensive and amazed at how its skin changed colour and its eyes followed her without any motion of the head. She would watch, mesmerised, as it deftly caught insects with a tongue almost as long as its body. Pat brought it inside to put on a houseplant in the lounge, fearing the birds would attack it, but Stephen the houseboy didn't like it and tried to avoid going near it.

"Aiwa, they are bad muti (medicine), madam."

One morning I woke with a severe headache, vomiting and diarrhoea. I started to sweat, cold as ice one minute, roasting hot the next. Les Merrifield did not like the look of me and took me home, where at some stage I passed out. When I woke up the house was deathly quiet and in darkness. I lay in the spare bedroom's single bed, my pyjamas clammy and wet. I got up to go to the toilet and take a shower, but my legs wouldn't hold my weight. I crawled into the bathroom with teeth chattering ten to the dozen. I knew then this was not a common cold. Pat telephoned Dr Forbes in Chingola, who examined me and took a blood sample. He gave me Paludrine and told me to drink plenty of water and wrap myself up warm.

"The symptoms tell me you might have malaria," he said in his Scottish lilt.

Dr Forbes returned the following afternoon and confirmed that I had a mild strain.

"I hope now that you and your family will take precautions by taking Malaprin daily while you are living here," he warned.

Two days later a gang of council workers came round to the house and cut down all the banana trees. They explained that bananas have tubular leaves when young and retain any moisture or rain; a pure breeding ground for mosquitoes. Old car tyres bottles and cans or anything that collects water had to be got rid of.

After four days off work, Eddie my boss came round to see how I was. He handed me a bundle of engineering drawings.

"I hope you won't mind taking a look at these. It's going to be a big job, Peter - we need it. Just see if we can handle it. Give me a ring in the morning and I'll call back to-morrow to see how you are getting on."

The client wanted four Pachuca tanks fabricating and at 80ft high x 30ft in diameter and conical shape, designed in the form of a silo with a girder-supporting structure. If we got the work, it would be the biggest steel fabrications we had taken on for a small workshop. I was looking forward to the challenge.

"We haven't the machinery to form the cones," I told Eddie over the phone.

"Then we'll get the right machines. Write down what you want and I'll see if I can get it. I am flying down to Jo'burg this afternoon and if I need more information I will ring you. Just get better, hey? We need this work."

I pondered over the details the following days and drew sketches and a list of gear we would need. Against Pat's advice, I went into work to discuss with Ted Hageman what I would need to do the work and together we came up with a quotation. Ted asked our secretary Mary to type it out ready for Eddie's approval; he later added a substantial extra sum to our figures. In the meantime, Eddie had made enquiries while in South Africa and to the UK. Within two weeks, we had brochures of machines, ½-inch plate guillotine, bigger plate rolls, a Sedgwick 8ft folding press and various other hand tools we required. However, the mines wanted these tanks 'yesterday,' as it were.

I told Eddie we could start the work with our old machinery with a few modifications. We submitted our price and won the order over stiff competition. It was not the steelwork that Eddie wanted, but the electrical contract that went with it. Ted explained to me what this new project was about: extracting copper from the tailings by using an electrolyte process.

Time passed quickly as it does when one is working hard and I was spending fewer hours underground. With this new contract imminent, I needed to be in the fabrication shop for the Pachuca tank project.

We had ordered all the steel plates and steel girders for the job and the yard resembled a steel supply company. I had already worked out the conical sizes for each tank. As no one else in our company had fabricated conical tanks this size before, let alone in 10mm thick plate, I took over the work myself. I told Eddie and Ted I would be kept busy for the next six weeks. By then we had all the plates cut and rolled to form all the cones.

Without boasting, it was no mean task, I can vouch for that. Using practically antiquated plate-rolls, it was the hardest piece of fabrication I had ever undertaken. We had everything ready for site erection and welding by another company in Chingola. Between them, Alf Drinkwater, Les Olivett, Tony Pereira, Ozzi Seagars and Eno Barratello, fabricated all the tank's main support structures, besides other work for Konkola Mine.

In the meantime, Pat had come to know Margaret, a Scottish woman whose husband Bill was a shift boss on Konkola Mine. We became close friends for many years to come, even after they left Zambia. Several years older than us, Margaret was like Pat's big sister Renee, full of fun and energy. Margaret and Bill Ramage were much older with a teen-age daughter in boarding school in Scotland. Pat first met Margaret in Smartwear where she served behind the linen counter for Mr Patel. Margaret was a good communicator, bringing people together and the life and soul of any party. Bill, on the other hand, was the quiet type; he would sit immersed in a book, or smoking a cigarette while he listened to Gilbert and Sullivan.

Smartwear, like any Indian-owned emporium, sold all types of packaged and canned foods. By now most of the South African varieties of canned food were being replaced by the inferior Chinese Mai Ling products, due to the sanctions imposed by Zambia against South Africa and their continued trade with Rhodesia.

Our Sunday afternoons took a new turn visiting Margaret and Bill Ramage, who lived at the posh end of Chililabombwe. Tracey loved it there, playing in their garden - a different garden means different games to children, it seems, and we'd all join in the fun of badminton or swing-ball.

After Pat showed her interest, it wasn't long before Margaret introduced her to the Women's Fellowship at the United Church. Pat was soon into flower arranging for the church, and beforehand we would go into the bush to pick wild orchids, daisies and foxgloves. Pat and Tracey attended church service every Sunday morning and, depending on my workload, I would also show my face. I liked the Reverend David Cruise, who was not much older than Pat and me. His wife that same year gave birth to their first child. David was a friendly person, not only because he was a priest; it seemed to be his nature and he had become the rock of our community.

I heard one tale, whether true or not, that slipped out during a Women's Fellowship meetings. A member's young child attending the infant school told her mother that her teacher didn't wear knickers. Obviously this gave the elder women members something to talk about, but they did not know how to handle the situation. A senior member volunteered to have a quiet word with the teacher, a young married woman not long out from the U.K.

Like most of the newcomers she wore the skimpiest of mini-skirts, referred to as pelmets, fashionable at the time. Caught one day washing her car, her stretching up made it patently obvious she was wearing the appropriate undergarments. With a sigh of relief, the older woman bid her good morning and walked away.

The town did have a reputation for wife or girlfriend swapping especially after party nights at the Bongo Bar disco. After all, this was the era of 'free love,' the height of the swinging 60s and 70s. While I was attending a karate competition, a fellow from another Copperbelt town remarked, "Ah, you come from Peyton Place. What's it like on Saturday nights?"

I had not the foggiest idea what he was talking about until a work colleague told me about the infamous TV series.

"It looks like you missed out on that, Pete," he smiled, "and Bancroft does have a reputation."

I later found the TV series was of a small New England town in America, whose quaint charm masks a complicated web of extramarital affairs. It brought to mind a tale that went around Chililabombwe of 'the woman in the basket' who hid in the clothes basket so she wouldn't be caught when her lover's wife arrived home early.

-28-

Rhodesian Odyssey

We had been in Zambia almost a year when I decided it was time we had a holiday. We planned to tour Southern Rhodesia before Easter 1969. I sold my Volkswagen 411 to an English couple, nicknamed 'Tatties and Onions' after their English county's famous recipe, Lancashire hot-pot. They intended to drive down to Cape Town, a journey of 2,500 miles, then take the car home to England aboard the Union Castle to Southampton.

Wanting a more powerful and comfortable car for the Rhodesia trip I bought Steve Oelofsen's father's 3.0 litre Vauxhall Velox. Only four years old, with bench seats and a huge boot, it was exactly what I wanted. My only problem was how to get hold of extra petrol-rations in Rhodesia, as the country was in the early stages of world sanctions due to its 1965 Unilateral Declaration of Independence (UDI.) Ian Smith, the Rhodesian Prime Minister, was still at loggerheads with the British Government led by Labour's Prime Minister, Harold Wilson.

Once again, my old faithful AA Southern Africa Touring Atlas came in handy as it had done for our first long African road trip to Durban when we lived South Africa. Our journey south along the backbone of Zambia to Livingstone would be roughly 580 miles. My friend Ted Hageman, himself a Rhodesian, advised us it would be safer driving during the daylight hours and to cross the border into Rhodesia before 4pm.

Two hours before daylight I lifted Tracey into the car's back seat.

"She will be fast asleep for another two hours at least," Pat said.

Two hours later at Ndola, I stopped at another police roadblock, our third that morning. Police and army militia, all armed, milled around my car and inquisitive black faces peered through the car windows. One has to be careful to show respect on such occasions. As usual we all had to get out of the car. Pat lifted Tracey out and, still half asleep, she stood between us holding our hands. The men searched the boot and the interior, peered under the bonnet and asked for I. D. cards and passports after I told them our destination. The twenty minutes we stood under the sun seemed an hour before we were allowed to move on.

I filled up with petrol at Kapiri Mposhi, once a small settlement that with the construction of the 1,000-mile Tanzam rail link, Zambia to the Port of Dar es Salaam, had grown to a busy town. In return for building the rail link, Chinese goods and food such as tinned fruit and many other products that once came from South Africa flooded the shops. I had to push on to make the border crossing before 4pm, though progress through Kapiri Mposhi was extra slow as the road was pockmarked with deep potholes.

Outside Lusaka, the Zambian capital, a roadside placard showed a full-size President Kaunda brandishing his trademark, a white handkerchief, with the slogan below 'One Zambia, One Nation.' I only stopped long enough to top up with petrol and check the oil and water.

After Lusaka the Great North Road led us through the town of Kafue that takes its name from the nearby river. This snakes down over 900 km through the heart of industrial Zambia and discharges into the Great Zambesi at Chirundu, another border post with Rhodesia (now Zimbabwe.)

Well away from the town of Kafue, Pat suggested we stop for a picnic lunch and soon after, just before Choma, she spotted a pleasant, tree-lined glade, with stone picnic tables and benches. It was almost noon and stifling hot with no threat of rain though April, being near the end of the rainy season, was often unpredictable. While Pat and I pondered over my road atlas Tracey busied herself playing with her dolls. That was one thing about Tracey, bless her; she was always content to amuse herself.

As the miles dragged on the scenery changed, with thick bush giving way to the more open farming country. This was where the tobacco, maize and sugar estates of southern Zambia lay. The road traffic was noticeably busier with charcoal burners pushing carts and bicycles loaded with sacks of charcoal, and dilapidated tractors, buses, and taxies full to the roof. Occasionally someone would wave as we passed them, and arms hung out of the windows seeking cooler air in the over-crowded buses.

Bush shanty towns were around almost every bend, easily discernible by the rusty corrugated iron roofs held down with rocks. The houses were made from timber from packing crates, cardboard or anything else the Africans could find, with clay to keep them watertight. We sped past these familiar scenes with their smoke spiralling up into the windless air from hundreds of cooking fires and charcoal bonfires. Painted on dwelling walls was the usual One Zambia, One Nation or UNIP, the people's party - United National Independence Party.

By now we had been travelling a little over ten hours and noted that we had almost completed our journey. We stopped for a last flask of tea and another toilet break; hopefully, the last squat in the bush. The sign showed twenty miles to Livingstone, where I knew I must remember to fill my petrol tank before we went into Rhodesia. My first indication that the falls were near was about ten miles from Livingstone. The Eighth Wonder of the World displayed her tell-tale column of spray like a plume hundreds of feet above the forest. Mosi-oa-Tunya, the Smoke that Thunders, was living up to its name.

I parked my car outside Zambian Customs and Immigration Post, where we were told to present ourselves with our passports. In the meantime, another officer walked around our car and demanded I open the boot. Satisfied, he waved to his companion who raised the barrier. I took a moment to marvel at the construction of the Falls Bridge, built in 1903 by the Cleveland Bridge & Engineering Company of Darlington, England. Little did I know then that one day I would be working for that same engineering company?

Moments later we were at the Rhodesian border post. Once inside a polite white customs officer in a pristine white uniform asked where we were heading and for how long. He gave me a ration book of petrol coupons after calculating the mileage we would be covering and a few over the top for good measure.

I had pre-booked two nights at the Victoria Falls Hotel, the oldest of its kind in Africa. Overhead fans cooled our room on the ground floor annexe with mosquito nets above the double and single beds. In the last hour of daylight, Tracey was first in the pool alongside other children while Pat and I sipped a tall ice-cold gin and tonic each after our long journey. I am not a gin person, but since my malaria scare did have one occasionally. Gin for a good night's sleep and the tonic's quinine is a deterrent against malaria - an old colonial excuse!

After showering and a change of clothes, we feasted on a sumptuous dinner in the hotel restaurant and a bottle of Cape Cabernet Sauvignon.

After tucking Tracey in bed with her favourite doll, Pat and I relaxed on the veranda surrounded by Africa's night sounds - crickets, frogs and the monotonous rumble of the falls.

Next morning we were up early and after a good old English-style breakfast, donned our plastic raincoats. With hoods up, we trod through the rainforest, where towering trees of all kinds flourished, festooned with creepers and adorned by a rich variety of pink and red flowers, and ferns on the forest floor. Particularly noticeable was Zimbabwe's national flower, the flame lily (*Gloriosa superba*) with its large red and yellow flowers, and Pat's particular favourite. Wild game that included bush pig, duiker, guinea fowl, francolin and baboons roamed freely around, though we hardly saw enough to bother us.

Tracey had been naughty so I took her back to the car to sulk, then Pat and I walked to the edge of the main gorge. As we got closer a continuous roar shook the ground like an express train. Glancing down proved an unforgettable experience, witnessing the immense ribbon of water as it tumbled 347feet down the precipice, at 60 million gallons a minute, into a broiling cauldron of water.

We were only gone a few minutes and returned to find Tracey wasn't in the car. Panic gripped us, and after some time wandering through the rainforest shouting her name, we set off in opposite directions to try and find her. The misty spray from the falls did not help. After what seemed like an hour, a young German couple came towards us with Tracey in hand. They had found her wandering around, dripping wet, and were about to take her to the hotel.

Before leaving the falls I took one last look and shot more film of Pat and Tracey with the cascading water and bridge in the background. How lucky we were to be standing where Dr David Livingstone might have stood in 1855 when he named the falls 'Victoria.'

The following morning after breakfast, it was back to my AA map to familiarise myself with the next step of our journey. Once away from the falls and thereafter the roads were mostly made with a continuous twelve-inch strip of tarmac set like railway lines. This was a cheaper way of building roads than full tarmac over a vast area of Rhodesia. When another car came towards you or was overtaking, both vehicles moved over with one set of wheels on the dirt as they passed. Scary at first and much safer to opt for a lower speed. A good thing too, as sometimes animals would bring us to a standstill, especially the elephants. Several miles to the right of us lay the Wankie National Game Park, which could have accounted for the elephant dung dotting the road like deflated footballs.

Suddenly the strips were gone and the road widened into a normal tarmac surface as we approached Wankie and the country's biggest coalmine. We crossed bridges over many rivers: Gwaai, Shangane, Bembezi and Umgusa, feeding lush farmlands. We drove alongside tidy grass verges, woodlands, tobacco farms and ranches with herds of cattle spread over vast areas.

Bulawayo was bigger than I had first thought it might be, making towns on the Copperbelt tiny and mundane in comparison. Typical of Africa, the shops had roofs built out over the pavements as shelter from the blazing sun or torrential rains. The town's roads were the widest I had seen anywhere, allowing parking in the middle and angle parking at either kerb. They had been planned by the early settlers to allow an ox-wagon team to make a full turn. We booked into the Cecil Hotel for one night and ate in their restaurant. It was past mid-afternoon and extremely hot, so it was heavenly to sit under the cool whoosh of overhead fans with a cold beer to hand.

The bar with its swing doors like a cowboy saloon in a Western was almost empty. The barman, who spoke with a hint of Gaelic twang, told me the Matopos Hills National Park was the place to visit, where the burial place of Cecil Rhodes was sited. Rhodes at that time meant nothing to me: I didn't even realise Rhodesia was named after him. How ignorant could I be? That afternoon I made a point of visiting his statue in Main Street.

Cecil Rhodes died of heart failure in Cape Town aged 48 in March 1902. His body was taken to Rhodesia by train and entombed in the Matopos Hills at the place he called 'The View of the World.'

The following day, Good Friday, we set off for Fort Victoria, 190 miles from Bulawayo and hopefully our next overnight stop. As I had not made prior arrangements, I was eager to arrive early and find a hotel, but it turned out my assumptions were once again wrong. By the time, we arrived at Fort Victoria it was late afternoon and all the hotels were full. The town was buzzing and we were lucky to find a small cafe where we could have a decent meal.

Whilst in the cafe I saw my first photographs of the Great Zimbabwe Ruins. I must admit we are not archaeology-minded, so the pictures had little appeal for Pat or me. Not enough to entice us to spend time walking around ancient stone-brick walls and circular conical turrets under an African sun. With no room at the inn, we had to sleep in the car, Tracey cuddled along the back seat with her mother. After the Victoria Falls Hotel this was a definite come-down.

After an uncomfortable and almost sleepless night, I decided to move on to the Birchenough Bridge Hotel, but not before we had a good breakfast at the cafe. As we left Fort Victoria the road snaked it way through verdant mountainous hills. Upon reaching the highest point, Moody's Pass (5,000 feet), I stopped so we could take in the breath-taking views. The air was cool in spite of the cloudless sky and glaring sun.

On our descent, the arched back of the suspension bridge came into sight as if rising like a silver rainbow out of the forest and thorn scrub. The bridge, built in 1939 by Dorman Long of England, spans the Sabi River. The engineer was Ralph Freeman, who also designed Sydney Harbour Bridge and the Victoria Falls Bridge we had crossed earlier.

The Sabi Hotel proved a good stop for viewing game. In the evenings before dusk we could sit outside and watch numerous waterbuck, impala and sable antelope at the water's edge, dainty and sure-footed, yet always wary of the unexpected. They knew that crocodiles patrol these waters, lying in wait beneath the surface that with one swift lunge could pull under any careless prey. Hippos floated with only their ears, eyes and nostrils above the water. At nightfall we heard them snorting and bellowing during a fight or as they munched on the grassy banks.

The following day we left for Umtali, a 70 mile drive through the Eastern Highlands past good irrigated land, apple orchards, and coffee and tobacco plantations. All around the scenery was of an unparalleled beauty, the Vumba Mountains reaching heavenwards to 7,000 feet. Glistening crystal waterfalls cascaded into lakes and clear rippling streams glittered as if with sequins in the morning sunlight. We called in for mid-morning tea and home-baked scones with cream and jam at the Trout Beck Inn; almost like being back in England, except for the weather.

While Pat and I stretched our legs with a stroll through the gardens, Tracey disappeared to play on the swings, soon calling to me to push her higher. The Inn was a thatched roof cottage of some considerable size. We had tea in the shade of the terraced veranda overlooking the gardens and the backdrop hues of the Vumba Mountains and the border to Mozambique. I could have stayed forever and I knew Pat was of the same mind, but Umtali called!

We were five miles out from Umtali when a rattling noise vibrated under the car. I stopped and checked under the vehicle to find that the prop shaft was at a queer angle. There was nothing I could do except continue; luckily it stayed in one piece until Umtali.

As it was Easter Monday, I parked near our hotel. The following day the mechanic told me the Hardy-Spicer (a universal joint on the prop shaft) had almost seized up. He had no spares and told me it would take two days to get them. We were booked into the Cecil Hotel for two nights so I asked him to contact me when the job was done. It left us with no transport so we made do by browsing the shops, relaxing around the hotel's swimming pool, visiting the town's sights and cafes. Although the country was in the grip of world sanctions there seemed to be no shortage of goods. Umtali has since been renamed Mutare and this border town with Mozambique and Zimbabwe is now Rhodesia's fourth largest city, nestling in a valley at an altitude of 4,000 feet between the Vumba and Nyanga mountains.

With the car fixed we set out for Salisbury (now Harare) a day later than planned. The capital of Rhodesia is one of the best cities I have visited in Africa. I had booked a room in the Meikles Hotel as recommended by my boss Eddie Reed and I could see why. The only thing wrong is that I was paying the bill. Built for the rich, it had nonetheless to put up with a common boilermaker from Grimsby for two nights.

Meikles, built in the early part of 19th century, still held its old world charm with a gold-braided doorman, waiters in white uniforms and gloves and a smartly outfitted lift bellhop. Sparkling crystal chandeliers hung in reception, up and down the corridors and even in our bedroom, which was on the fourth floor facing Cecil Square. There the first pioneers ran up the flag of the British South African Company in days gone by.

Above the single bed and double bed a tent of mosquito netting added to this typical African setting. Paintings of the old city, Victoria Falls, Berchenough Bridge and Zimbabwe Ruins hung on the walls. The following day we spent the morning at Lake Mcllwaine where we had a picnic and watched the yacht racing and the anglers fishing for bream and carp.

The following day I drove north to Chirundu 214 miles from Harare and the final leg of our journey around Rhodesia. En route we stopped at Sinoia (now Chinhoyi) with its historical caves and Sleeping Pools, sinkholes filled with water. Craggy steps hewn out of the rock-face and walls overgrown with vines led to the largest cave 60 feet below ground level. These are limestone and dolomite caves and history has it that the Shona tribe used them to hide from warring tribes and they are said to have a spiritual presence; once used to throw in sacrificial victims. One had to be careful not to slip as you peered down into three hundred feet of crystal clear water that gave a blue hue to the caverns. These were similar to the Blue John Caves in Derbyshire England, colourful, dank and mysterious.

At Chirundu we crossed into Zambia over the Great Zambesi River again, then back to the Copperbelt repeating our outward journey through Kafue, Lusaka and Kapiri Mposhi. We had completed a full circular route of over two thousand miles. Our Rhodesian journey had lasted almost two well-spent weeks. On our return it was disappointing to find all four reels of 35mm still films printed out blank. The chemist in Bancroft told Pat that not one frame had turned out in all four reels, due to a shutter malfunction that was not repairable in Zambia. The camera ended in the rubbish bin. Luckily, our Rhodesian excursion was fully was recorded in my notes and captured on our Canon Super 8 Cine-camera.

Two months after our holiday Pat found out she was pregnant. Was this another coincidence since a similar event happened while we were in South Africa? We were on holiday in Durban and Tracey was born nine months later. I blamed it then on the sea air. This time I blamed the conception of our son Damon on our visit to Victoria Falls.

-29-
Damon

On my return from our Rhodesian holiday, I opened our post office mail box to find a telegram from my sister Irene telling me my father had died on Easter Sunday. Our family came to accept his sad last years and the long expectation of death. My father's life had been full of misfortunes of his own doing, but he did not deserve the existence he lived in his latter years, nor my mother hers. The last time I saw Dad was when he was in the care home in Cleethorpes before we left again for Africa. Now I was upset at not being able to attend his funeral.

At the time the telegram arrived in my post-box, I was staying in the Birchenough Bridge Motel in Rhodesia. I opened it now and read: "Father died peacefully on Easter Sunday. Letter to follow. Love, Irene." That letter from Irene was rubber-banded with the telegram and three weeks old. She wrote mainly about the funeral, who was and was not there.

"The big shock for me, Pete, was our Uncle Jim, Aunty Lily, Uncle Will and family not being there."

Sadly, like me, my brother James was also overseas in the RAF in Cyprus. Both of us sent Irene a £10 bank draft for a wreath, the least we could do in our circumstances.

Six months later another letter came from Irene with a £150 Barclays Bank draft, a seventh share from our parents' estate after father's funeral costs and the sale of their house. I never knew my parents had bought 69 Yarborough Street, the house I grew up in for twenty-one years. I left there when I married Patricia in June 1957. So much had happened since.

Pulling myself together, I settled back into work and filled my evenings with a vigorous weight-training routine. I made a personal vow it would be my last competition. I soon tired of travelling to Chingola to train, and somehow got permission to set up a basic gym in the old Bancroft Scout hut. Two others trained there, mainly for fitness, but my intention was solely to keep in shape to enter the forthcoming Mr Zambia competition to be held in Chingola. Somehow, I won and became the new Mr Zambia - no competition really, with only six of us in the line-up, four from Kitwe and one from Chingola as far as I can recollect. The trophy, a plain copper 12-inch cup set on a black Bakelite stand, inscribed Lexington, Mr Zambia 1969, stood proudly on our sideboard in Chililabombwe until we left Africa. In later life, it was stored among dozens of my other trophies in a box in the attic until I gave them to my grandson Jack.

We had been in Zambia a year and were coming to the end of the rainy season. I could never tire of the rains and the Africans jumped for joy and gathered under the streetlights to capture flying white ants or termites. Immediately after a rainy season, these creatures would be attracted to the glow of the street lamps and flutter around in circles until their wings dropped off. Some with only one wing would spin helplessly around drop like sycamore seeds. They would carpet the ground, squirming like maggots. The African considers them a delicacy and fries them in groundnut oil; the insects are immensely nutritious for their size, apparently packed with protein.

During the winter months, the dry season from May to September, the daytime temperature drops to a more comfortable 60 degrees and a transformation takes place. The shoulder-high bush grass and trees lose their verdant lustre as they turn to dry tawny browns.

We started spending our Saturday nights at the Theatre Club with Steve and Judy followed by drinks in the Bongo Bar. Here the management would put on a disco with Mike Harl, Derek Hatton and Pete Smedley playing all the latest music hits to keep us in tune with the outside world. The town's theatre society, the Bancroft Players, produced some wonderful plays, both serious and comedy; without them life would have been unbearably dull. One of their best productions was Boeing-Boeing, which always reminds me of my Zambia days.

There were other clubs in the town all with bars: cricket, rugby, flying, gymkhana, golf, rifle and bowls Most had their 'jolly' nights throughout the year, organising dances, braai (barbeques), children's Christmas parties and even Guy Fawkes Nights complete with bonfire and a fireworks display.

In this small town with its rapid turnover of expats coming to work in the mine, or leaving for home, you would meet new people almost every week. One such was Margaret Edmondson, a pleasant young woman whose husband Bob, worked in the Boma, the town council and district administration offices. BOMA (which originally stood for British Overseas Military Administration.) Whenever I touched on the subject of work, Bob would avoid discussion as if his was top secret. Other than that he was a pleasant enough fellow.

Patricia and Margaret got on well and became good friends, more so than Bob and I, possibly due to our vastly different employment roles.

The women saw each other every day as Tracey and Margaret's boy Lee both attended the same infant school. Margaret's ten-year old daughter Lee-Anne attended the Sacred Heart Convent in Chingola, a privately funded school.

Although we had been to Rhodesia (Zimbabwe) earlier in the year, I suggested we have another holiday before Pat got too uncomfortable to travel while carrying our second child. I proposed that we go to Lake Kariba over the Zambian Independence Day weekend and asked Bob and Margaret if they wanted to come. Bob seemed a bit sceptical of this plan, as the political feelings between Zambia and Rhodesia was worsening, and the hotel I booked us into was on the Rhodesian side of the lake.

As it was a holiday weekend, I booked three nights at the Lake View Hotel on the Rhodesian side of Lake Kariba. After the 360-mile drive, we passed through Zambian customs after waiting in an endless queue at the border. Driving across the Kariba Dam's spectacular 120ft high wall dividing the great Zambesi River was a spectacular experience. The politeness of the white uniformed customs officers and the colourful show of bougainvillaea growing up the whitewashed walls – was a pleasant comparison to the Zambian style.

"Good afternoon, gentlemen. Would the ladies like to take a seat? This will only take a few minutes. Where are you going and for how long are you staying in Rhodesia? We have to assess your petrol rations."

"We are staying at the Lake View Motel for three days," I said, "so we won't be using much fuel and I have enough to get us back into Zambia, thank you."

Bob and I completed the formalities of passport control and the barrier rose to let our car through. It was only a fifteen-minute drive to our hotel from the dam wall. The heat of the day at its highest seared through my clothing. Sweat was running down my back and I was more than ready for a shower and change of clothes, but not before an ice-cold lager.

The construction of the Kariba Dam started in the late 1950s and was completed in 1960. The scheme was brought about during the Federation days between the British-ruled Northern and Southern Rhodesia, now Zambia and Zimbabwe. The lake built on the Zambesi River at the time was the largest man-made lake in the world at 200 km x 40km (125ml x24ml). The project was aimed to provide electrical power to the whole of Zambia and Rhodesia.

The clearing of forests and the rescue of wildlife in the Zambesi valley was called 'Operation Noah,' in itself an enormous task that involved saving and relocating over 6000 animals, reptiles and insects. Even the local tribes who inhabited the valley had to be housed on higher ground around the lake's shores. The lake now provided plentiful amounts of fish and in the following years a lucrative fishing industry was established.

Arriving at the motel we were shown to our holiday chalets built in the style of the African hut, complete with conical thatched roof and white-painted mud walls. Inside were two rooms with single beds, under mosquito nets, prepared with white crisp linen, a shower, a table and chairs.

Tracey and Lee, Bob's lad, were the same age and played well together as the hotel had a good pool and a children's play area. Lee-Anne reluctantly tagged along with us grown-ups rather than with our youngsters.

We took a two-hour boat safari along the south side of the lake. Elephants waded in the river to play in the shallows, trumpeting and spraying each other. Baboons seemed to follow the craft from tree to tree, as we glided along, sometimes just sitting and watching. Herds of majestic sable antelope wandered through the sparse forest that fringed the lakeshore.

We spent our late afternoons and evenings by the pool or sitting on the restaurant veranda, to view the unforgettable sunsets. One morning we ventured further up the rocky escarpment to view the dam from a different angle. On Kariba Heights was the St Barbara Roman Catholic Church with a towering cross on its roof, and located in an awe-inspiring and entirely befitting setting at the summit, where it overlooked the lake and dam.

I was humbled as I walked around the church's circular walls built as archways around the perimeter. Inside were seventeen stained glass windows, one for every dam worker who had died to make life easier for millions. To make it more impressive its outer walls were painted a brilliant white and the grounds planted purple and white bougainvillaea and flamboyant jacaranda trees.

The church interior was well set-out with several rows of pews and an altar with the cross of Christ in the background. I had a lump in my throat as I filmed. On our return after our Kariba Holiday, Eno Barratello, an Italian colleague, told me that some of his workmates were entombed in the dam's concrete wall.

Soon after our Kariba holiday Margaret and Bob moved to another government posting in Botswana. For a while Pat and Margaret exchanged letters, but finally lost touch with each other.

We had more bother with the Velox and I later exchanged it for a black Ford Zodiac, which gave me even more trouble with overheating. Steve Oelofsen, now back at Reed's, had it over the firms pit in the garage and showed me where the engine block was cracked. He had Robson, our store man, mix up a bowl of mealy porridge. Steve then fed it into the radiator to temporarily seal the crack, which worked for a while. However, I wouldn't let Pat drive it as every five to ten miles water had to be added to the radiator to prevent overheating.

The big test came when I drove the 40-odd miles to Duly Motors in Kitwe as their Chingola branch did not take trade-ins. I borrowed more money from Eddie my boss and traded the

Zodiac in part-exchange for a Ford Cortina E 1600cc, the first new car I had and a dream to drive. It was azure blue with chrome trim and inside walnut panels around the dashboard. With its 'lollipop' gear stick and wide ground-hugging Lotus suspension, I was Stirling Moss. Best of all it was the only one of its kind in town where everyone is known by the cars they drive.

Pat wanted the Ford Zephyr V6 she had seen in Duly Motors in Chingola. Instead I came home with a Cortina!

"That's not big enough," she blurted out. "You said we could have the Zephyr. You can take it back."

"I can't. I had to pay cash for it with trading in that heap of rubbish."

"Heap of rubbish! That Zodiac was the best car we've had, roomy and stylish."

Pat only liked it because the actors in the TV police series Z Cars drove them.

"Style doesn't get you from A to B safely, love. Anyway it had a cracked engine block and I had to carry two gallons of water every time we used it.'

By this time, Pat had joined the Women's Fellowship at the Kamenza United Church here after meeting Margaret Ramage. The Women's Fellowship had a good many women, Pat had noted in her diary. Lal Swartz was the eldest, along with Jean, Jayne, Ida, Norma, Esther, Joyce and others who helped cater for most of the town's major functions. Burns Night, St Patrick's and the Mason's Ladies Night, to name a few. I would often come home from work to the smell of hundreds of eggs, each one with the pointed end facing downwards in buckets on the boil.

"This method stops the yolk ending at one end of the egg" Pat had told me.

The worst job was to peel the eggs. Pat would end up with sore fingers and finally let Boniface try. From his long face I thought he'd rather be digging the garden. Pat usually preferred to prepare all the food herself. Oh, the smell of baking especially when Pat made her speciality rum babas – mmm, mmm. The aroma drifted enticingly throughout the house.

Pat kept herself busy on other days with dressmaking, as fashions changed from the sixties to the seventies. She'd buy the latest fashion patterns from Patel's or Solanki's General Store in Chingola and - being adventurous, as in most things she undertook – Pat would alter the pattern to suit the latest styles she'd picked up from overseas magazines. She would sit deftly sliding swathes of fabric through her fingers, the Bernina whirring as it ate up the shapeless cloth and magically turned it into long evening dresses, catsuits or those delightful mini-skirts. Now she was pregnant she made her own maternity wear. Pat was a dab hand at creating anything from patterns shown in women's books and at altering ready-made garments for friends. She had a list of women she made for, not as a business, but for pleasure and the delight of seeing her own creations worn by others.

For me work became more hectic as we expanded, installing new fabrication machinery and employing more white artisans from South Africa. My boss called me into his office one day and said that we had a new boilermaker starting and that I had to meet him at Ndola Airport. Manfred was an Austrian and had been working in South Africa for two years. He was the untidy sort, as broad as he was high, with unkempt mousy hair resting on his collar. A well-creased, rumpled shirt hung loosely outside his khaki shorts and his black ankle socks did not suit his fat hairy legs. Manfred had a reasonable command of the English language, but like most Germanic people I've known, tended to shout and get frustrated if not immediately understood. They seem to want to hammer a conversation into you and Manfred was no exception.

Nevertheless, I found Manfred to be hard-working, although crude in his fabrication methods and with a bullish attitude towards our Zambian labour. There were times that I had to pull him up on that, as we did not want labour trouble and UNIP breathing down our neck.

Manfred told me that he had a wife still working in Swaziland, but they had to leave. That was why he had come here and his wife would follow if he liked it in Zambia. It turned out that his wife was a black African from the Transkei in South Africa and a highly-qualified nursing sister. We all knew that whites could not hold hands with, let alone marry, a black person in South Africa under the apartheid laws. In Zambia, it didn't matter, although many whites, especially the South African and Rhodesian nationals, still frowned upon it.

Our second Christmas was a quiet affair as Pat had only two months to go before her due date. Times were changing fast in Zambia since independence and many Afrikaners were leaving and other European nationals coming in, many from England and central Europe. As it turned out Manfred's wife Joyce soon got a job in the mine hospital, being well qualified in her profession. They set up home in the Copperfield flats as Des Pienaar and his family had returned to South Africa.

On February 7th 1970 Pat gave birth to our son whom we named Damon James. Pat chose Damon from one of the actors in The Champions, a popular TV series at the time, and James after my late father. I was down Konkola No 1 shaft at the time and somehow word came from the surface that Pat had given birth. I caught the next available cage to the surface and rushed to the mine hospital where I had left Pat the night before. The wife of the town's MP Paul Chandra delivered him and pronounced him to be a fine 9lbs boy. The Reverend David Cruise christened Damon six weeks later at Kamenza United Church in Chililabombwe. David Cruse was good-natured, and a proud family man himself. Following the christening, we held a braai for this occasion to wet the baby's head.

Eddie Reed bought Chingola Air Services, a private company that had been in service many years. The company had two light aircraft and a hangar that we had worked on to smarten up until we built the new hangar. Some months later at the Mufulara Air Show Peter Barlow, a passenger in one of the planes, was killed along with the pilot. It took some time for everyone to take this tragedy in, especially Eddie. Although our staff included Mary, our young English woman secretary, Peter, who was studying to be an accountant, had helped in our office. He was a fine young man in his early twenties and eager to get his pilot's licence.

Peter had told me a few weeks earlier that Eddie took him to Duly Motors in Kitwe to get information on the delivery of the new Rolls Royce he had ordered, concerned after reading Zambia's new import tax laws could adversely affect the price. The manager told Eddie that he would be paying 105% import tax under the new luxury items levy. Eddie immediately told the manager to leave the car at Durban as he would collect it personally. As he was exiting, Eddie saw a new Jaguar in the showroom, a gleaming chocolate-brown Mark 10 series.

"Is that for sale, man?" Eddie asked in his typical South African manner.

"Er, no, not really, Mr Reed. I have a customer interested in it who is due here this afternoon."

Eddie jumped in with both feet.

"Put a battery in and get it ready for the road. I want it. How much is it? Fetch my cheque book, Peter; it's in the glove compartment!"

That same afternoon Eddie drove into the works yard with the new Jag followed by Peter in the bakkie.

After that fatal plane accident Eddie sold both old Cessna aircrafts, bought a Baron Queen Air, a luxury 11-seat aircraft, and employed another pilot called Dave who was a trained South African Air Force pilot.

-30-
Prohibited Immigrant

Eddie threw his annual Christmas party for the African workers the day before the firm closed for the two weeks' Christmas holidays. Several braai fires were set up and the white staff, including Eddie, served the food to the 'boys' and one drink of chubuku, the African maize beer. Crates of Fanta orange, Coca-Cola and Seven-Up were guzzled as if we were about to run out of stock.

The workers eagerly consumed beefsteaks, ribs and boerewors - the Afrikaans farmer sausage as long as a man's arm - and dozens of loaves and roasted corncobs. At the end of a feast that lasted all afternoon, the boys were each given a Christmas 'hamper' - a cardboard box of food for their family with sweets, jars of jam, chocolate, powdered milk, sugar, cooking oil, cornflour and other foodstuffs.

Our own Christmas party, held in Eddie Reed's new aircraft hangar, was also a great success. The inside was transformed into Santa's grotto and with a Christmas tree festooned with trimmings. The party, the best we had ever had in Africa, lasted from morning to dusk and Father Christmas arrived in Eddie's new Cessna plane, his sack loaded with presents for the children. There was food and drink in abundance for young and old alike. Father Christmas was George Sammons, aptly dressed in red and white fringed robes and black Wellingtons, with a curly white beard and a hood to mask his mop of sandy hair. George was one of our young electricians, but he didn't fool our Tracey.

"You're not really Father Christmas, are you, Uncle George?" she said as he handed her a present. Damon, at the crawling stage, pulled at his beard to finally reveal who he was, though he did have a real beard of sorts, albeit ginger.

As usual we celebrated New Year's Eve 1970 at the Bongo Bar and Theatre Club where there were disco dances to all the latest tunes, and a pantomime for the children. Over the years, we saw Boeing, The Goon Show, The Gang Show and Variety shows. Those wonderful actors helped to keep us sane.

Late one afternoon in January 1971 a white Land Rover stopped outside my front gate and three well-dressed black people climbed out. The driver of the blue Land Rover behind was a uniformed police officer, who rattled the gates. I had only been home from work half an hour and was relaxing as I watched Tracey and Damon play on the front lawn with the dogs.

Jesse's ears pricked up and he approached the gates head down with his hackles up, growling low. The smart-suited officer shouted across when he saw me. I got up as Jesse dashed towards the gate, snarling as he always did at strangers, especially Africans. Sally, a more placid type, sat back on her haunches, watching. With her wet pug nose raised, she sniffed the air. A Boxer, she seemed the more ferocious of the two, with protruding front teeth and permanent strings of saliva dropping from her mouth.

"Are you Mr Peter Pratt?"

"Yes. What is it you want?"

'Suited' thrust a sheet of paper at me with its National Emblem heading the page, a shield with heavy black wavy lines depicting the cascading water of the Victoria Falls. On either side stood a black man and woman with a pick and hoe and above was the African fish eagle and the nation's motto 'One Zambia, One Nation.'

I read on, but couldn't take it in. This was an official notice to Prohibited Immigrants to Leave Zambia (Act, 1965). It said, "Peter Pratt of Grimsby, England is inimical to the country of Zambia and has 48 hours to leave Zambia. He has a choice go through Immigration at Lusaka Airport or the Churundu border."

Why me, and why am I a prohibited immigrant? I stood confused under the late African sun.

My question, "What is this about?" fell on deaf ears and my heart skipped several beats.

I had heard of similar incidents, read about them in the *Zambian Times,* of people deported almost weekly. These scenarios could happen at any time of the day or night and you ignored them at your peril. Some offenders had been locked up until the Zambian authorities made up its mind when to deport them. "Why me?" was always a challenging question.

"We are only doing our job, to issue you this document and stamp your passport. You are now a prohibited immigrant," he said. "Not your wife or children; just you."

Pat stood by, bewildered, as I told her what this meant. She went quickly inside, gathering up the children, and told Boniface he could go home. Stephen, our houseboy, had left earlier. I asked Alan, my friend from next door, if he would come in with me and translate if needed.

I unlocked the metal gate and beckoned them into the house, hoping to find out how this accusation had come about, and to be out of sight of inquisitive servants and passers-by. With no further explanation why or what this was about I read again the paper heading: 'Notice to Prohibited Immigrants to Leave

Zambia' (Act, 1965.) With a touch of sarcasm one of them had the gall to demand I pay stamp duty of K2 (£1.)

When asked what for, he smiled.

"For your temporary 48 hour permit allowing you to wind up your affairs in Zambia before you leave."

"I'm giving you sod all. You mean to tell me that I have to pay to be deported? Get out my house."

The police officer suggested I sit down and think about it. Out of the trio, he seemed to be the more polite.

Alan, my neighbour, had already come over. He nudged me.

"Peter, calm down, and listen to what they are saying or you will end up inside."

I paid the two kwacha and then signed the deportation forms. I looked at my watch and asked the customs officer, "What time do I have to be out of Zambia on the sixth?"

"If you are not at the Zambian border before the 6pm deadline then you'll be in serious trouble. The authorities will come looking for you and you will be jailed."

He turned to Pat, smiling.

"Your wife and children can stay as long as they like, sir. They are not being deported, only you."

His unmoving jet-black eyes held a hint of contempt. I had a strong feeling he was enjoying this confrontation; now he had the power over the bwana. I did not answer him and showed them the door.

At the Chililabombwe Police Station my British passport was stamped Prohibited Immigrant. After that ceremony as I stood up to go back home, the suited officer held out his hand, which I ignored. As the police constable who drove me home pulled up at our house, he held out his hand. As I shook it, he said, "Very sorry, bwana," and drove off.

By now dusk was falling fast; the entire episode had taken only one hour. The clock had started ticking. I had only 47 hours to wrap up and go. There was no more to do now but telephone my boss and ask his advice.

"Inimical," Alan clarified, "means you're an enemy of the state.' Peter, you should do everything these people ask of you or they will bang you up. If you leave through the Chirundu border into Rhodesia, I will phone my father to meet you in Gwelo as he lives in Selukwe and he will look after you. From there you can decide what you want to do. Blimey, Peter, this is ridiculous, but we have to make a plan tonight."

"What are we going to do now?" Pat was trying to hold back the tears. "What is this all about?"

"I haven't the slightest idea, love. I've been going over any incident I can think of but I can't make any sense of this. My mind's a blank. Everything has happened so fast."

I put my arm around Patricia as she started to cry in earnest, which made the children cry, too. She lifted Damon, barely a year old, into her arms and hugged Tracey close, then put them to bed.

Knowing Eddie was in South Africa, I telephoned Ted Hageman, my manager. He was flabbergasted at the news and said he would contact Eddie.

Ted rang back an hour later.

"Eddie will speak to his solicitor in Lusaka first thing tomorrow, Pete. He gave me the man's home telephone number so I could put him in the picture. I will ring you back later. How is Pat taking all this? Tell her one way or another we shall sort this mess out."

Alan suggested I call round to see Paul Chansa, who lived nearby, and was a councillor and the town deputy mayor. Mr Chansa opened the door, a napkin tied around his neck.

Obviously he was eating his evening meal, by the fishy aroma kapenta, the little silver fish mixed with maize flour and boiled as a kind of piscine porridge. This was the typical Zambian daily diet; even, it would seem, for those in high places.

"Yes, what can I do for you?"

I apologised for disturbing him at this late hour and told him what had taken place. After some moments, he said, "This issue has nothing to do with me; it has obviously come from Lusaka. I suggest you see a solicitor to make an appeal if you have not done anything wrong."

When Alan and I got back it was to a full house where friends and neighbours had come round to see if we needed help. The jungle drums had done their work.

Over a few beers, Alan and I made a list of things for me to do the following day. First, I had to get the Barclays Bank clearance letter, and one from the tax department, both addressed to Zambian Immigration to be handed in at my arrival at the border. Inoculation certificates had to be updated by the hospital.

The night brought little sleep to Pat and me. I was awake most of the night listening to the thunder and lightning as it crashed overhead and heavy rain played its staccato tune on the house roof. The rain eased only to give room to the annoying drone of mosquitoes and other night creatures, killing any restful silence I might have had.

Reading Alan's list of priorities I must have fallen asleep in the chair, waking up stiff in the early hours. At 6 a.m. a tangerine streak split the eastern skyline and now it was quiet. No dreaded buzz and the rain had stopped and steam rose from the front lawn. I sat watching our friendly gecko. The agony of waiting for daylight was over.

I still could not fathom what I had done to cause this turmoil that seemed to be a bad dream. Our friendly gecko, eyes black as coal against a pink transparent body, regarded me as if to say, "You can't do this." Clinging upside down, adhesive toes gripping the ceiling as it darted for another quarry, it must have had a good night's hunting. Now its tummy was full, it disappeared into a wall crack.

At 7am Stephen, our houseboy, knocked on the back door. Boniface was already here tending to his vegetable patch. Sally and Jesse, our two dogs, came in for their breakfast. The children were up for breakfast as Pat emerged from the bathroom red-eyed.

"I am sorry for this upset," I said as we clung to each other.

The phone rang and Ted Hageman told me the firm's solicitors were going to meet me in their Lusaka office at 10 am tomorrow morning, knowing I had to be at the border that day before 6pm if things go wrong.

"They are arranging for you to meet Mr Changufu, the Zambian Minister for Home Affairs at 11am," he went on to say. "If you have a good case they may get you a suspension for an appeal."

The following morning and the day before my assumed deportation would, I knew, be hectic. I went to the bank and explained to the manager what was happening, and then to the tax office in Chingola. Pat had asked the mine's hospital if we could have our inoculations that afternoon as it was so urgent.

The Chingola Income Tax office was the worst, a degrading, drawn out affair. Nothing would budge their routine. I had forms to fill in while the Zambian clerk eyed me as if I were some kind of criminal. He wanted to know why I was leaving Zambia. I showed him the pink slip I had to leave in my passport with PI emblazoned across it, and his attitude changed immediately.

"You wait. I have to attend to others first. You come when I call you, OK?"

It was mid-afternoon before I got back to Chililabombwe, hot and exhausted. I had to give my tax clearance certificate to Barclays Bank Manager before they would give me their letter of bank clearance. Next stop was the Bancroft Mine Hospital for our injections and to get our medical books updated. As I drove down Kamenza Way the frangipani, flame and jacaranda trees were in full bloom. The usual afternoon cricket match was in progress with the revellers, beer glasses in hand, milling around the clubhouse.

As news got around the town of what had happened we had more friends round that last evening. David Cruise, our minister of the Free Church, and his wife Susan came to see us. Our two neighbours Iona and Judy stayed practically all day keeping Patricia and the children occupied. Iona arranged that if we were deported, they would see that all our important items were boxed and sent to Alan's father in Rhodesia. I don't know what we would have done without our friends.

I spoke quietly with Alan asking him to see that our two dogs went to a good home or were put down. Together we went over everything on the list that Pat and I had to take with us, especially clothes enough for a long stay. Finally, the car was fully loaded ready for a 3am start for the 260-mile journey south to Lusaka. I was not looking forward to it. There would be police roadblocks outside every town and a full search and I had to allow extra time for this.

I was to meet the firm's solicitors at 10 am at all costs and confidently put forward my appeal to the Minister of Home

Affairs at Government House. Could this be the nail in the coffin of our love affair with Africa?

I could not think of anything that might have triggered this situation. I had read where others had been deported after extreme verbal abuse of the President or for beating their house servants. Had I been too hard on the 'boys' at work or my two house servants? I had sworn at them, but never threatened them or called them munts or kaffirs. I was aware of the consequences of such actions. This affair was bewildering.

I took what might be one last look at our house, its colourful garden, cropped lawn, deep purple bougainvillea hedge, hibiscus, tall orange cannas and frangipanis. We had said our farewells to our friends the evening before - our two servants Boniface and Stephen were staggered by this event. As our two children were in a sleepy stupor Pat and I hugged our dogs and told them to be good. Alan next door came to see we were both OK, and wished us luck, again giving me his father's address and telephone number in Rhodesia.

On reaching Lusaka, we were invited to stay with friends who used to own the chemist shop in Bancroft and invited that night, if not deported, to stay overnight before returning home to Chililabombwe the following day. I left Pat and the children with them until I returned after making my appeal with the solicitor.

The solicitor was a pleasant young Zambian who spoke better English than me. We arrived at the Minister of Home Affairs' office and told that Mr Changufu was away but his assistant is prepared to see us. My solicitor told him the details and handed him the deportation notice along with my passport. After some moments, the assistant took out a file; after reading it he looked up at me, then at my passport. The chair groaned as he lent back.

"You are to go back home and within two weeks Ndola Customs will contact you."

We shook hands and left swiftly. Although I wanted to know how this had come about I was scared to ask too many questions. Before leaving the solicitors, I was told it could all be a mistake and not to worry too much now. I immediately telephoned Ted Hageman with the good news and to let Alan Goddard know we shall be returning home.

Although we put the house back in the order it was before, for the following two weeks I was on tenterhooks. After three weeks, I was exonerated as a Prohibited Immigrant and immediately applied for a replacement passport at the British Embassy. I was determined to leave Zambia after all the worry this had caused and told my boss I would only stay another six months.

"Peter, you would be foolish to do that. Give it time and you will have forgotten all about it. I have big plans for the future and I would like you to be here," Eddie said. "You can take two weeks leave in the UK for Christmas, providing you agree to stay on for two more years."

Pat was not too happy, but financially we had little choice. If we stayed a further two years we could at least afford to buy outright a decent house back in Cleethorpes.

"Anyway, Pat, I couldn't pass up Eddie's offer or let him down, especially after all the help he has given us."

Margaret Ramage came round one afternoon laughing and showed Pat the letter from her daughter Eileen in Scotland. In the envelope, she had sent a news clipping taken from one of the English national newspapers headed: 'Monkey' charge against Briton. It read as follows:

'A British pilot went on trial today for calling Zambian President Kenneth Kaunda a monkey. Peter Pratt (40), from Nottingham has admitted making defamatory remarks about the president to police who found him in a car parked in the middle of a Lusaka street.'

Although that little titbit made me angry, it also clarified matters. I had been mistaken for *another* Peter Pratt. With my boss Eddie employing a pilot to fly his Cessna aircraft and with my three-year employment permit sent to Immigration for a further three years' someone had confused the two of us, explaining the mystery of why I was singled out for deportation.

With my escapade over but not forgotten, the company suffered a major setback. Ted Hageman told me that Eddie and several other prominent businessmen had been arrested during a police raid on their homes. Marie and her two daughters were left bewildered and fearful for Eddie's wellbeing, not knowing why or where they had taken him.

This was a great shock and we wondered how it would end, as others arrested in similar circumstances had been known to go missing. It was a further three months before we had any news of Eddie's whereabouts, and it was still a mystery why he'd been arrested.

-31-

A Family Visit

Soon it was time to arrange our Christmas holiday in the UK as promised by Eddie before he was imprisoned. Pat and I dropped in to see Marie, Eddie's wife, in Chingola. I didn't know then if she was aware of the promise Eddie made to fund our airfares. Although I had hardly seen Marie since the first time in South Africa almost four years ago, she knew of our impending holiday.

Marie made Pat and me welcome and asked Pat how she was bearing up. She was pleased that I was not leaving the company. I told her that I would stay in their employ at least until the situation with Eddie was over. At that time Marie had a lot on her mind trying to get Eddie released and holding the company together.

"At least we have a loyal workforce in both Chingola and Chililabombwe," she commented. "I am sure everything will turn out right."

"Thank you, Marie. I hope by the time we come back Eddie will be released."

On our flight to England, we stopped off in Cyprus to visit my brother James and his wife Joy. I had written a letter telling him of our intentions and he suggested a hotel to stay in at Famagusta. James was still in the RAF and asked permission for us to visit them for a day at the Akrotiri RAF base. I hired a car to get there. When we arrived at the barrier post after a three-hour drive over almost arid landscapes, I had to park outside the base in a special visitors' compound.

I reported to the guard on the barrier post and within minutes James appeared. He took us to his house were Joy was preparing lunch. It was three years since we had seen each other by our father's bedside in Cleethorpes. Not one for children, neither of them made a fuss over our two. After a light lunch, James took us all to the pebble beach and to see the Vulcan bombers fly out over the Mediterranean. After a pleasant afternoon tea, we said our goodbyes. With James being fifteen years older than me and away for long stretches and during World War II we never had had much in common.

However, we had five relaxing days in Cyprus and toured its historical sites. Tracey and Damon had a wonderful time on the beach and it was fun to watch Damon's first reaction to the sea, as he jumped the waves; falling, he would surface spluttering and go back for more.

The last two days I hired a Turkish taxi driver called Emile to take us around Famagusta Old City and around Othello's Tower and Gate. After an hour, Emile took us up winding country roads around mountainous hairpin bends barely the width of the Mercedes. He parked in the shade of olive trees dotted with picnic tables and seats. Kantara Castle loomed above us, 700 or more metres high and built in the Karina Mountains. From the turrets, we had clear views of mainland Turkey. Before leaving, Emile fed us lunch from his hamper: Turkish breads, salami, sweet cakes topped with scented Turkish delight, fresh apples, grapes and a bottle of wine.

Emile spoke English well and was smartly dressed in a suit and white shirt and tie; it was obvious the heat didn't bother him. The following day he took us though small villages where we bought a camel stool and leather belts and beaded necklaces. The highlight was the medieval Bellapapis Abbey before a final tour of ancient Salamis with its massive amphitheatre and marble pillars. It was all too much to take in especially with two children in tow; nevertheless, I took cine-films for us to view when we got bored with Zambian television.

Our VC10 landed at London Heathrow on a cold December day. Slate grey clouds and drizzly rain reflected the traffic on the roads amid a sea of bobbing black umbrellas crowded the pavements. We got to Kings Cross railway station and were about to pay the cab driver when Tracey said she had lost her Barbie case, a small brown school case she kept her dolls in. The cab driver saw Tracey was upset, with tears rolling down her face.

"Never mind, love. I am going back to Heathrow I will enquire if it has been handed in and if it has I will post it to you. How's that then?"

I gave him Pat's sister's address in Grimsby and pushed a ten-pound note in his top pocket.

"There's no need for that, guv."

He bent down to Tracey. "Father Christmas will see you all right."

After the train left London, I went to bring something to eat and drink from the buffet car. I shoved my way through the idle talkers propping up the bar and ordered what I wanted. I recognised a face I had not seen for many years; my cousin 'Little' Jimmy. At 6ft 4in and almost as wide, he stood far above most. We looked at each other a brief moment until the penny dropped.

His face lit up and his massive form shouldered its way towards me and almost lifted me off the floor as we hugged and shook hands. The two of us must have been the biggest and tallest in the bar. We made our way back to where Pat and the kids were, with arms full of sandwiches, potato chips, cool drinks including beer and a bottle of Red Label whiskey in

Jimmy's pocket. Pat didn't look so pleased, as she had never liked him because of his bawdy past as a drunken fisherman. We had a lot to talk about nevertheless. He was now in the Merchant Navy and had jumped ship at Beira in Portuguese East Africa. With several others, he joined a group of South African mercenaries to make some money. He proudly showed me two purple scars across his chest and others on his arms. The old scars on his face were possibly from bar room brawls. Sadly, two months after our unexpected reunion, Irene wrote telling me Little Jimmy had been lost overboard in mid-Atlantic.

The train steamed into Grimsby on a winter afternoon and we said our goodbyes to Little Jimmy. The taxi stopped outside 313 Heneage Road where Pat's sister Renee lived, our base whenever we visited Grimsby. It was twilight and Damon was wide awake as he stood there holding my hand under the frosty streetlights. It didn't seem three years since we were last in Renee's living room, a rabbit hutch in size compared to ours in Africa. I sat in the fireside chair by the small coal-fire, as it was icy cold outside and Arthur, Renee's husband, was not home yet to claim his chair.

Renee made a fuss of Tracey and Damon, as she always did with any children. Arthur came in his usual cheerful self, flat-cap, trousers bottoms gripped in cycle clips. He lit his pipe and supped his tea with Damon on his lap, our son probably wondering who he was. Tracey was used to Arthur who had played games with her before we returned to Africa.

We were only home a week when the postman delivered a parcel wrapped in brown paper addressed to 'Miss Tracey Pratt.' Tracey knew what it was before she opened it; she thought Christmas had come a week early. She counted how many were in the case, her little world of dolls restored to her.

"I never thought we would see them again," Pat told Renee, reading the card. 'Have a wonderful Christmas, your London cabbie.' Later Renee walked Damon across the road to the sweetshop for a treat of his own.

Back in Grimsby and Cleethorpes we visited demanding relatives. Whether you are just up the road or a few miles or 6,000 miles away, family do not seem to realise how tiring such visits can be, thought it was great to see them all again and introduce them to Damon and Tracey. Family gatherings erupted instantly over every doorstep with biscuits, cakes cups of tea, or hard liquors especially from my East European in-laws. There were additions to our brothers and sisters expanding families to add to our two.

Questions were fired at us from all quarters especially from my brothers-in-law. Basil, a Ukrainian, asked, "Is there plenty of work in the mines? What do you do and how much they pay you, Pete. You no get me down them - especially with them darkie fellers."

"What type of food do you eat over there then," Doreen asked. "Is it like curry?"

"What's that place called, Pete? It's not on my map."

John had his world atlas open at Africa. I showed him where Chililabombwe was with an x near the Congo border.

"Well, it's in Africa somewhere, isn't it, our Pete?" Brenda chirped. "Stop asking him so many questions, you John, let him get his tea!"

"How do you get on with them black buggers?" John asked again in his guttural German accent.

I didn't let on that we had two servants or about my near deportation escapade. To give them an idea where and how we lived I hired a cine-projector to show them film of Victoria Falls, Lake Kariba, our house and the children playing with our dogs and their birthday parties. I was about to put the third reel on when Pat nudged me. She could sense they were getting bored and so could I, especially when I heard somebody whisper, "Coronation Street's on next door."

Before leaving Grimsby again, I made a special mission of taking my eldest sister Irene to visit our parents' grave. On that bleak frosty morning there was hardly a living soul in the Grimsby Cemetery. The polished black granite headstone with their names in gold lettering was a fitting tribute to our mother and father.

The weather was kind to us, cold with hardly any rain or snow, and that made our visits easier as we traversed Grimsby and Cleethorpes visiting relatives and friends. This scenario took up much of our time as each visit was expected to last half a day with tiring questions fired from all quarters.

I was disappointed that none of our friends made any effort to meet us. If it were not for Pat's sister Renee and husband Arthur, our trip from Africa would have been dull. We had Christmas and New Year's dance nights at the workingmen's club where Arthur and Renee were members.

We visited Pat's 74 year old mother Minnie who was living with Joyce, Pat's other sister, in Phelps Street, Cleethorpes. Minnie had not altered much, just as thin, and sitting quietly by the living room fire puffing on a cigarette. Tracey had seen her before but Damon hadn't; she didn't make a fuss of him either. I had a lot of time for Minnie, knowing she had had a hard life fending for her children while working well into her late sixties. Besides, she and Alex welcomed Pat and me to live with them when were first married. It was a comfort to us that she was well and being looked after by one of her own.

As I drove my hire car through Grimsby's bleak and old streets, I knew I wouldn't be able to settle here again. I was looking forward to our return to Africa.

The 'crucifix' tree, Chililabombwe

Typical termite mound in Zambia

Pat with Bob & Margaret Edmondson
Lake View Motel, Kariba (1969)

Santa Barbara Church, Kariba Heights (1969)

Kariba Dam, Zimbabwe and Zambia (1969)

Mosi-oa-Tunya – 'The Smoke that Thunders'
Victoria Falls (1969)

Tracey, Sally & Jessie (1969)   Damon's christening (1970)

Damon (1970)   Reed's Christmas party (1971)

Bill & Margaret Ramage   Noel & ChristineOelofsen
with Damon & Tracey (1972)

The Edinburgh Hotel, Kitwe:
Bernard & Betty Harris, Pat, Steve & Judy Oelofsen (c1971)

With Alan & Iona Goddard. Bancroft Mine Club,
Chililabombwe (c1972)

Farewell dinner at the Kitwe Chinese Restaurant
with Pat and Malcolm Campbell (1973)

Patricia far left, back row with the cast of Kemenza Church joint
production of Jesus Christ Superstar and Godspell (1975)

Far right, front row after gaining my Shotokan 3 Kyu brown belt.
Kenny Henderson, my senior instructor, second left back row (1975)

My membership club card (1975)

-32-
Crocs, Hippos and Golf

We had been back in Zambia a few weeks when Pat telephoned me at work to say that Tracey had something in her hair and she had called the doctor. When I arrived home Dr Forbes told us that Tracey had putzi-fly larvae on her head and neck.

"The putzi-fly lays its eggs on damp earth and leaves. Sometimes they settle on clothes hung out to dry and if not ironed properly, the worm can burrow under the skin and eventually it erupts into a pimply boil. The maggot eventually wriggles out and turns into a fly. Whatever you do, you don't squeeze the pimple as that leaves part of the worm inside and cause more infection."

Forbes smeared Vaseline on the infected areas.

"Now the worm cannot breathe and squirms out gasping for breath. In future make sure you or your house servant irons everything," was his parting advice.

Tracey was not her usual pretty self with her golden locks greasy with Vaseline. We kept her from attending school until after two weeks she was back to normal. Not a pleasant experience for any of us.

And finally my boss Eddie was free after almost six months in jail. Marie's unrelenting efforts and pleas had paid off. It was believed that the Reverend Colin Morris had spoken to President Kenneth Kaunda personally to secure Eddie's release. He was obviously unwell, drained and tired. For weeks he had been unable to stomach the prison food. With hardly any clean bedding, he suffered sleepless nights due to no air-conditioning, the flies and sharing a toilet in the cell with several others. It was only when Marie was allowed to visit him that he started to eat, the story emerged, as she took him food parcels.

After his release, it was almost a year before Eddie was back to his normal self. Between him and Ted Hageman, the business began to pick up again and everyone felt safe in their employment. Eddie bought a truck mounted hydraulic 65 tonne P&H crane, something the company needed as hiring cranes was expensive. This crane was one of biggest of its kind in Zambia. The mines all around the Copperbelt, from Konkola to Bwana Mkubwa at Ndola were soon queuing up to hire its services. Although under the ever-watchful eye of Johnny Sweet, who was in charge of all lifting operations, Eddie had to employ another experienced crane operator in Tony Kirkham. As far as I can recall no African drove the crane. During a heavy lift, one of the out-riggers that stabilised the crane collapsed. The chassis twisted putting the crane out of action for over a year awaiting repairs. Luckily, no one was injured.

Eddie had not lost his business acumen and within a year of being back in charge, the company had gone from strength to strength, winning bigger contracts below ground and on surface installations. Anglo American had decided to extend their Nchanga Mine to extract copper from the 'tailings' (mine dumps) Nchanga brought in American and UK companies who designed the system and other contractors to build the main installations for the new Leaching Plant. Besides the Pachuca tanks, we fabricated, the site had stainless steel Kennecott cone tanks, concrete thickeners and additional concrete tanks lined with stainless steel.

Specialist tradesmen from England and America were brought over to install the hundreds of metres of pipelines and other associated specialist work. Our own workload increased as the main contractors needed the local engineering companies to help in its construction by providing materials, plant, African labour and skilled tradesmen. This enormous project started producing copper from the 'tailings' after two to three years.

Before I left Zambia, some of our electricians were working in the electro tank-house. I asked the production engineer if I could keep one of the pure copper droppings that lay in a bin. I chose an unusually-shaped piece about 16inches square and as delicate as lace. I did not realise until later it was similar in shape to the map of Zambia. I showed it to Kenny Henderson, my karate teacher, who was the Konkola Mine Model shop supervisor and also renowned in the town for designing and producing semi-precious jewellery. He made me a wall clock, fixing the copper on green Perspex, and using malachite to fashion the clock face numbers. Kenny fitted a clock mechanism to drive the hands. Pat fell in love with it, as did many friends seeing it on our lounge wall. We had it for forty years before donating it to our son Damon when we moved to New Zealand.

By this time I had almost put aside our Prohibited Immigrant unpleasantness, especially after hearing what cruelty Eddie had gone through. He reassured me that the rift between Zambia and Rhodesia over UDI would settle down, it didn't. Political tensions worsened between Zambia and Rhodesia after talks with the British government failed at the negotiating table. This resulted in armed army and police roadblocks outside every town. Everyone had to get out their vehicles while they searched them from bonnet to boot. We heard stories going around of Rhodesian farmers fighting off insurgents from across its borders coming from Mozambique. This did not affect us adversely, apart from the roadblocks and some food shortages.

It was almost Damon's second birthday and he was growing into a fine boy. Our house servants Boniface and Stephen would push him around the garden as he sat on his toy pedal car. He would play out in the garden almost all day chasing Tracey and the dogs with the hosepipe or dangling upside down from the Jungle-Jim climbing frame – Damon was fearless. He had no fear of heights, but once came a cropper climbing the low wall that surrounded our veranda. He slipped and crashed down the other side to a five-foot drop. He landed onto the stone storm gulley and blacked both his eyes and nose. Pat rushed him to the mine hospital for a check-up. Luckily, no bones were broken, but his face was a mess, swollen with extensive bruising. People stared at him tut-tutting, giving Pat dirty looks as if she had battered him.

Alan Goddard, my next-door neighbour and work colleague, asked if I wanted to try my hand at golf. He took me on the Bancroft Golf Course two miles out of town near the mine farm, gymkhana and rifle club. The nine-hole course was designed around a natural lake fed by the nearby Lubengele Stream, a tributary from the Kafue River. The Kafue, only a quarter of a mile from the golf course, is one of the longest rivers in Zambia, ploughing south through the sub-Saharan bush to the Zambesi, a lifeline to Zambian towns and villages alike. Though hippo and crocodile-infested it offers great fishing.

"A word of warning, Peter," Alan said as we parked in front of the clubhouse. "The course has crocs, hippo and deadly snakes, so don't go foraging for your golf ball in the water, and be careful searching for them off the fairway."

The clubhouse was a sprawling brick-built building, surrounded by a spacious veranda. Around the side, several young African golf caddies dressed in vest and shorts milled around the clubhouse, hoping for work. Alan spoke to them in Chickabanga and selected two before we entered the clubhouse.

"Friday," he shouted to the golf club's barman, "come here, man. We want a couple of cold beers."

Though it was only 7.30am, it was already hot and sticky as we were still in our humid rainy season. Friday's real name was Laswell; he was a happy-go-lucky man who took all Alan's banter jokingly - they had known each other for years. Laswell lived in a kaia (house) at the back of the club with his wife and children and, among his others duties, acted as night watchman.

The membership fees were high enough to discourage all but a few Africans from joining, a tradition from the old colonial era upheld by most sporting clubs on the Copperbelt.

The 9-hole course, one of the world's toughest, and a standard scratch par 73, measured 3,843 yards; official club matches are played over 18-holes. The longest fairway was number four, a par 5 that stretched 620 yards to the green and once boasted the longest par 5 in Africa.

I managed to acquire a copy of the original architect's drawing dated 18th April 1959, detailing the 9-hole fairways, tees and greens around the lake. It must have been some task laying out the fairways on what was once a forest of teak and mopane bush-veldt. The fibrous rough of the kasensi grass, one to two feet high, reminded us of the most important reason to hit straight. Pyramid-shaped termite mounds 20ft high x 30ft wide at the base dotted the surrounding landscape.

On one such mound, whose top had been scalped to form a flat plateau, Alan showed me how to tee off. Being a keen sportsman, I was soon able to hit the ball straight if not far under Alan's tuition using mid-irons only. Teeing off from this unique location was certainly worth the effort; if not for the golf, for the view of the lush fairway ahead.

Many birds could be heard around the course and Alan pointed out the fork-tailed drongo that wags as it sings, the carmine bee-eater or go-away-bird and the crimson-breasted bush shrike. The lake was home to a resident fish eagle and flocks of white egrets – a bird watcher's paradise.

The lake's placid water was also home to 10-foot crocs who sunbathed on its banks. Hippos came from the nearby Kafue River attracted by the new sewerage ponds built alongside the Lubengele Stream. Sometimes turtles could be spotted should one dare venture nearer the lakeside. One early morning we saw a wonderful sight; dozens of newly hatched turtles hobbling en masse across the 4th fairway towards the lake. I captured two no more than the size of a newborn baby's hand and gave them to Jack Sammons, the club captain, for his garden pond.

On my first outing, Alan, perhaps unaware it might put me off golf, warned me again to be careful not only of the occasional croc that might be dozing in the bush, but also of the resident snakes. He reeled off names: the highly venomous spitting cobra, boomslangs, mambas, puff adders and gaboon viper - none giving much chance of survival after a bite. Then, smiling, he offered me a swig of the lager he carried in his golf bag.

During my first few games, I learnt as much about the course's wildlife as about the fundamentals of golf. Alan, being born in Africa, was a mine of information, and one of the most pleasant persons one could wish to meet.

Bitten by the golf bug, I soon became a member, as I liked the challenge of the game, the club atmosphere and the banter at the 19th hole – the bar. The club captain, Jack Sammons, whom I knew from dealings with him as the mines mechanical services engineer, signed me in without hesitation.

Hippopotamuses were much loved and frequent visitors to the course. But three-ton hippos are no ballerinas as I soon found out when I picked my ball out of a four-inch deep footprint. One of the club rules was that if your golf ball landed in a hippo footprint you were entitled to a penalty-free drop.

A legendary incident was when Jimmy McCabe and Tony Mack beat off a six-foot crocodile with their golf clubs after it attacked them on the course. The pair arrived in the clubhouse well over par! The incident ever since is remembered as 'The Bancroft Bogey,' and was highlighted as such in the *Zambian Sunday Times*.

I had given up my weight training after winning the Mr Zambia competition and needed something else to do at free weekends. As a family we shared many happy times at the golf club's braai (barbecue) and weekend social nights, together with our neighbours Alan and Iona. The children were excited to see the hippos frolicking in the lake, a memorable and most unusual sight to witness around a golf course.

I enjoyed the challenge of golf, but with my karate grade due, I had to concentrate more on that to attain my brown belt, which Ken Henderson, our principal Second Dan, assured me was just around the corner.

-33-
The Campbells

Soon after our Christmas in England, Margaret and Bill Ramage introduced us to Malcolm and Patricia Campbell. Margaret and Bill were staying in a leave house before returning to settle in Cowdenbeath, Scotland. Nearing retirement, they wanted to spend their last working days in their homeland. We both missed them and Pat especially, who had taken to Margaret as if she were her big sister.

After Margaret and Bill left, we began to cement a long and lasting friendship with the Campbells. People in the town thought the two Pats were related, as they did look somewhat alike. Malcolm, known as Mal, was a fitter and turner in the Konkola Mine machine shop. They lived on Ibis Road, where the garden included an immense avocado tree that dominated everything and produced fruit sometimes a quarter the size of a rugby ball - one weighed almost 3lbs. Bruno, their bull terrier was a fearsome-looking brute, who daily gorged on the fallen avocados. Damon used to play with Bruno, even trying to climb on his back.

The Campbells came from Middlesbrough in the north east of England, sailing from Southampton to Cape Town on a Union Castle Line vessel. They brought their new 1969 Ford Capri with them at the mining company's expense as part of their travelling deal to Zambia, as many did. Mal drove the 2,000 miles from Cape Town to Zambia, taking several days to sightsee along the way. The highlight, Mal said, apart from places in South Africa and Rhodesia, was the Victoria Falls.

It was strange that we had not noticed Pat and Malcolm Campbell before as they had been in town a year and drove the only Ford Capri around. Now it wasn't long before we all became good friends, a friendship that was mutual, happy and constant and would last for many years thereafter. As the months passed, Pat Campbell told Patricia that she hoped Malcolm would not sign another contract. This must have broken Malcolm's heart because of the opportunities and activities he so much enjoyed in Zambia, like water skiing and scuba diving. He had a boat of his own in England before he came to Africa.

Because of his interest in water sports, some weekends we'd all go to the river Kafue Pump Station, a popular place for boating and skiing. Malcolm knew Bokki Nel, Norrie Smith, Dick Bierling and Jake Koekomore, all of whom had motor boats. I never let Tracey and Damon near the water, fearing the odd rogue croc might be lurking, but that did not seem to deter the water skiers.

One Sunday afternoon Mal assured me we would be safe riding in Jake's boat as it was big enough to take six. We all piled in, Tracey and Damon screaming with excitement as Jake towed Mal on the skis. Nearing the end of the ski run an almost hidden bank of rocks brought Mal off. It was too late for Jake to turn and the boat rode across the rocks, pulling the prop off. The boat took in water and started to sink. Luckily we were only ten feet from the bank and were able to get the children and women safely ashore. Mal was left high and dry standing on the rocks, shouting for a lift from another boat and to ferry us back across the river.

In our almost two years together the four of us shared an active social life, mainly at weekends and in our own homes. We did go to the town's theatre club on dance nights or had the occasional evening out at the Edinburgh Hotel in Kitwe with Alan and Iona our neighbours. The six of us got on well together.

With Pat's dressmaking our house at times looked like a women's fashion store. I would arrive from work to elegant garments hanging from pillar to post around the house or to the music of the Bernina sewing machine as she sewed even more.

Knowing we had plans to leave Zambia, I sold my 1971 Cortina E to our neighbour, a black Zambian and manager of a brewery in Kitwe. With hardly 10,000 miles on the clock, within a month he had written it off. Luckily for me, he had paid cash for the car. To replace the Cortina I purchased a second-hand Ford Zephyr Z6 from a mine worker who was leaving. Being an expert on cars, Mal soon noticed one of the front suspensions was dipping. He gave it the once over and found the MacPherson strut was knackered. We tried all over to get a replacement.

"Lena, the wife's mother will be arriving in four weeks," he reassured me. "She will bring one with her."

She did too, although she had one hell of a time convincing the South African Airways staff what it was wrapped in hessian and cardboard. Persuading them with her old lady charm that it was indeed for her son's car, she managed to get it on as extra airfreight, albeit at the cost of twenty English pounds. Mal fitted it easily within a few days and the car was as good as new.

That July, before Mal and Pat were due to leave Zambia, he asked me if I wanted to go on a hunting trip. With meat in short supply it sounded like a good idea. In the brief time I'd known Malcolm I had found out that besides being a good car mechanic he was keen on shooting. His stories abounded with times he'd been hunting as a boy with his Dad on the Yorkshire moors and how he had taken part in the British Army shooting team at Bisley on his National Service.

Bert Rocha, a man who looked to be in his mid-sixties and who worked in the mine store, had asked Malcolm if he wanted to go game hunting over the long holiday weekend. The first time I met Bert, he stood tall and gangly with his sweat-stained felt hat shading a face burnished to leather. With his felt-skin boots and the hunting rifle he was cleaning he certainly looked the part of the big game hunter. We all agreed to share the costs of fuel, food and hunting licences, which were costly.

Preparing for a hunting trip takes careful planning with each animal you intend to hunt duly noted on your hunting licence. The rules are strict and if you were caught with an animal in your possession not on the licence you could find your equipment and vehicle impounded and yourself perhaps in jail. You had to have the right equipment, a reliable vehicle such as a four-wheel drive like a Land Rover with a winch, rifles and ammunition, a 44-gallon drum of fuel, fresh water, tarpaulin, freezer and portable generator, food and cooking equipment.

Although I had been fishing on Lake Tanganyika, Lake Kariba and the River Kafue, this was my first real journey into the bush on a hunting safari. How often does an ordinary person like me have this chance of a lifetime? Thrilled to the core, I squeezed in the front of the Land Rover with Bert and Malcolm, while our two African trackers sat on the back among the provisions.

Bert drove steadily westward along the wide and gravelled Solwizi Road. This was not my first time on African dirt roads, but here the scenery all around was dense forest thickened by acacia thorn scrub. We had covered about 80 miles before we turned southwards near the river Lunga. The bush trail led us into deep miombo woodlands and the natural vegetation of

Zambia. This district near Kasempa was well-known to Bert who was born into a hunting dynasty. With the Kafue National Park some 60 miles to our south, I was in the real Africa.

Stopping for refreshments and to let the Land Rover's engine cool down, we also hid the 44-gallon drum of fuel for our return journey. It was getting dark when Bert said we should make camp and shoot something for the pot. Alex, Bert's house and cook-boy, stayed with me to set up camp. We tied tarpaulins sheets between trees for our nightly cover and made a fire. Half an hour before dusk fell Bert and Malcolm came into camp carrying a duiker. The boys expertly skinned it and within the hour, we had stew for supper and a few beers before we turned in.

Every night on our trip I lay awake to the night sounds of Africa: crickets and the whoop-whoop-whoop of wild dogs breaking the stillness... Were they waiting for something to happen? Sometimes I thought I saw dark shapes in the forest. I must admit that first night I was a bit frightened and had to will myself to sleep.

I woke up before dawn to the welcome aroma of breakfast cooking. We had fried liver from yesterday's kill, with eggs, tomatoes, slices of bread and beans. After a strong black coffee and before the dew had started to dry on the grass we left camp to scout the area for game in the chill of early morning. There are no roads in the bush, only animal trails and we threaded our way around towering trees and anthills, some twice the size of our vehicle.

Suddenly Bert stopped, turned off the motor and whispered, "Hartebeest grazing across the dambo."

This was a vlei, a treeless grassy depression. These open pans can be a mile long and a half mile wide. Bert had told me earlier that two months previously he and his son Otto came out with some Africans to carefully burn the grass, knowing new shoots would grow and attract the game.

"Luckily we are up wind," Bert whispered quietly. Cautiously he stepped out of the Land Rover, indicating that Malcolm should do the same. I stood in the back of the vehicle, not daring to move. Malcolm lay prone by a fallen tree, sighting his rifle, and seconds later there was a loud report. Through my binoculars I saw one of the hartebeest trot a few yards, then topple forward onto its face. Bert's shot then stung my ears and a second beast momentarily faltered and keeled over.

We drove across the dambo, taking care there were no boggy patches. Bert told us the two beasts were fine specimens, with hides and horns worth keeping. Using a block and tackle hung from a sturdy tree, Bert showed Malcolm how to skin and gut them. No sooner had Bert started than bees swarmed around us, attracted by the blood.

"Light a couple of cigarettes for me and Mal," said Bert, "and then the bees will not bother us."

He laughed. "Best you start smoking, too, Pete."

My arms flayed like a windmill as the buggers swarmed around me. I ran for the shelter of the vehicle and closed the windows. I only smoked a cheroot at Christmas while having a beer with the lads, but now I lit a cigarette and more for Bert and Mal until they had finished the skinning.

Over the four days we bagged two hartebeest, two bushbuck and three bush pigs, well within our licence quota. Hunting was more for the meat than for trophies, but Mal could not resist claiming his hartebeest horns. I saw them on the wall in his garage years after while visiting him in England.

During our last few weeks with Pat and Malcolm we spent our weekends by Jake Koekomore's pool rather than down by the Kafue Pump Station. Jake was a good host and liked to have plenty of guests around. He had a young duiker roaming the garden as well as a vervet monkey, a civet ringtail cat and a 17ft python. He only had the python a few weeks before it died after disgorging the remains of a dog and being unable to eat anything else afterwards.

Three weeks before December '73, Pat and Malcolm left Zambia as his three-year work contract with the mines had ended. I think Malcolm would have liked to stay another three years, but his wife had had enough of Africa and missed her mother.

"I didn't want to come here in the first place," she once told us.

I drove Malcolm and Pat to Ndola Airport, taking my young son Damon with us for the ride, which made their farewells even harder as they loved him to bits. The Campbells left a big void in our life along with the many other friends who had left.

Patricia and I sat down to review our own situation in Zambia. We did not want to go down that road of subjecting our children to a boarding school lifestyle. We had no alternative but to return to England as previously planned after surviving the Prohibited Immigrant order.

Although our dear friends and neighbours Alan and Iona Goddard had decided to go back to Rhodesia, I knew in my heart that-that move for us was out of the question. The terrorist war was escalating, with stories of whites carrying guns and it was no longer safe to travel on rural roads. Terrorists were crossing the Mozambique border into Rhodesia on a daily basis, it seemed.

Nor did I want to go back to South Africa, as it would only be a matter of time before that country will have to change- for better or worse, no one knew. The whole of Southern Africa seemed so uncertain. A few years later my assumptions proved right and for once I had made the correct decision. I loved Africa, but I was not prepared to subject my children to any risk.

Pat wrote to Renee to send us details of any new houses around the Grimsby and Cleethorpes area. By the following month, we had the addresses of local estate agents to write to, and Pat had also kept in touch with the Campbell's, who knew we were thinking of returning home.

I got permission from my boss Eddie to take my overdue leave and I booked our flights for end of May 1974. Eddie knew I was going to England in the hope of buying a house and that I'd leave Zambia at the end of 1975 when my contract expired.

We had a surprise visit from George and Jennifer Batty who lived in Ndola. George was a long-time family friend as my sister Pauline used to look after him from being a baby in a pram to becoming a young lad. It was George's parents who owned Battys' fish and chips shop on Corporation Road, Grimsby.

George rolled up in his new Land Rover and told me they had decided to return to England by road. It was to be an epic journey taking them across Africa and Asia eventually to Europe and the UK, over 11,000 miles. In a way envied their courage and wished them well. They returned to Rhodesia before it became Zimbabwe and still live there.

It was about this time I was approached by Horace Holmes and Bernie Lloyd who asked me if I might be interested in joining the Freemasons. I did become a member of The Bancroft Lodge 7549 (E.C.), mainly out of curiosity. I knew Bernie as he was foreman in the mines boiler- shop and Horace was also a mine employee and attended our church; both men were well thought of in the community.

-34-

House Hunting in England

We arrived at London Heathrow and flew by British Midland to land at Teesside Airport where Pat and Mal Campbell met us. Although only 150 miles from Grimsby, Pat and I had never been that far north before and we found the Yorkshire countryside inviting. After spending two weeks with Pat and Malcolm, meeting their relatives and friends, we saw the house we wanted, a three-bedroom home in Ormesby, an ideal choice near to junior school for Damon and a comprehensive for Tracey.

Mal acquired a good second-hand Austin 1100 for Pat and me that enabled us to thoroughly explore the Middlesbrough area. At the end of our second week in Teesside, we drove down to Grimsby to Pat's sister Renee. Knowing we would need many items to set up home again, Pat over the past year had ordered various essentials posted to Renee's address in Grimsby.

On our arrival we told her we were buying a house in Middlesbrough, which came as a shock at first; but Renee did come to understand why we didn't want to settle back in Grimsby or Cleethorpes. Her front room was like a shop with everything ready for us to load both our car and Malcolm's to store in his house in Middlesbrough until Patricia finally arrived home the following year.

Before we left, we visited Pat's mother and sister in Cleethorpes, and other visits to my own sisters, and lay flowers on our parents' grave before we left Grimsby. Both our relatives in Grimsby and Cleethorpes couldn't understand why we would not be settling back there and took some convincing of the whys and wherefores.

Before we left for Africa, Mal took me round the Middlesbrough industrial sites: ICI Europe's biggest chemical plant, and shipyards that no longer built ships, but offshore oilrigs for the growing North Sea oil fields. The work prospects for me seemed endless, better than I had hoped. I managed to get a mortgage with the Middlesbrough Council, laid down the required mortgage deposit, and signed an agreement for us to move into the house the following summer. That suited the present owner and left time for me to wrap up our affairs in Zambia.

I had two surprises soon after arriving back in Zambia. Eddie had appointed a new general manager - Jim Burgess, an Australian mechanical engineer, who was taking over from Ted Hageman. We also had to move out of the bungalow on President Drive to live again in Copperfield Flats. Eddie wanted to cut his rented accommodation and as we were leaving the following year this suited him. Pat asked Boniface, our garden boy, if he would take on Stephens's duties in the house. Boniface's face lit up as he knew he'd get an increase in pay and would only have to work part of his day in the garden.

We settled in Copperfield Flats again, where our neighbour Peter Farrelly turned out to be a newly-appointed electrician at Reed's. Peter and his wife Sue were much younger than Pat and me, and came originally from Wales. Sue took to Tracey within days of moving in next door and Tracey spent all her free time at Sue's. Pat didn't see much of Sue during the week, after Sue came home from work, but at weekends we all spent time around Jake's pool with the children or went shopping in Chingola.

It was about then that Damon made friends with the African children next door by exchanging toys. Damon had a big red fire-engine he would push around the garden, and he swapped it for a wire car he'd often seen them playing with. Another time he went missing for several hours. I was underground and Pat called several friends for a search. Because of his silver-white mop of hair, he was soon spotted playing with the African kids up Kamenza koppie (Afrikaans for rocky hill and a favourite retreat for snakes.) Pat reached me to tell me the search had been called off only after I came up from underground.

Soon after our UK house-hunting mission the children started back in the routine of school. Tracey went to the Sacred Heart Convent in Chingola, travelling fifteen miles by school bus. Six months later five-year old Damon also started at the Sacred Heart Convent, travelling with Tracey and the other schoolchildren. School could not come soon enough for him and now at least we knew where he was.

Yet school was a challenge for Damon and for his teachers. It took weeks for him get used to the bus travel and settle to the strict school routine enforced on the children by the nuns, who soon put paid to his antics. Erik Trytsman's company Bodwin Engineering daily maintained the school bus. Erik himself serviced it tirelessly to ensure the bus was in good fettle. He took on carrying thirty-odd children the fifteen miles there and fifteen back each day was a big responsibility.

The year passed quickly. Christmas came and went, and before we knew we was sorting out our belongings for shipping to England. One day Pat rang me to tell me that her wristwatch was missing. I came home and we both searched the flat. I asked Boniface if he had seen the madam's watch.

"No, bwana."

He kept his eyes on his feet and I knew he was lying, but not how to prove it.

"It wouldn't be him, surely?" said Pat. "Boniface has been with us seven years. No, it must be lost; it can't be Boniface."

The following day I came home unexpectedly before lunch. Boniface was sitting in the garden under the paw-paw tree. When he saw me he stood up abruptly, I asked him again if he had seen the watch.

"No, bwana."

I had asked Robson, our works clerk, to come with me and now I called him over. Robson Ngwani was Eddie's faithful employee, and had been with the firm for many years. He acted as interpreter and mediator in all such matters or during industrial disputes. Almost all the Africans around knew who he was as he had a younger brother who was a member of UNIP and employed by the Zambian Government. Robson knew of Boniface, stared at him with his one good eye, and took Boniface to one side to talk sternly to him. Boniface's face by now bore a greyish pallor.

Robson came back to me.

"Boniface thinks he knows who might have the watch and will bring it back for the madam to-morrow."

The following day the watch was back where Pat always hung it in the kitchen. I sacked Boniface on the spot and told him not to ask for a reference.

A week later I woke up in the early hours thinking I heard a noise. The time was three am. Without disturbing Pat, I grasped the pickaxe handle I kept for protection against would be burglars, got out of bed and listened hard. A slight rustling noise came from down stairs. I peered out from behind the window curtains. The night was dark except for the streetlights further up the road.

From the top of the stairs, a faint strip of light fell across the lounge floor. I knew then that the front door was open. I kept still, not daring to make any noise. A pair of bare black-feet appeared as if to climb the stairs. I quickly switched on the landing lights, yelling as I ran down the stairs with pickaxe handle held at the ready. The room was empty, the door wide open. The burglar had fled as fast as lightning, and I glimpsed him scaling the six-foot wire fence.

With the shouting and commotion, Pat and the children were awake and our next-door neighbours Sue and Peter called to ask if we were all right. On walking round the perimeter fence with Peter, we saw several piles of fist-sized rocks. These are to throw should anyone follow the culprits and, believe me, an African can throw a rock with deadly accuracy.

We found that the burglar had removed the fly screen from our window close to the front door. We had made the mistake of leaving a door key on the lounge coffee table for them to hook by the infamous pole method. We were fortunate that nothing was stolen and that the burglar was not armed as in the most recent spate of robberies in the town.

We found our two dogs, Jesse and Sally, drugged in a state of semi drunkenness in the back garden. Sally was so ill I had to let the vet end her life and Jesse was also put down a month later, because of what the vet told me was a kind of canine venereal disease common in Africa. To fill the void our dogs left behind, we got from Bill Davidson at the karate club a six-month old puppy a crossbreed Doberman-spaniel with a pug face that we named him Churchill.

Soon after, Damon was even more adventurous for a four-year old boy. He knew where I worked, as sometimes I took him with me at weekends in the bakkie. He decided to see his father at work and walked, barefoot as always, up Kamenza Way to the

Konkola Industrial Estate. How he remembered the route amazed us. For company, he took Churchill, with him.

Luckily Pauline, our secretary, saw them and brought them to my office at work The first thing he said was, "Can we have a drink, Daddy?" I could have wrung his neck for the worry he had caused. When I called Pat to let her know Damon was with me, there were sighs of relief both ends of the phone.

Although Churchill came to us so late before we departed, he gave us some happy days. When the time came to leave and find Churchill a new home, Pat gave him to a young English couple she knew at the church.

To kill the remaining few weeks Pat and the children, along with Sue from next door, spent more time at Jake's garden pool, a good size and surrounded by poinsettia, frangipani, fig, banana and paw-paw trees. There Damon and Tracey could feed Bambi the duiker, and watch the snakes and vervet monkeys Jake kept in nearby cages. Besides the animals, the children could let their hair down and enjoy the pool, especially after a hot morning at school. We also had Pendleton Pool on the mine side of town.

With his three-year contract ending, our friend Richard Johnston and his wife Sheila were also due to go, and were booked on the same flight to London as Pat. Richard and Sheila were regular members of the same church fellowship group as Pat. Dick played King Herod in the church's production of Jesus Christ Superstar and Godspell, a combination of the two shows. Pat was Mary Magdalene as one of a cast of fifteen, including Reverend David Cruise.

David's trainee minister Stephen produced and directed the show and designed the props. A great hit in the town, the show was invited to tour the other Copperbelt towns. Pat made the costumes with the help of Sheila and other members of the cast. The show was a kind of farewell for us, and many more who took part in it.

June 1975 was the beginning of yet another era in our life as I waved goodbye to Patricia and our children, the second time I would be without my wife in Africa. At least this time Pat had a house to call her own. I had highlighted our new home and county on the England map as 'Pratt's Castle,' because, as the proverb goes, an Englishman's home is his castle. There would be no need for steel burglar bars at 28 Welburn Grove, or a steel chain and padlock around the front gate and no need for guard dogs. In England, one can go shopping or drive anywhere without the thought of police roadblocks or a fear of being car-hijacked, robbed or killed.

Our friends Malcolm and Pat Campbell met Patricia and the children at London Heathrow and thereafter help them settle in. Although Middlesbrough is in England, at first it would be almost as much a foreign land to us as Africa when we first went there. Settling in takes time and patience but nothing Pat could not handle, especially with good friends just around the corner. There would be new neighbours, new environment, a new town and a new school – yes, a strange dialect, but still forever England.

Alas, I had to settle down to six months as a bachelor again before completing my contract with Eddie Reed. As we'd sold up all our furniture and car, I stayed with my karate guru Ken Henderson and his wife Carol whose three boys were in boarding school in the UK. I stayed with the Hendersons two weeks before my intended safari and after Kenny left for Italy. He asked me if I would look after their house on my return from the bush as Carol was leaving then for the UK.

Three of my evenings while at the Hendersons were spent practising at the Chililabombwe Karate Club. Bill Davidson was our stand-in tutor until Ken came back. We had a good attendance at the club so this cured most of my boredom. I did not want to fall into the trap of propping up the bar again at the theatre club every night as before; truly, that was not my scene.

Everyone seemed to know we were leaving. I cannot remember why or when Ted Hageman left the company to go to Rhodesia. Before Ted left, he and I used to have the odd round of golf and even now, forty odd years later, his words come rushing back: "Shall we have a game of 'dammit,' Pete?" Ted was great fun on and off the course. Sometimes as I was addressing the ball he would say, "Have you heard this one…?" After Ted Hageman left Reed's, the place wasn't the same again.

I heard years later that, shortly after I left Zambia, Jim had had a fatal car accident while travelling on the dirt roads over the border in Zaire. I vaguely remember that just before I left he had been urging Eddie to take on work at a copper mine there. Sadly, it was not long after that Eddie Reed was also killed in a similar accident near the Chingola flying club.

-35-
The Last Safari

I rode in the lead Land Rover with Theo, and Max his African cook rode in the back. I would be lying if I said there was no boyish excitement. Jake followed in his much bigger long-wheelbase Land Rover with Robson and Benson, his two African employees. Both vehicles towed a fully loaded trailer with the usual gear for such a trip. The most important commodity besides the shooters were the 44 gallon can of fuel, fresh drinking water, a box-freezer loaded with ice and portable generator.

Before reaching Kasempa, Theo slowed and took a right turn off the main road onto what appeared to be an old bush trail; similar to that which Bert Rocha had followed on that earlier safari I had with him and Malcolm. We threaded our way around and beneath the tall drooping trees, teak, mopane and acacia thorn scrub. It was an hour's drive into the forest before the first wave of invaders attacked us from all quarters.

"Tsetse," Theo shouted as he slid his door windows shut. I did the same and Theo switched on the windscreen wipers to sweep away the marauding flies that settled on the windscreen. Luckily, we had put on the overalls that Theo provided for this very reason. He told me a tsetse sting could penetrate normal clothing.

Theo stopped the vehicle and lifted the tarpaulin. He told Max to get into Jake's Land Rover with Robson and Benson until we passed through the tsetse belt. Usually there are manned stations that spray all vehicles coming in and out of these areas, but we had not passed through one; perhaps another Zambian loss of control.

We zigzagged through the bush unable to break speed limits as we pushed forward. Elephant spoor clotted the track. Theo stopped to poke with his boot at a pile of droppings the size and shape of deflated footballs. Robson, Jake's tracker, examined some, sticking in a finger to sniff. He glanced up.

"A day maybe two, bwana," he said.

All around trees were shredded and stripped of their bark. We drove around a marula tree robbed of its succulent fruit, much favoured by the elephants. Theo warned us they might be drunk on that, and to keep our eyes open for more elephants. We moved on.

The thought of being so close to these enormous and fascinating creatures unnerved me, yet I wanted to capture them on cine film. Whoever would believe otherwise that I had taken part on a real safari? Jake and Theo checked their hunting rifles, Jake his 375 Remington and 12-bore shotgun and Theo his Winchester 243 repeater.

Soon after, the Land Rover came to a halt with a shudder. Theo sat up, startled.

"What's up?"

"I think we have a problem. The temperature gauge is in the red."

Steam billowed from under the bonnet and the acrid smell of radiator fluid filled the cab.

Theo was first out.

"Shit! The radiator's punctured."

He continued to shout and blaspheme in Afrikaans. By now it was dusk and I shone the torch on the tree branch that had punctured the radiator.

It took the best part of two hours for Theo to take off the radiator and repair the damaged section under torchlight. Patiently he nipped the damaged radiator veins and sealed them with epoxy-resin. He stood up, satisfied that it should do the trick, but didn't want to refill the radiator until the glue had set to his satisfaction.

As the epoxy-resin would take several hours to set Theo decided to make this a temporary camp for the night. Robson made a fire to boil water and Max helped Benson prepare our site. After we had quenched our thirst from the cooler box, the boys handed around sweet tea as we opened packets of sandwiches and ate them around the fire.

Theo and Jake mostly spoke in Afrikaans, forgetting that I could not understand the Taal (Afrikaans language.) They apologised when they realised. Like most local gatherings, the South Africans who had spent their lives in the Rhodesias talked of the good times before independence came; of how things used to be. Such times were fast becoming history. The typical Afrikaner spoke of the Union, meaning South Africa.

"We will never give in to the Kaffirs down there; we are too strong in the Union."

Deep down I always suspected they hated the English, a hatred that stems from the Anglo Boar War and has been passed down the years. After reading *Rags of Glory,* the historical novel by South African author Stuart Cloete, I fully understand how the Boers' ill feelings originated.

That first night as we sat around the campfire until tiredness took hold and I lay there thinking of Pat and the children as the usual night sounds took over: cicadas, night-jays, wild dogs or perhaps a hyena. I fell asleep but not before thinking of Jake's advice as he handed me the 12-bore.

"Don't wander from camp by yourself or unarmed. The bush-veldt can be deceptive. Walk four paces and turns around several times and you will not remember north from south."

At first light we breakfasted and, with the radiator back in place, moved on. The track became worse the deeper we headed south along rutted tracks. Our first real hazard came as we crested a steep rise. Theo stopped the Land Rover below a stream some ten feet wide flowed at a steady rate. This surprised him, as we were into the dry season. Max and Benson waded up to their knees to cross.

"We will make a bridge," said Max.

The timber scaffold boards had been brought for such an occasion, and several good trees cut to ford the river. It took the best part of three hours to build the bridge. I recorded most of this on my cine-camera. Jake's Land Rover came across without mishap. Theo's Rover ran off the edge with wheels slipping as a scaffold board cogged just before the front wheels could grip on the far bank. Jake, already across, unhitched his trailer and attached the winch wire to tow Theo's vehicle up the incline.

On foot, Jake and I followed Theo and Max down a track and into a clearing. Outside a crude beehive dwelling almost hidden with tree branches, a scrawny ragged figure of some considerable age stood in the open doorway. He held a rifle of sorts over his shoulder as he came warily towards us. Jake greeted him, but he did not seem understand. Theo called Max over to see if he could understand the old man.

Max greeted him.

"He says he is alone and lives here after travelling many miles."

He pointed north.

I sat in the shade of the vehicle as, cross-legged on the ground, they held their indaba (discussion), shaking heads as they scratched maps on the earth.

Jake stood up.

"The old man says hunting here is no good. We should head further west. That will take us past the Lunga Game Reserve and nearer the Angola border.

"That I don't like," he added.

We set out following the direction the poacher told us. Theo, with the old man and me, took the lead following a narrow trail for at least five-miles. We made camp leaving Max and Robson to set things out away from a small dambo and in the shade of tall teak trees.

While the poacher sat in Theo's open-back Land Rover with me, I indicated I would like to look at his rifle. I knew nothing much about guns, but this weapon, an ancient flintlock muzzle-loader was much longer than any we carried. There was an unreadable inscription on the metal trigger guard; surrounded with fancy scrollwork, and etched above that was the date 1889.

On our return to camp I gave the old man two cans of Coca-Cola along with some bread, which he gratefully accepted. Jake told me the old African would make ball-shot with the cans. We watched him empty the gunpowder from the two 12-bore cartridges Jake gave him into a small bag. Before Theo and Benson took the poacher back to his camp, he gave me a metal ball that might once have been a tin can.

The following morning at first light, we upped camp again and headed south-west where Theo said he had hunted two years previously. This was also to get as far as we could from the poachers camp, as we didn't want to be accused of helping him if the game rangers caught him. We found a clearing that would be sufficient for our permanent campsite and last three days with a stream nearby.

"Will we catch bilharzia?" I asked Theo.

"No problem. This will be ideal for washing as it's running fast." Theo was laughing. "Just don't drink it or sit in it as if there is anything in the water it will get up your arsehole."

We followed the stream for half an hour. On foot, you are simply another animal in the African bush, so you have to be aware other eyes might be watching you. The stream ran into the Lunga, a river some ten to fifteen yards wide, but shallow in places with central sand banks. We saw no evidence of crocodile or hippo, but knew they might be there somewhere as Theo had warned. Back at the stream, it was cold and refreshing but no amount of scrubbing could remove five days' dirt from our pores and under our nails. After drying myself I sat quietly, fiddling with my cine-camera. Theo was catching some sleep, still hugging his rifle. I saw flashes of turquoise as a kingfisher took turns with its mate to dip into the stream.

We were out hunting every day before sun-up and back in camp by early afternoon. Whatever was shot was instantly skinned and divided into manageable chunks, put in plastic bags and stashed among the ice in the freezer - the little generator had done its job.

"I think we should try the other side of the area while the boys pack up the camp," Jake said.

An hour later Theo quietly stopped the Land Rover behind a towering anthill from where we could watch the movements of several sable antelope nonchalantly grazing. Theo whispered that we should fan out; that he would take his boy and I should go with Jake and stay low for, say, fifteen minutes from now. I checked my watch as Theo left at a crouching stride through the trees, his boy following.

Jake picked a good spot behind one of a dozen 6ft high, knobbly termite mounds two hundred yards from the nearest bull. The sable stood proud like a black thoroughbred racehorse with two females by his side. We crawled on our bellies through the light scrub, my knees scratched by dried grass and the thorn-scrub that tugged at my clothing. The bull was a fine specimen, black with a snow-white belly. His scimitar annulated horns swept over his shoulders, almost touching the middle of his back. Jake handed me the 375, whispering, "Take him in the shoulder."

I took aim with my heart pounding. I wanted this beauty, yet felt guilty for what I was about to do to the majestic creature. Nevertheless, I squeezed as Jake had shown me at the Bancroft rifle range. I heard the thud as the soft nose struck, then another shot rang out and another immediately after. My ears stinging, I winced from the pain, not yet realising that Jake had taken the rifle from me.

The following two days brought us to the end of a magnificent hunting safari, an experience I will never forget and had thankfully recorded on 8mm film. It was only after two days since shooting the sable that the finest meat was selected for biltong and marinated in a brine: vinegar, salt, pepper and spices, a special recipe of Theo's. (Biltong is a sun-dried delicacy that the Boers made during their long treks and handed down through generations). Earlier I had helped Theo string out the roll of 10mm metal chain between trees like my mother had hung up her washing line. After two days marinating and using opened paper clips as hooks together we hung the strips of raw meat to dry for several days. During the winter, the cool air is dry and generally, there is no fear of flies. I had often heard from my South African friends how to make biltong, but not realised the work involved until now.

The boys were busy skinning and cutting up the two hartebeest we had shot on our last day. Robson came and warned us that four people were coming armed with sticks and pangas, though luckily there was not an AK-47 in sight. Nevertheless, Jake and Theo stood with rifles under their arms on watch. Jake told me to get on the back of the Land Rover with the loaded shotgun in easy reach, but out of sight of our visitors. I had a good look around the way they had come and could not see anyone else, but then the African is hard to spot in the African bush.

Robson spoke to Jake who nodded and looked at Theo and then me, raising his eyebrows as if to tell me to be ready. I felt behind me for the reassurance of the 12-bore.

Robson approached them and spoke to the four natives in Bemba, which it appeared they did not understand. After much jabbering, they pointed towards the west. Robson told Jake that he thought they were from Angola. Only one of them spoke and understood Robson in Bemba. Robson sat down with them in the shade of a tree, and so their story went...

"They have been hunting for many days with no luck and are hungry with families to feed."

I saw them eyeing up the half-skinned beast hanging on the pulley blocks. Jake instructed Robson to give them the offal, head and feet from one animal as a gesture of good will. Our boys were disappointed as this was their meat ration, but Jake said we would make it up to them.

Our uninvited visitors laughed with excitement at this gesture and started to dance around us, holding out their hands in friendship, with their two dogs jumping up and barking. Two of the group had crudely made bows and 3ft long steel-tipped arrows; something I had never thought to see in the real. None of them had rifles, only roughly made axes, pangas and longbows. They were a ragged lot, in dirty vests or shirts and trousers torn from days in the bush. They agreed I could film them on my cine-camera wielding their bows and axes.

Before leaving, they gave us a sack that contained a half honeycomb complete with a few dead bees in exchange for the meat. We accepted it as a gift as they did ours to them and watched them melt into the forest.

Over ten-days, we had completed a full circle of the area, filling the freezer box. After three hours driving, we came across the first dambo that we had passed on the fourth day; a herd of sable antelopes were grazing along the far edge. Theo wanted to shoot one for a trophy and chose for his target a bull with horns, the biggest Theo had seen. He made us stop, but the entire herd immediately took off like greased lightning.

Walking through the shoulder-high grass back to our Land Rovers I saw a movement to my right. Max, Jake's African tracker, grabbed my arm and pulled me back. We had disturbed a leopard from its kill that now sprang up as if from a trampoline and bounded away in a flash. The leopard's unmistakable yellowy-orange and black spots were a perfect camouflage in the dry grass. If alone, I would have been easy prey armed only with a camera. Jake at my side lifted his rifle to fire, but too late; the leopard was gone. I will never forget how close I was to death if the leopard had stood its ground, a vision that has lingered.

We were heading home after almost ten days of washing in streams, sleeping under canvas and cooking on open fires. Except for the many francolins and guinea fowls that had made a fine feast and a change from the usual fare there were not many birds to be seen. I had only one sighting of the infamous lory or go away bird that Theo had pointed out to me. These little birds are the bane of the hunter, warning game of our presence, fluttering, chirping, and squawking 'Go 'way! Go 'way!' - an inbred alarmist.

Over the week, we had bagged a roan antelope, two sable antelope, a reedbuck, two hartebeest, a warthog and a few guinea-fowl. By his standards, Theo was disappointed. He thought we would have got more game or a buffalo even. I consider myself lucky to have experienced a real workingman's hunting style safari, thanks to Jake and Theo and their Africans, Robson, Max and Benson. Nevertheless, I do not consider any of us being the Hemingway type as a means to gain prowess. I would rather impress using a camera as, in most cases, they don't lie. The game-hunters I knew here did not hunt for any trophy, but to feed their own families.

We were all caked with dust from head to toe, when Theo and Jake dropped me off at the Hendersons' house after the long ten-hour drive back from our last safari.

-36-

The Final Goodbye

I was longing for a good hot bath, shave and clean clothes, a cold Lion Lager and a sample of home cooking. Carol was a good cook, although I had only eaten there occasionally before going on my hunting safari. It was common practice in Zambia to have someone live in and look after your house while you were on holiday, thus referred to suitably as 'a leave house.' After Pat left Carol and Kenny asked me to stay with them in their home and continue living there while they were on holiday in the UK. Kenny knew I would be at a loose end with nowhere to stay until I left in November.

Before she went, Carol reeled off a list of instructions.

"Don't forget to feed my cat one meal a day in the evenings. Chock the kitchen window open with the piece of wood for her to get in and out. The dogs are to be fed twice a day, first thing in the morning and evenings about six and not before. OK, Peter?"

Before I could answer, she continued in her firm and lively Scottish lilt. She would have made an excellent teacher.

"Now, Peter, don't forget my wee dogs. Sandy, that's the big one in the kennel now."

(Sandy was a full-blown Rhodesian ridgeback bred to hunt lions).

"Sandy stays in the garden day and night by the kennel and make sure my houseboy tops up his drinking bowel, as he tends to forget. Feed wee Bessie the same time as the cat."

357

She opened a cupboard stacked high with tins of cat food and a sack of dog food.

I knew all this, as I had been staying with Kenny and Carol for the past two weeks. When I came back from hunting Kenny left for Italy for his second dan karate black belt grading. I had the feel of the house by now and was used to the dogs, if not the cat.

I think the houseboy Michael was a bit wary of me as his bwana for the next few weeks as after a few days he knew I would not stand for any nonsense. Michael was getting on a bit, grey-haired and with the kind of old African face I had seen on cheap wooden carvings. He was from the Bemba tribe, Kenny told me, and can be trusted. I could tell Michael liked his drag of dagga (marijuana) by his bloodshot eyes and lazy gait around the house.

Carol went on and on about the do's and don'ts.

"Wee Bessie, Peter, is to stay in the kitchen especially if you go out, and during night-times. Make sure the door is shut before you go to bed, as she tends to chew things if left alone."

"Like what?"

"Shoes, slippers, magazines and papers, even the rugs. She gets bored."

Carol pointed to the chewed rug on the floor.

"If she makes a mess, which she sometimes does, mind, Michael will clean it. He starts at 6am every morning. He'll cook you breakfast if you want, won't you, Michael?"

"Yes, madam, if the bwana wants, madam."

He did not because I would not let him.

Carol had been gone three weeks when Michael rang me up at work as soon I arrived. Before he could say anything, I tore a strip off him for not being at the house before I left at 6.30am.

"Water, bwana, there is maningi – much water, bwana, all over the madam's house. Checha lapa kaia." (Hurry.)

I looked out of my office window but there was not a cloud in sight so it was not rain.

Thinking the house had been burgled, I took Peter Farrelly, our electrician, and four African labourers in the bakki. As I drove up the drive water was cascading down the veranda steps like a miniature Victoria Falls. I stopped the pick-up in the drive and told my African labourers to put down their weapons and help Michael drag furniture from the house. We laid stuff out on the lawn. Some of the smaller rugs were already hanging on the clotheslines.

I went into the lounge where Bessie was plodding around and yapping with excitement at the bleb hanging from the ceiling that was about to explode. Luckily, water had found another outlet – the ceiling's centre light fitting, and Peter had already switched off the electrics.

I went into the kitchen but the valve was not where it should be under the sink. I asked Michael were the water stopcock was so I could turn off the water. He scratched his head.

"Stopcock. What is this, bwana?"

I phoned the mine's services department, who said it was in the garden and promised to come round. I found it just in time as the water by now was creeping along the passage towards the bedrooms. A mains pipe that fed the header tank had burst in the false roof almost bringing the lounge ceiling down. It took a few hours in the sun to get the lounge suite and carpets relatively dry, though shrunken and faded. Within two days the ceiling was replaced, the electrics checked and everything back to normal.

The following week the cat went missing; she wasn't there for her evening meal. Michael said he had not seen her for three days. Then I noticed the kitchen window and asked Michael if he had shut it.

"No, bwana."

His heavy lidded eyes, bloodshot from smoking too much dagga, stared at me in innocence. I propped the window open with the wood. Tufts of bloody fur were stuck on the bottom ledge of the window, which could only mean one thing - the cat might have had its tail guillotined.

Another week passed with no sign of the cat and in three weeks Kenny and Carol would be back. I got up early one morning to go to the toilet. I had been in a drinking session in the Bong Bar with Jimmy Crabbe until the early hours. At 5am it was still dark and my head was thumping like a steam hammer. I made coffee before going into the lounge to listen to the morning radio. The door was ajar and little Bessie ran out to jump up at me and fuss around as dogs do. It was the bits of white fluff stuck on her nose that made me realise she should not have been in here. I switched on the lounge lights and quickly sobered up!

The white fluff had turned the lounge into a winter wonderland. I sat down on the settee, my head still pounding from last night's liquid supper. Taking in the mess, I realised to my horror one of the arms on Ken's recliner had been chewed through to the wood as if ravaged by a crocodile.

"Bessie, you little bitch," I yelled at her."

I swung my leg almost giving myself a hernia and Bessie a hysterectomy. This was all I needed. Water everywhere last week, the cat lost and maybe tail-less and now this. Carol's new suite. I phoned the mine's service department again. They took the armchair away for repair and returned it a few days before Carol and Kenny were due home. The only drawback was that whoever did the repair had stitched a double seam on top of the arm for all to see. The carpenter told me, "There was a shortage of matching material."

"But why a seam on top for everyone to see?"

He shook his head.

"That's Zambianisation for you, Pete."

Eventually the cat turned up with its tail only an inch shorter.

On their return, I went through the events with Carol and Kenny over dinner and reported that Bessie had changed her diet from slippers to suites.

"I thought there was something different about that arm; it's a lighter colour too."

Carol ran her finger along the seam as I told them about the chair, the flood and the poor cat surviving the guillotine. We all had a good laugh over wine to celebrate Ken gaining his second dan in shotokan.

Soon after I left as their boys were due home, and I had to start making my own flight arrangements. I moved in with Jimmy Crabbe for my last week, and managed a final game of golf at the Nchanga course with Johnny Sweet and Jan Fourie. Then it was time to thank everyone at OK Flats and say my last goodbyes. It seemed impossible that it had been only seven-years since Peter Hageman met us at Ndola, yet so much had happened between then and now.

Soon, I was airborne as the homeward flight began. The plane, a British Airways Boeing, took off in the coppery gloom as the sun slowly dipped over the Zambian bush. The twelve-hour flight was uneventful and we landed at London Heathrow in a flurry of sleet. I caught the domestic flight to Teesside Airport in north-east England without any complications. I realised this was the first time I had ever flown over the heart of England.

In early winter a light fall of snow dusted London's suburbs, villages and fields below. The dark patterns of country lanes, roads and rivers broke the monotony of the whiteness before the plane rose into dense cloud. Immediately forgotten were the sleet and rain the moment I saw Patricia with our children waiting for me at Teesside Airport. Pat and Mal Campbell were also there to welcome me and drove us through North East Yorkshire and our home in Middlesbrough. I stood a while on the pavement in the cold crisp November air, looking at 28 Welburn Grove. I had accomplished what I set out to do, own a 'castle of my own.'

With Africa still burning in my mind, I paused. Would this mark the end to my nomadic roaming? Only time would tell.

Epilogue

Two weeks after our return to England and once we were settled in our house in Ormesby, Middlesbrough, it dawned on me that we should take the road south to Grimsby before Christmas to visit our families.

Besides, I wanted to see the old town and the iconic Dock Tower; to walk once more down my old street. I telephoned my sister Irene to let her know we'd be coming down.

"You'll not recognise it, Pete," she said. "All the houses in our street have been knocked down and they've built modern homes. They call it Yarborough Place now."

Tracey and Damon were both settled in school and making new friends. Patricia had a part-time job merchandising with Pat Campbell and was getting to know people.

Our friends Pat and Malcolm had helped us settle in. As they only lived a few streets from us, we saw each other almost daily. It was almost like being back in Zambia - except for the weather and the pervasive smell of wood-smoke. And we didn't have to chain and padlock our front gates every night!

We had chosen a good place to live; Captain Cook country, as Malcolm proudly called it. I hadn't the faintest idea who Cook was until he told me about this famous sea captain and took us up the road to where Cook was born.

At weekends during our first six months Malcolm took us out and about, with drives over the Cleveland Hills and Yorkshire Dales to Whitby, excursions to Cumbria and the Lake District National Park. Only twenty-minutes away was Redcar, Middlesbrough's seaside resort, another favourite haunt of his and always popular with the kids.

Although I had a foreman's job, I missed the challenge of management and that sense of responsibility Eddie Reed had instilled in me. Restless, I began to scour the daily newspapers as I had in Brighton before we departed for South Africa.

William Press Engineering was advertising for senior supervisors to work in Bahrain. That was tempting, as I had met some of their management team on the Nchanga Tailings Leach Plant before leaving Zambia.

We had achieved our main purpose – to earn enough money abroad in order to buy our own home. Yet here I was, I admit, a little restless and curious to know what opportunities might be on offer.

When Pat found me hunched over the dining room table with the world map spread out, she knew immediately what I was up to.

"Oh, not again, Peter," she said. "Will you ever stay put? As soon as we get settled you want to be somewhere else."

She was right – and the Arab world that was soon to open up to me was completely different to that world we'd known in southern Africa. Perhaps I will continue my long road from Grimsby by recounting next my further adventures in Bahrain, Abu Dhabi, Saudi Arabia, Egypt and the Sultanate of Oman.

And yes, I did manage to stay put eventually, fortunately with my dear wife still beside me, and together watching our grandchildren grow.

New Zealand is our home now, and I am settled in this beautiful country, content at last with good memories of our life's journey, some of which I've shared with you.

Acknowledgments

Grateful thanks are due to the following:

- My wife Patricia. Without her, this journey would not have been so successful. This story belongs to us both.
- My daughter Tracey and neighbour Chris Taane who read the manuscript with keen eyes, contributing suggestions and amendments.
- Our families – brothers and sisters and their children – with love and appreciation.
- Malcolm and Pat Campbell. Thank you for your generosity and our lifelong friendship.
- Yarm Writers in England and Tauranga Writers in New Zealand for sharing their knowledge, constructive criticism and advice.
- The teachers at South Parade Juniors and Armstrong Street Comprehensive school - my respects and thanks.
- My work colleagues while serving my apprenticeship at the Humber Graving Dock and thereafter.
- My school friends, especially Bernard Kendall, David Holmes and George Batty (now in Zimbabwe.)
- Grimsby Health Studio friends: John Dent, Colin Bush, Steve Farman, the late Geoff Doncaster, Terry Brown, the late Bill Turner and John Brown - and their

wives who kindly kept in touch with Patricia and me over the years. Love and appreciation.

- The many characters of Grimsby and the West Marsh. Heartfelt thanks for what you added to my story.

- The editors of the *Grimsby Telegraph* who published earlier articles on family in their wonderful historical Bygone's supplement.

- Derek and Louise Manthorpe of the Manorbe Health Studios in Brighton and members.

- Dear friends made in South Africa: Archie and Edie Mackay, Alan and Monica McMasters, Bert and Betty Lecky who made our stay there memorable.

- Eddie Reed in particular, who gave me the opportunity to prove myself as a supervisor and instilled in me the principles of workshop management.

- To the many helpful colleagues and friends at E. W. Reed Engineering in Zambia: Steve and Judy Oelofsen, Ted and Peter Hageman and families; the Fourie's, George and Jack Sammons, Mavis and John Sweet, Les Merrifield, Alf Drinkwater, Mary and Bill Flavell.

- The many employees of Konkola Mine.

- Special thanks goes to Carol Henderson and her late husband Ken and the Chililabombwe Karate members.

- The Bancroft Theatre Players and the Daisy Disco for keeping us sane with music and laughter.

- The Rev. David Cruise who christened our son Damon at the United Church of Zambia, Chililabombwe.

- The Kamenza Women's Fellowship members, with appreciation.

366

-   Anne Harris, Lincolnshire artist, for her kind permission to reproduce the print of the Grimsby Dock Tower for the front cover. [www.anneharrisart.net]

-   Mike Whittaker: photograph of The Grimsby Royal Dock and Tower.

-   Rod Collins: photograph for the Grimsby Fisherman's Memorial. [www.Rodcollins.com]

-   Chris Mackay, George, Western Cape, South Africa: photograph of Kamenza Way, Chililabombwe, Zambia.

-   Reg Hann Tour SA Travel Pty Ltd [travel@toursa.com.] Maps of South Africa and Zambia.

-   Special thanks to my editor Jenny Argante of The Little Red Hen Community Press, for being so patient and meticulous.

-   The minds and hearts of many people, family and friends have gone into this book and I thank you all dearly.

Bibliography

(2004) ZINSSER, W. *Writing About Your Life A Journey into the Past*. Boston, Da Capo Press.

(2004) FODEN, G. *Mimi and Toutou Go Forth: The Bizarre Battle for Tanganyika*. London, The Penguin Group.

(2003) LEONARD, B. *Cleethorpes and District Remembered*. [The Changing Times Series.] UK, The History Press.

(2002) CROSSLAND, G. J. & TURNER, C.E. Turner. *Great Grimsby A History of the Commercial Port*. [With the assistance of Associated British Ports.] UK, T & C Publishing.

(2002) LEONARD, B. *Grimsby Remembered*. [The Changing Times Series]. UK, Tempus Publishing.

(1999) HOFFMANN, A. *Research for Writers*. 6th rev ed. London, A & C Black (Publishers) Ltd.

(1999) SPARKS, A. *The Mind of South Africa: the Story of the Rise and Fall of Apartheid*. London, Wm. Heinemann Ltd.

(1998) LEGAT, M. *An Author's Guide to Publishing*. 3rd rev ed. London, Robert Hale Ltd.

(1997) SMITH, I. *The Great Betrayal: the Memoirs of Ian Douglas Smith*. London, Blake Publishing.

(1996) THOMAS, A. *Rhodes: The Race for Africa*. London, BBC Books Worldwide.

(1994) MANDELA, N. *Long Walk to Freedom*. UK, Little, Brown & Co.

(1992) PACKENHAM, T. *The Scramble for Africa*. London, Weidenfeld & Nicolson.

(1989) THOMAS, F. P. *How to Write the Story of Your Life*. USA, Writer's Digest Books.

(1955) MORGAN, H. *The Toughest Job in the World*. UK, The National Fish Friers Federation.

Made in the USA
Charleston, SC
14 September 2016